Women's Radical Reconstru  *n*

Women's Radical Reconstruction

The Freedmen's Aid Movement

CAROL FAULKNER

PENN

University of Pennsylvania Press

Philadelphia

10   9   8   7   6   5   4   3   2   1

First paperback edition 2006

Published by
University of Pennsylvania Press
Philadelphia, Pennsylvania 19104-4112

Library of Congress Cataloguing-in-Publication Data

Faulkner, Carol.
   Women's radical reconstruction : the freedmen's aid movement / Carol Faulkner.
      p. cm.
   Includes bibliographical references and index.
   ISBN-13: 978-0-8122-1970-8 (pbk. : alk. paper)
   ISBN-10: 0-8122-1970-8 (pbk. : alk. paper)
      1. Freedmen—United States—History—19th century. 2. African Americans—
History—1863–1877. 3. Reconstruction 4. Women social reformers—United States—
History—19th century. 5. Radicalism—United States—History—19th century.
I. Title.
E185.2.F28 2003
973.7'14—dc21   2003051227

For My Parents,
David and Joanne Faulkner

Contents

Introduction

In July 1863, Cornelia Hancock, a New Jersey Quaker, volunteered as a nurse for the Army of the Potomac at the Battle of Gettysburg. As the wounded soldiers recovered, Hancock looked for other ways to aid the Union cause. During the winter of 1863–64, she traveled to Washington, D.C., where hundreds of Northern women had gathered. In the District, women offered aid to former slaves gathered in camps around the city or worked as nurses in the local military hospitals. Hancock spent the rest of the war as a Union army nurse, but her winter in Washington inspired her postwar career. After observing the situation of former slaves in the city, Hancock formulated her ideas for the protection and elevation of freedpeople. She envisioned a government bureau, independent of the military, led by men "with living souls in them large enough to realize that a contraband is a breathing human being capable of being developed."[1] These men would appoint "good energetic, anti-slavery persons who will have an interest in the improvement of those under their charge." Finally, Hancock imagined a "National Sanitary Commission for the Relief of Colored Persons," an organization of abolitionists and other reformers working with the bureau to alleviate the condition of former slaves.[2]

In the same year, Josephine Griffing, an Ohio feminist acting as an agent for the National Freedmen's Relief Association of Washington, D.C., petitioned Congress to give Northern and Western women responsibility for the "care and education of these freedmen."[3] Like Hancock, Griffing believed that emancipation's success required continued government involvement. Although Hancock referred vaguely to "anti-slavery persons," Griffing's plan was more explicit. She suggested that Northern *women*, with government authorization, be deployed to provide relief to former slaves. During Reconstruction, both Hancock and Griffing saw much of their vision achieved, if only temporarily.

Hancock and Griffing were just two among many Northern white and black women who devoted themselves to freedmen's relief during the Civil War and Reconstruction. This book examines the different ways these women tried to shape Reconstruction policy, and the methods they employed to aid former slaves. It also seeks to illuminate the lives of individual women in the freedmen's aid movement, as their personal histories informed their strategies. Many of these women participated in the antebellum antislavery and women's rights movements, while others seized the new political and economic opportunities provided by the war and emancipation. As the proposals of Hancock and Griffing indicate, women in the freedmen's aid movement viewed the federal government as a vehicle of reform. To advance the rights of both women and former slaves, women lobbied the government, worked as agents of the Freedmen's Bureau, founded freedmen's relief societies, toured the country raising money for freedmen's aid, bought land to sell and rent to freedpeople, started common and industrial schools for freedpeople, and moved permanently to the South to act on their commitment to justice and equality for former slaves.

The successes and failures of these women are largely absent from most histories of the freedmen's aid movement, which often portray the "Yankee schoolmarm" as the prototype of Northern women's activism.[4] Historians describe the freedmen's aid movement as a male preserve, led by the abolitionists of the American Freedmen's Union Commission, the evangelicals of the American Missionary Association, and the military officers of the Freedmen's Bureau.[5] But, as in the antislavery movement, women were the "great silent army," without whom the movement would have foundered.[6] The efforts of white and black women appear in the records of aid societies and the Freedmen's Bureau, in abolitionist and suffrage newspapers, and in published pamphlets and personal accounts. Though evidence tracing African American women's contribution is scant, black newspapers such as the *Christian Recorder* and the published writings of Frances Harper, Charlotte Forten, and others reveal the extent of black women's involvement in the freedmen's aid movement.

In addition to revising the history of the freedmen's aid movement, this examination of women's participation in freedmen's relief shows the profound intersection of Reconstruction and women's reform. Women addressed issues that dominated Reconstruction politics, including race, labor, dependency, and political and civil rights. But rather than viewing these issues as separate from the women's rights movement, abolitionist-feminists maintained a broad definition of social reform that linked the struggles of former slaves with the struggles of women. During Reconstruction, women in the freedmen's aid movement urged the federal government to include both women and African Americans in the national polity.

Black and white women in the freedmen's aid movement articulated an ambitious platform for Reconstruction. Like the most radical of the Radical Republicans, they argued for universal suffrage, land confiscation and redistribution, and an activist federal government.[7] Anticipating modern arguments in support of affirmative action, reparations, and a national apology for slavery, they argued that the nation owed former slaves for their years of involuntary labor. They suggested that Americans repay this debt, and thereby absolve the national sin of slavery, through the private benevolence of Northerners and the public protection of the Freedmen's Bureau.[8] Abolitionist-feminists believed that this assistance would enable freedpeople to become self-supporting citizens, while sustaining widows, mothers, children, the sick, the elderly, and others who could not survive without some aid. Finally, abolitionist-feminists asserted that women's participation in the war effort had earned them a right to participate in the reconstruction of the nation, both as administrators and as voters.

Many of the abolitionist-feminists' goals failed, in part because most Republican politicians and Freedmen's Bureau agents embraced a different vision of Reconstruction, one that prized economic freedom and independence over the repayment of social debts and equal rights. The male politicians and reformers who experimented with freedom in the South were principally concerned with reviving the Southern economy and creating a free class of African American laborers; they believed that a free-market economy would inevitably correct the racial and economic inequalities in Southern society. These policymakers asserted that diligent wage laborers could achieve upward mobility, and that only laziness and incapacity limited workers' opportunities. Historians label this Northern worldview free labor ideology, a system of beliefs that pervaded their economy, society, and culture.[9]

Free labor ideology shaped Northerners' policies toward former slaves. Politicians, military officers, and reformers initially introduced wages and employment contracts into the existing plantation system. In 1865, Congress established the Freedmen's Bureau to temporarily oversee the transition to free labor and protect freedpeople's interests. Though political and civil rights became an important component of the Republican plan for Reconstruction in the late 1860s, politicians presumed that once freedpeople had won these rights, they could assert them unaided. Most Americans stigmatized those who relied on others for their support, and they associated dependence with an ineligibility for the privileges of citizenship. To accept the help of the state was to be childlike, subordinate, and feminine. As a result, freedpeople could not seek help in claiming these rights without having those very rights called into question.[10]

Reconstruction policymakers worried about the potential for African American "dependency," an issue that came to dominate policies concerning former slaves. Similar anxieties had long accompanied manumission throughout the Atlantic world, as they were tied to questions of labor, race, and social order, but they reached new heights following the emancipation of four million slaves in the South.[11] Northerners feared that Southern blacks would turn to Northern whites and the federal government for support and guidance, thus remaining wards of the nation rather than becoming self-supporting laborers. Racism also influenced Northern attitudes, as they suspected that African Americans might not be capable of economic independence and full citizenship. In response to these concerns, Freedmen's Bureau agents curtailed the distribution of relief, believing charity would encourage African Americans' dependence on the government; freedmen's aid societies established common schools to foster an independent character among Southern blacks; and, instead of giving away donated clothing and food supplies, reformers sold these items to former slaves so as not to encourage pauperism. In addition, the military and the Freedmen's Bureau strongly encouraged and coerced freedpeople into signing labor contracts.

The egalitarian promise of free labor ideology was tempered by both race and gender. As field laborers and domestic servants, freedwomen were central figures in the operation of the plantation economy, and both Northern and Southern whites desired that they continue in these roles. But reformers and bureau agents believed strongly in middle-class notions of the family and viewed freedwomen as the legal dependents of their husbands. They also wanted to insure freedwomen's rights to remain with their families, after the violent severing of men, women, and children in the slave trade. As a result, reformers struggled to balance freedwomen's family life with the demands of free labor.[12]

The free labor vision of Reconstruction predominated, but it did not go unchallenged. Freedpeople fought to become landowners in order to make themselves truly independent of whites. When wage labor seemed inevitable, former slaves tried to shape plantation labor to suit their own needs. Freedpeople resisted white authority over their work and family lives at every opportunity.[13] Northern blacks also viewed Reconstruction as their opportunity for equal citizenship and fought for suffrage and civil rights. They formed their own freedmen's aid societies and demanded that the government and the Freedmen's Bureau consult them regarding policies toward former slaves.[14] Both former slaves and free blacks resisted white notions of black dependency and sought to shape freedom on their own terms.

Women's activism in the freedmen's aid movement also challenged the free labor values expressed by politicians, male reformers, and military personnel, but their radical plans caused conflicts within the freedmen's aid movement. Though the divisions in the movement cannot be defined neatly along gender lines, male and female reformers disagreed over organization and policies. Abolitionist women believed they had an important contribution to make to Reconstruction, yet they were deliberately excluded from the leadership of the American Freedmen's Union Commission, a national organization founded by abolitionists and Republicans to aid the Freedmen's Bureau. Free labor advocates singled out women reformers for criticism, voicing their concerns about women's methods to the government and male leaders of the antislavery movement, often in gendered terms. As one Massachusetts businessman noted, "women with misery around them see a little too much through the *heart*."[15] These conflicts represent the clash of women's political culture with a new style of benevolence that emerged during the Civil War.

Women's activism in the freedmen's aid movement grew from their participation in antebellum charitable and reform societies, illustrating the continuity between that network of women and an aggressive postwar women's political culture. Historians define women's political culture as the "organized public activity" of women, including the "values associated with women's participation in the public domain as well as their actual behavior."[16] Although historians agree that the antebellum era provided a solid foundation for women's reform, the postwar development of women's political culture inspires debate among scholars. One school sees the rise of scientific or organized charity, informed by social science methods and requiring dispassionate investigation of social problems, as a conservative development which bound middle-class reform women to male elites rather than to other women. The Sanitary Commission, formed during the Civil War to work closely with the government and the army in supplying the needs of soldiers, was the beginning of this new professionalized and state-sponsored benevolence.[17] Other historians see the Sanitary Commission as the foundation of a national women's political culture. The Sanitary Commission and its branches, they argue, placed women in prominent public positions, and strengthened connections between charitable women around the country.[18]

Though some aspects of the freedmen's aid movement, particularly the American Freedmen's Union Commission, fit the first pattern, women's involvement in freedmen's aid, women's rights, charity organization, and other reform movements demonstrate that women's politics entered a dynamic period after the Civil War, in which female activists asserted their influence in local communities, on the national political scene, and with the government.[19] The freedmen's aid movement in particular proved an important stage in the development of postwar women's political culture. Women eagerly sought the assistance of government in their efforts for former slaves; they also relied on the financial and emotional support of other women. As in the Sanitary Commission, women's efforts to shape national policy and politics met with opposition, often stemming from their perceived resistance to male authority and the new style of benevolence.

These women also participated in the Reconstruction debate over race, sex, and universal suffrage, adding another dimension to the history of women's reform in this period. For scholars, the birth of an independent, but divided, women's rights movement has overwhelmed other aspects of women's activism in the Civil War era. Following disappointing attempts to secure both African American and women's suffrage, Elizabeth Cady Stanton and Susan B. Anthony formed the National Woman Suffrage Association in 1869. They left the American Equal Rights Association, founded by abolitionist-feminists in 1866, when the association endorsed the Fifteenth Amendment, giving African American men the right to vote. During this schism, Stanton and Anthony used racist rhetoric to argue that white women should have the vote before black men, thus arousing the lasting ire of many abolitionists.[20]

But the focus on the racist origins of the NWSA obscures other important factors in the development of the women's rights movement during Reconstruction. Many women, notably Lucretia Mott and Josephine Griffing, were committed to the NWSA platform, though they did not condone the racism of Stanton and Anthony. African American women also participated in the split in the women's rights movement, as African American men stressed the connections between emancipation and the assertion of black manhood. While some black men supported women's suffrage during Reconstruction, others relegated women to subordinate roles in the domestic sphere. Roslyn Terborg-Penn has found at least six African American women who joined the NWSA (as opposed to nine who affiliated with the opposing American Woman Suffrage Association). Others, like Sojourner Truth, adopted a more neutral position on the split.[21] The allegiance of these women indicates that abolition, freedmen's aid, and women's rights remained part of a broad platform of social reform supported by suffragists. Members of the National Woman Suffrage Association encouraged the women who assumed leadership positions in the freedmen's aid movement and praised their efforts on behalf of former slaves. These suffragists believed that the social and economic problems of Reconstruction reinforced the need for women's suffrage as well as an activist state.

Though not all women in the freedmen's aid movement participated in the organized suffrage movement, they endorsed a broad definition of women's rights. Most supported themselves as career reformers, committed to social justice; once agents of antislavery societies, they now worked as representatives of freedmen's aid societies. They belonged to networks of like-minded women throughout the North. In addition, most of the women in the freedmen's aid movement were single by choice or circumstance, and thus unusually independent of men. In their own lives, they challenged the notion that women were "dependents."[22] Finally, most, if not all, of these women expressed a commitment to the expansion of women's sphere or expressed dissatisfaction with the limited opportunities open to women. The critics of women's involvement in the freedmen's aid movement undoubtedly realized the connections between freedmen's aid and women's rights, and feared the expansion of women's public power.

The freedmen's aid movement also provides an important site for examining the racial beliefs of feminists in a formative period in race relations and national politics. Rather than simple paternalism or racism, the freedmen's aid movement reveals a more complex picture of women's relationship with former slaves.[23] Women's gender, race, class, marital status, and regional and religious identities all affected their choices and strategies. Because of their own experiences as women, they interpreted freedpeople's poverty and dependence as a result of specific historical circumstances, rather than as an innate racial characteristic. They rejected the pejorative definition of dependency, seeing that condition as inevitable in an unequal society. Instead, women's efforts acknowledged the real privation of freedpeople and endeavored to ameliorate it by public and private charity.

But as middle-class Northerners, white women's defense of freedpeople also exhibited many of the same prejudices and paternalistic attitudes of their associates. They believed they had a special connection to freedwomen, but found that their ideas about work, marriage, and family clashed. Influenced by their own struggle for economic independence and access to professional employment, white women emphasized the importance of wage labor, which ignored freedwomen's desire for autonomy from whites and the right to put their families before work. Furthermore, white women portrayed freedpeople as dependents on their aid or as supplicants for their help, thus placing freedpeople in an inferior position. In many ways, women's independence rested on the neediness of former slaves.[24] Yet even with these important caveats, white women criticized the inadequacies and injustices of Reconstruction, expressing their empathy for former slaves, when few others did.

African American women had different motivations for joining the freedmen's aid movement than white women. Their class position, religious background, and educational level set them apart from freedpeople, but free blacks recognized the ties that bound them to former slaves. As Northern blacks argued for education, suffrage, equality, and civil rights for freedpeople, they also demanded these things for themselves. Anticipating the "lifting as we climb" motto of the National Association of Colored Women, black women in the freedmen's aid movement became mothers to their race, offering instruction and guidance in the transition to freedom. In addition, they reminded white suffragists and the government that they had not yet met their obligations to former slaves. By positioning themselves as social and cultural leaders and public advocates for former slaves, however, middle-class black women also affirmed the class and cultural differences between themselves and freedpeople.[25]

The history of women's activism in the freedmen's aid movement illuminates the debates over race, sex, freedom, and equal rights during the Civil War era. Arguing that government intervention and material aid were necessary components of emancipation, women presented a vision of Reconstruction based on justice and national responsibility, rather than free labor and independence. Their radical support for federal and Northern intervention were the beginnings of a new mode of women's reform closely linked to politics and government. Though stymied in its time, their philosophy of federal responsibility and action remained a strong current in women's reform for the next century.

Chapter 1

Dependency, Gender, and Freedmen's Aid During the Civil War

The freedmen's aid movement began in November 1861, when the Union army took control of the Sea Islands and the area around Beaufort, South Carolina. This Northern victory provoked a mass exodus of white Southerners who left behind their plantations, their houses, and their slaves. Hearing of an area controlled by the Union, slaves also left inland farms to seek safety and freedom on the coast. The government and the army enlisted the assistance of Northern missionaries, abolitionists, and businessmen, led by Edward L. Pierce, to aid them in the care of former slaves and the reorganization of labor on abandoned plantations. This group of reformers, known as "Gideon's Band," a name reflecting the religious and antislavery zeal of their endeavor, initiated the "Port Royal Experiment," which tested the possibilities of freedom for former slaves.[1]

As the Union army occupied more Southern territory, freedmen's aid reformers followed closely behind, distributing food and clothing and reporting back to the North on the condition of former slaves. Sympathetic Northerners established freedmen's aid societies as religious missions, as auxiliaries to antislavery or soldiers' aid societies, and as independent "commissions" intended to work closely with the government in aiding slave refugees. All these groups had roots in the antislavery movement, and most of their members either belonged to antislavery societies or, at the very least, opposed slavery.[2] Women were especially active in the freedmen's aid movement, sewing clothing in the North, traveling south as teachers, working as agents and officers of Northern aid societies, and distributing relief to freedpeople in the South. In addition, women sought to shape the policies of the movement and the government. In so doing, they confronted social tensions over the nature of benevolent work and women's public activism.[3]

From the moment these experiments began, reformers, the military, and government officials debated how to best assist former slaves. They discussed the wisdom of charity and the most effective means of introducing free labor values to freedpeople, grappling with their own preconceived ideas about former slaves. Male and female abolitionists, anxious to prove the capacity of African Americans for freedom, agonized over the place of direct relief in the transition to free labor. But women more frequently expressed empathy for the poverty and exploitation of former slaves. From the first experiments with freedom, a uniquely female perspective on freedmen's relief developed. Indeed, the introduction of female agents often frustrated military officials and heightened their opposition to charity, which they already viewed as unmanly. Thus, in the early stages of freedmen's aid movement, gender shaped the conflicts over freedmen's aid.

The nation was watching the Sea Islands, where reformers conducted the first experiment in emancipation. Members of Gideon's Band wanted to convince the North that former slaves could develop into productive and independent free laborers.[4] But abolitionists also had to reconcile the establishment of a successful free labor system in the South with the need to ameliorate the poverty caused by the upheaval of the war. Like other Northerners, many reformers feared that former slaves could not be independent from whites. As a result, the early reports of individual abolitionists and freedmen's aid societies contained contradictory messages of independence and dependence, free labor and humanitarian prerogatives, and antislavery egalitarianism and racial prejudice. These early tensions between charity and free labor shaped the direction of the freedmen's aid movement at the end of the war.[5]

Members of Gideon's Band hoped to demonstrate the progress of former slaves to a skeptical North. Abolitionist Edward Hooper, Edward Pierce's personal assistant, frustrated that Northerners viewed former slaves as idle paupers, wished that "some fair-minded and disinterested person" would come and "carry home a stock of correct information & who would also be believed by respectable people at the North."[6] The themes of freedpeople's industry and self-support remained central to the freedmen's aid movement. As the American Freedmen's Inquiry Commission emphasized in its final report, "Upon the whole no fear is more groundless than that the result of emancipation will be to throw the negroes as a burden upon the community."[7]

While reformers defended the independence of freedpeople, they also believed that former slaves needed a brief period of guardianship. "The more I see these people the more I think them capable to take care of themselves—to be their own masters," Hooper wrote. But he added: "They need to be educated, &, for a time, to be specially protected from money makers, whiskey sellers & bad men generally."[8] Hooper feared the consequences of freedom for a people unschooled in the Protestant work ethic or moral values such as temperance and frugality. The antislavery

Educational Commission also voiced their concern that former slaves had been conditioned to dependency by slavery: "the life of dependence which they had so long led had unfitted them, for a time, with few exceptions, for independent action on their own account."[9] Reformers concluded that former slaves required the guidance of Northerners and the government.

But Hooper and other reformers at Port Royal also worried that the relationship of former slaves to the government could potentially be disastrous to their experiment. Hooper wrote that former slaves needed every opportunity to become industrious and self-supporting, for "even a single year of idleness & eating Govt. rations would make these laborers a terrible burden to themselves & the community and would perhaps greatly defer the satisfactory social question which we now confidently hope for."[10] He presumed that freedpeople would easily slip into dependency if allowed. But in order to allay Northern concerns, Hooper wrote that "where the Government has been obliged to support destitute 'contrabands' it has issued only such portions of the army ration as were absolutely necessary to support life. No fair-minded man acquainted

Figure 1. Group of freedpeople, Cumberland Landing, Virginia, 1862 (photographed by James F. Gibson). Courtesy Library of Congress, Prints and Photographs Division, LC-B811-0383.

with the facts of the case, would say that the 'contrabands' in this Department have so far been 'a great burden' to such a Government as ours."[11]
With his eye on the North, Hooper juggled freedpeople's poverty with
his commitment to aiding the transition to free labor.

Hooper and other reformers at Port Royal viewed freedom of contract
as the ultimate right, which, combined with their racial preconceptions,
shaped their prescriptions for African American free laborers.[12] Ideally,
reformers believed that African Americans would move from wage labor
to economic independence through land ownership. Until that time, they
urged former slaves to support themselves and their families through
paid labor on Southern plantations. Reformers wanted freedpeople to
be independent, but they established an economic system that denied
them opportunities for advancement, and kept former slaves subordinate to whites.[13] In the Sea Islands, former slaves became employees of
the Northern white investors who bought up confiscated Confederate
land. As former slaves worked long hours on the cotton plantations, they
were forced to abandon their efforts at self-sufficient farming and turn
to stores established by Northern reformers for clothing and molasses,
sugar, and other staples.

Reformers saw freedpeople's independence from charity as an important outcome of emancipation, and their policies aimed to guarantee
freedpeople's self-reliance through wage labor. Susan Walker, one of the
first women at Port Royal, noted the education in free labor that work on
abandoned cotton plantations provided: "Many are well-disposed and
work willingly when made to understand that the corn, which they so willingly plant, is to furnish them food, but the cotton must also be planted
for Government and for this planting, wages will be paid them and with
their wages they must buy clothes." Though she acknowledged that former slaves had not yet achieved independence, Walker believed former
slaves had the capacity for self-support: "Some are lazy and others are
grasping. Are whites less so? I think the latter trait justifies faith in their
ability to take care of themselves, now that they are relieved of the necessity of supporting their masters' family." Walker's assessment illuminates
the antislavery perspective that blamed slavery and racial prejudice for
the panic provoked by black dependency, and she remarked upon other
signs which she thought proved African Americans' potential for "self-care
and provision for the future."[14] Both Hooper and Walker articulated the
tensions over free labor, charity, and race encompassed in the Port Royal
Experiment.

Abolitionists shaped policies that they felt would prevent pauperization and demonstrate to the North that they were teaching former slaves
the value of self-support. For example, reformers hoped to encourage
independence by selling donated cloth and clothing to former slaves, or

using it as payment, instead of giving it away. Edward Pierce instructed Port Royal missionaries that "New garments must be paid for in their labor, to cherish in them feelings of independence."[15] From Helena, Arkansas, Maria Mann, the niece of Horace Mann, explained to Northern supporters her policies regarding the selling of clothes: "I have been querying whether some persons reading that report will not see objections to the fact that a portion of the articles have been sold. I see them, did at the first, but I saw stronger ones against making free gifts of all at my disposal & greater advantages in opening a system of compensation for favors & donations."[16] Ann B. Earle of the Worcester Freedmen's Relief Society articulated this policy again in 1864. Freedpeople should, if they were able, "pay something for the clothes they have." Earle believed that "they will value the articles more will learn self reliance and will feel more self respect than if they depend entirely on charity."[17] Similarly, the American Freedmen's Inquiry Commission recommended the establishment of stores for freedpeople.[18]

Even as abolitionists worked to inculcate independence, they were also struck by the enormous poverty of freedpeople. From a contraband camp on Craney Island, in Virginia, Lucy Chase wrote, "Woe rests on her who holds the key to the store-house on Craney Island! She knows the gift and power to give are hers, and the Islanders know it also. She knows that the needy are many and the greedy and lying are more, that she may withhold where she should give; and that error in judgement may work mischief." Chase's fear of encouraging idleness was countered by the knowledge that her decision might be a life and death matter for the poorest refugees: "When one pair of shoes is in the store-room, and one hundred feet go bare, she wonders which of the fifty, will, next week, walk into her grave, because her feet are unshod:—wishes she knew today, as well as she will know then."[19] Chase's statements reveal a great demand for relief. Although Chase recognized destitution, like many reformers she also adhered to the "discourse of idleness." As she stated, "we must strive so to regulate our charities as not to educate paupers."[20]

Chase's sister, Sarah, also believed in encouraging freedpeople's self-reliance. "I always talk *self dependence* to the people, and strive to show them how to 'go alone,' & help each other."[21] As an abolitionist, Chase blamed slavery for freedpeople's dependence, but her "talks" also condescended to former slaves. Sarah resolved to stimulate industry among freedpeople so as not to encourage pauperism: "The colored people will need little help except in helping themselves. We are not going to make beggars of them. Will you please consult with your Society in regard to getting a box of straw & materials for braiding—and yarn & needles & other material for manufacture." The Chase sisters' concern with preventing freedpeople's dependency grew in part from their zeal to show the success of emancipation to a critical North. As Sarah Chase stated, freedpeople had to "prove their worthiness" of freedom.[22]

While abolitionists emphasized free labor values, however, they retained their commitment to material aid. During the Civil War, freedmen's aid societies openly acknowledged that their associations were established for the *relief* of former slaves. The members of the Barnard Freedmen's Aid Society of Dorchester, Massachusetts, believed that "To the relief of the freedmen the public are called not only by the demands of true political economy but by consideration of justice to a race which for so many years has been the victim of oppression, and by the dictates of common humanity towards brethren in need."[23] The Friends' Freedmen's Relief Association of Philadelphia was established "for the purpose of assisting in the work of relieving the wants, providing for the instruction and protecting the rights of the freedmen of the South."[24] In 1865, the Pennsylvania Freedmen's Relief Association proposed to "relieve the pressing necessities, moral and physical, of the freed people whom the progress of our armies or the policy of the Government have thrown, or may throw, upon the generosity and sense of justice of the country." The Pennsylvania association also acknowledged the pitfalls of pauperization and the realities of freedpeople's poverty. Their function was "not to degrade the black man by regarding him as a pauper; but to elevate him by acknowledging his ability to take care of himself and so treating him. We should not, of course, underestimate the present distresses of his lot. His condition should be fairly stated. It is pitiable enough without exaggeration."[25] Though reformers worried about the effects of aid on the morals and work habits of freedpeople, they did not deny that such relief was just or imperative.

Freedmen's aid reformers viewed relief as "justice," "generosity," and "necessity", but the New York National Freedmen's Relief Association (NFRA) remembered its work at Port Royal as widely unpopular: "Few heard the freedmen's sigh; few that heard it heeded it. He was regarded as a hopeless vagabond, who had no health in him, and whom it would be foolishness to attempt to aid. Some said the money would be thrown away; some said it would be worse than thrown away, for it would go to perpetuate pauperism."[26] The fear that charity had corrupted former slaves governed the opinion of most Northerners. The NFRA also reported that "one gentleman of large experience, great sagacity, and proved earnestness" wrote, "'It is my honest conviction that your efforts will do more harm than good. I feel sure that, while you will benefit individuals, you will, in the broad careless views which the world will take, exhibit a disastrous failure.'"[27] Such opposition prompted the New York society and other freedmen's aid societies to adjust their policies to emphasize free labor ideology and self-support.

The tension between relief and dependency that governed freedmen's aid societies also took its toll on individual reformers working with freedpeople. Women seemed especially sensitive to their firsthand experience with freedpeople's poverty. Maria Mann begged Northern aid societies to respond to the situation in Arkansas: "it needs an exhaustless fountain to supply these demands. No class of charitable objects ever before appealed to the benevolent, where it required so much to accomplish so little, yet it must be done for will their moral & intellectual elevation ever commence until their physical natures are improved."[28] But Mann also wrote her aunt of the difficulties involved in her position as dispenser of charity. That destitution existed was unquestionable, but Mann's dilemma was how to respond to freedpeople's destitution:

Leaving out all that constitute privation at this strange point, as not worth naming, the weight of cares incident to this unsought sphere of duty, made mine by mere fortuitous circumstance, the weightier responsibility given by the public as the work enlarged with their knowledge of it, their benevolence, placing me so closely under their lawful scrutiny, these completely destroy the little self confidence I ever possessed, when I never needed so much.[29]

Mann and other abolitionists acknowledged the need for relief but responded to Northern pressure which questioned the implications of such aid for freedpeople. As more slaves fled to the protection of Union-held areas, the controversy over dependency increased. While racial ideology continued to shape the debate over freedmen's relief, the growing presence of female freedmen's agents and teachers created new conflicts between politicians, the military, businessmen, reformers, and abolitionists. These gendered clashes centered on the problem of direct material aid.

The career of Julia A. Wilbur, freedmen's agent of the Rochester (New York) Ladies' Anti-Slavery Society (RLASS), working in Alexandria, Virginia, reveals the gendered conflict over charitable aid to freedpeople. The Rochester Society hired Wilbur as their freedmen's agent in October 1862. Despite the ongoing existence of the Port Royal Experiment and other freedmen's relief efforts, the work of a freedmen's agent, especially a female freedmen's agent, was undefined. Previously, Wilbur had taught in the Rochester public schools, so she may have planned to teach, as Charlotte Forten and Laura Towne did at Port Royal. Wilbur traveled to Washington, D.C., and made contact with prominent men in freedmen's relief, including Mr. George E. Baker of the State Department, Mr. Hamlin of the Treasury Department, and Mr. J. Van Santvoord of the Patent Office, all members of the National Freedmen's Relief Association of the District of Columbia. Van Santvoord welcomed Wilbur's assistance, proclaiming, "it seems to me that God has sent you."[30] He informed Wilbur of the situation of slave refugees in Alexandria, and recommended she go there after getting permission from the appropriate military authorities. Wilbur reported to the RLASS, "It will be a great undertaking for me to go to Alex. but I do believe the Lord will help me through it. I am undertaking much more than I expected—I had not thought of being matron or Superintendent."[31] In addition to challenging Wilbur's self-perception, her experience in Alexandria transformed the Rochester Society's understanding of women's role in Reconstruction. Both Wilbur and the members of the RLASS concluded that women provided services to former slaves that men could not. Wilbur criticized military officials, ministers, and doctors working with freedpeople for their inhumanity. She and her backers believed that women's sex especially suited them to working with freedwomen and that their virtue and morality enabled them to advocate and provide aid for the needy.

The RLASS was founded in 1851 as an antislavery society, becoming a freedmen's aid society when members turned their attention to fugitive slaves in nearby Canada. The society expressed conscious commitment to free people of color, especially through their support of *Frederick Douglass' Paper*, and members worked closely with the Douglass family as well as other free blacks in Rochester and Syracuse.[32] One of their stated goals was to bridge the divisions among abolitionists, though their close association with Douglass and his British friend, Julia Griffiths (later Crofts), shaped the society's politics. They consciously formed a female society, initially a sewing society, keeping in the bounds of social propriety, but they also sponsored speakers, held fairs, sold copies of *Autographs for Freedom*, edited by Griffiths, and communicated with antislavery societies in the British Isles and throughout New York state to raise money for their cause.[33] Wilbur and her sister-in-law Charlotte (Mrs. Theodore) Wilbur were among the founding members of the society. By October 1862, the society recognized that emancipation had opened a new field of labor for abolitionists, "comforting, cheering, advising, educating, the *freed* men, women and children." Members of the RLASS shared a commitment to aiding former slaves "in the new condition of freedom" as well as a hope that the government would meet its obligations to freedpeople. Though they expressed confidence that "Government is in *earnest* in its emancipation policy," they believed that only when the nation "has heartily turned back from the sin of slaveholding" could "the freedman have justice done him."[34] As a freedmen's agent, Wilbur acted as an intermediary between the RLASS, former slaves, and the government and military, interpreting and analyzing the progress of emancipation.

In becoming a freedmen's agent, Wilbur pushed the bounds of women's voluntary and paid labor in the Civil War era. Prior to the Civil

War, Wilbur (1815–95), a self-described "old maid," searched for a meaningful life outside of marriage.[35] Raised an Orthodox Quaker, she grew up on a farm outside Rochester. In the mid-1840s she moved to Rochester and began teaching in the city's public schools; she also joined the New York State Teachers' Association. Her experiences as an underpaid teacher shaped her commitment to women's rights. In 1857, she proposed a resolution to the New York State Teachers' Association that "the practice of paying teachers one half or one third the salaries received by men for performing the same services, is unjust and inconsistent; and that if a woman does the same work as a man, and does it as well, she should receive the same pay for doing it."[36] Wilbur embraced reform life in Rochester; in addition to her work with the Rochester Ladies' Anti-Slavery Society, she also attended lectures by well-known abolitionists and feminists. But in 1858, her independent life in Rochester was "overthrown" by family troubles, and Wilbur moved home to Avon, New York. After several difficult years of living in her father's household, Wilbur jumped at the chance to become the Rochester Society's freedmen's agent.[37] Wilbur's involvement in freedmen's relief expanded her own commitment to women's rights and set her in direct opposition to government policy toward freedpeople.

The *Annual Reports* of the Rochester Ladies' Anti-Slavery Society impart Wilbur's impressions of the state of freedmen's relief in Alexandria, where she labored until 1865. Upon her arrival in Alexandria, the provost marshal authorized Wilbur "to act as 'visitor, adviser, and instructor'" to slave refugees. Located directly across the Potomac River from Washington, Alexandria became a depot for black and white refugees. Approximately 17,000 freedpeople passed through northern Virginia during and after the war. Wilbur informed the RLASS that there were 1,500 contrabands in Alexandria when she arrived.[38] While the government provided rations and some shelter for former slaves, they desperately needed clothes and blankets. "They need everything but food," she told Anna M. C. Barnes, the secretary of the RLASS.[39] Wilbur immediately wrote to benevolent friends for "bedding and clothing," "the next thing was to ask the President of the United States to provide a suitable shelter for these people, a physician, and medical stores." From the beginning, Wilbur recognized that the government had responsibility for the condition and care of former slaves. She reported that both of her appeals were met and "the hearts of the people were opened wonderfully."[40]

Wilbur secured clothing and bedding privately from benevolent Northerners, but she needed the cooperation of the government and military to obtain appropriate shelter for former slaves. Wilbur asked the RLASS and other antislavery societies for donations of shawls, skirts, aprons, and other clothing, and directed that all contributions be sent to her in

Figure 2. Julia Wilbur (undated). Courtesy Haverford College Library, Quaker Collection, Julia Wilbur Papers, Collection 1158.

Alexandria, where she would "distribute such articles according to their needs and to the best of my ability."[41] But Wilbur's pet project was the government barracks, where the most "helpless and destitute" "would find a shelter free of expense." When the military began to rent these rooms to former slaves, Wilbur was appalled: "A good plan, perhaps, if the only object of Government was to make money out of these poor people, who have been robbed all their lives."[42] She expressed concern that families remain intact and be allowed to live "by themselves." But Wilbur also wanted to protect young women and keep them separated from the soldiers who guarded the barracks. Her plans, she feared, would be foiled by rent-hungry officials.[43]

These policies discouraged Wilbur and her supporters in Rochester. As Barnes and C. E. Marsh, president of the RLASS, noted in their 1864 report, "it has seemed, at times, that opportunities for striking effective blows for Freedom have not been embraced by the Government."[44] Wilbur stressed the state's obligations to former slaves repeatedly: "The Government of the U.S. having sanctioned the robbing of these people, not only of their earnings, but of themselves through the long years that are past, it now owes them a debt it can never repay nor can it ever repair the wrongs it has done the colored race." Wilbur hoped the government meant to pay this debt to the extent that it could, stating, "In this hour of trial the liberated slave is well entitled to assistance from the Government; and I believe the Government means to deal fairly by them."[45] But Wilbur's expectations masked her criticism of government and civilian officials working with freedpeople in Alexandria. In private letters to Barnes, Wilbur bemoaned the state of freedmen's affairs, though she retained her hope for the future. Wilbur's criticisms appeared in mild forms, and without explicit mention of individuals, in the annual reports, because as she noted herself it would have been politically inexpedient to print them. She wrote Barnes, "I should exceedingly regret to have a word go from me to counteract or lessen any good influence they may exert. So please let what I said in relation to them pass as though it had not been said."[46] But Wilbur's conflicts with officials in Alexandria dominate her letters to Barnes and clearly shaped her perceptions of policy toward former slaves, as she lamented that she was the only white woman working among former slaves in Alexandria.

Wilbur emphasized the importance of a woman's presence, especially for freedwomen: "there are women here that need woman's care & counsel & kind words." She emphasized her opposition to white men, such as the Rev. Albert Gladwin, working closely with freedwomen: "there are none but white men to care for them & minister to their most delicate necessities. I was sick. I was disgusted." She told Barnes that the white men treated freedwomen with "coarse familiarity."[47] Wilbur used her moral authority as a woman to condemn Gladwin's presence as sexually inappropriate. The minister retaliated by accusing Wilbur of violating gender roles. Wilbur reported that Gladwin said, "'I am out of my sphere, & he does not like to see a woman wear men's clothes.'"[48] She berated Gladwin for his remark, but his criticism stung. Wilbur felt alone "in a large sense of the word." She thanked the Rochester Ladies for their constant support and encouragement—"you can hardly imagine how comforting it is"—but she also had a few military officials on her side. Captain Wyman, the provost marshal, told one minister, albeit with some exaggeration, that Wilbur had "authority from the President of the U.S. to take charge of these people."[49] Wyman lost his position shortly thereafter, however, and the provost marshal who replaced him was much less supportive of Wilbur's efforts. Wilbur fought to make her ideas heard, especially when military officials and ministers like Gladwin disparaged her abilities because of her sex.

While Wilbur, Gladwin, and military officials clashed over the treatment and care of freedwomen, they also disagreed over the distribution of relief and basic military policies, including the appropriate use of the barracks to house impoverished freedpeople. Wilbur wrote to Barnes that "Mr. G. has a great quantity of sheets but he does not give many of them out, I dont understand Mr. G.'s way of doing things." Wilbur did not comprehend why Gladwin would not give out sheets, especially when former slaves were "shivering & half-naked."[50] After Wyman's removal, Gladwin found an ally in Colonel H. H. Wells, the new provost marshal. Gladwin supported the policy of renting the barracks to former slaves, and Colonel Wells agreed. Wilbur told Wells that she "'was sure neither the Pres. nor Sec. Stanton intended these buildings should be rented; they were designed for the poor & helpless & widows & children, & I thought there would be enough of these to fill them.' Said he, 'It makes no difference to me what the Pres. & Sec. S. intend, the buildings shall be rented.'" Wilbur continued to plead with Wells, however, and he finally agreed to fill the barracks with the poor and rent the rooms which were left.[51] But this did not end the dispute between Gladwin and Wilbur; Gladwin continued to try to wrest authority and living space from Wilbur's control.

Wilbur also complained of the way that Wells, Gladwin, and other officials treated former slaves. According to Wilbur, Colonel Wells had no real interest in former slaves: "He shows no more regard for the decencies & proprieties of life, nor for the wishes or comfort of those people than if they were so many horses." Wilbur suspected that Gladwin, a Baptist minister, apparently sponsored by a black church, had been a slave driver. "He has said to me several times, 'Oh! Miss Wilbur, if you had been on the plantation as much as I have & knew these people as well as I do you wd. find there is no other way to get along with them.'"[52] Gladwin continued his attempts to rent the barracks to freedpeople by over-crowding rooms with families, each of whom had to pay rent. After one of his attempts to remove impoverished freedpeople from the barracks was foiled, "Mr. G. was so angry that he slapped Amanda's little girl."[53] Wilbur's principal complaint regarding both men was their willingness to "extort every cent" from freedpeople. Wilbur believed that the bar-racks met a necessity, a basic tenet of humanity, and at times it seemed to her that every individual working with freedpeople did not live up to the task.[54] She criticized Dr. Bigelow of the freedmen's hospital for his plan to remove all orphans to the "pesthouse," which housed small pox cases. Wilbur asked Barnes, "Would you think that such an idea could enter the head of a sane, Christian man, wh. he professes to be?"[55] She expressed her frustration with the military in general in another letter to Barnes, "It has come to this, that a man who wears shoulder straps, South of the Potomac, is to me an embodiment of evil."[56] Wilbur wanted abolition-ists and true humanitarians to be responsible for freedmen's relief. In Wilbur's view, the men in Alexandria aimed less at protecting former slaves than at generating profits for themselves.

Wilbur wrote directly to the secretary of war to protest the injustices she witnessed in Alexandria. She informed Secretary Edwin M. Stanton that Colonel Wells was a person of "little experience," and she hoped Stanton would use his influence to end the policy of renting rooms at the barracks to freedpeople, "I have not thought for a moment that either yourself or the President intended to extort from the Contrabands in Alex. $17 00 a year as rent for these rude barracks." She opposed Glad-win's appointment as superintendent of freedmen, calling him "alto-gether unfit" for the position. Although she did not presume that she could become the superintendent, she wrote, "I did think of asking for the position of *Assistant Superintendent.*" She went on to describe the im-portance of women's efforts in Alexandria, concluding that women also deserved to get paid for their work: "I could do still more were I invested with a little more authority. Although a *woman* I would like an appointment with a fair salary attached to it, & I would expect to deserve a salary."[57] Though a woman, Wilbur wanted her contribution to aiding former slaves recognized and valued. She realized her request challenged the idea of woman's charitable labor as voluntary, or at least limited to the private sphere. Nevertheless, Wilbur asked for both authority and a sal-ary from the government.[58] Her experience in Alexandria pushed her to demand greater responsibility for women in freedmen's relief. But the government refused Wilbur both a salary and greater authority.

The military had a different understanding of their disagreement with Wilbur. Wells reported that on his first day as provost marshal, Wilbur visited him and "at that interview she expressed considerable interest in the subject of control or influence." Wells told her that he would receive her at any time "with great pleasure," though he was solely responsible for the "proper discharge" of caring for former slaves. Wells defended his position regarding the barracks and claimed it was "calculated to benefit the colored people. and not render them more dependent and indolent than they now are." He responded to Wilbur's charges of cruelty against Gladwin and stated that her opposition to Gladwin was caused by her desire "to have the control, and management of the contrabands." Finally, he informed the military governor, he did not intend "to be directed by her."[59]

Wells's letter demonstrates both his visceral response to a woman's demand for authority and his ideological opposition to material aid, as he implied that Wilbur's policies would only increase the indolence of freedpeople and their dependence on the government. In another letter he wrote that Wilbur "seems to labor under the belief that the chief object is to make life easy, and obtain for them the largest possible grants from the Gov't." While he respected Wilbur's "goodness of heart, and broad benevolence" he concluded she was "interfering" and "troublesome."[60] Wells's criticism linked Wilbur's gender and her charitable tendencies, and condemned both. General John P. Slough, the military governor, concurred: "It too often occurs that these ladies in a mistaken zeal act as if they would usurp the whole power of Military Governor. Such a disposition is manifested by Miss Wilbur. As auxiliary to a male superintendent her services are valuable—she has done much good and I gladly second her efforts but must be permitted to prevent her attempts at encroachment."[61] Both Wells and Slough opposed giving a woman any power over contraband affairs in Alexandria. They were offended by Wilbur's violation of traditional gender categories through her work and her aggressiveness, but they also found her ideas about aid to former slaves, which she considered humane, indulgent and destructive.

The Rochester Ladies' Anti-Slavery Society supported Wilbur throughout her struggle with Wells, Slough, and Gladwin, printing her response to their accusations in the 1864 *Annual Report.* "It has been said that my only object is to see that the contrabands have an easy time, and in this light I have been *mis*represented to the War Department," Wilbur wrote. She defended herself by stating that she did support "teaching the liberated slaves to rely upon themselves," but that she would not "turn a deaf ear to their necessities and ignore their rights entirely."[62] She rebuked the men currently in charge of freedpeople, hoping that when Congress passed a Freedmen's Bureau bill they would stipulate that "Men appointed to take charge of the interests of the freedmen should believe in the capabilities of the colored race; they should be true philanthropists and honest withal."[63] Wilbur also defended Alexandria freedpeople from charges of "dependence" and "indolence." She reported that government required men and women to work two months before receiving any pay and that five dollars per month was deducted from the wages of the men as taxes to pay the expenses of the sick and destitute. The deduction paid all the expenses that the government incurred in Alexandria, so that Wilbur did not even view the Colored Hospital as charity. She emphasized that freedpeople were not dependent on the government: "Many of the Freed people have never received any assistance from Government. They have sustained themselves wholly and are justly proud of doing so."[64] But, she wrote, "It seems to me that the newcomers, and such as are disabled for a time, and the sick who are not fit subjects for the hospital, should receive rations until they have a chance to keep themselves." Wilbur criticized military officials for blindly fighting dependence: "Now, if cutting off or withholding rations is done to make it appear they are not needed it is a gross deception."[65] Despite the accusations against her, Wilbur concluded to fight on: "The situation of the Freedmen is so peculiar that many difficulties must be encountered in their struggle to live as becomes a free people. I hope I never shall be found adding one iota to their burdens, and I mean never to cease speaking in their behalf until they are in a situation to speak for themselves."[66]

Wilbur presumed to speak for freedpeople, positioning herself as their protector. But her patronage was less racial condescension than recognition of the poverty of freedpeople. This fact was suggested by her alliance with Harriet Jacobs (c.1813–97), the author of *Incidents in the Life of a Slave Girl*, who arrived in Alexandria in January 1863. At first the relationship was rocky, as Wilbur's insecurities and the racial politics of the RLASS stimulated a brief rivalry between them.

Initially, Wilbur was suspicious of Jacobs, who arrived armed with a letter from Benjamin Latham, a New York City Quaker, appointing Jacobs matron and authorizing her to distribute clothing and other items the New York Society sent to refugees in Alexandria. An addendum to the letter stated: "She [Jacobs] is to keep record of the names of all persons & list the articles furnished to them to prevent fraud or mistakes." Wilbur expressed her outrage over this letter to Barnes: "I dont know how this strikes *thee* but it struck *me* very unpleasantly. It seems almost like an insult to us."[67] Although Wilbur expressed her confidence in Jacobs's abilities, she thought that both Jacobs and Latham had an unrealistic perception of freedmen's relief in Alexandria. As she explained to Barnes, "We have but one room for the things, & that is not half large enough. We cannot spread them out & it is a great deal of work to look over a pile of things every time an article is wanted.—& to keep an account of every article wh. is given out, wd. take the whole time of one person. As far as we can we satisfy ourselves that persons are needy & deserving before we give them anything, & then give what is adapted to their wants if we have it. Nothing further has been required of me by those who have sent goods to me."[68] Wilbur was affronted by Latham's assault on her integrity and judgment, especially when she felt that she was the only honest reformer in Alexandria. But for Wilbur there was more at stake than freedmen's welfare, her position as a woman with authority was also in question. As she stated to Barnes, "I mean it shall be felt that mine is a respectable & honorable business."[69] Wilbur's solitary struggle had become a central part of her identity as a freedmen's agent and Jacobs's arrival threatened her position. The directions of Jacobs's sponsors also called into question her methods and achievements.

Race also figured into Wilbur's anxieties, as Julia Griffiths Crofts pressured the RLASS to send an African American woman to Alexandria. Wilbur had personal difficulties with Crofts in Rochester, stemming from philosophical differences and competition over elected offices in the society.[70] Soon after Wilbur informed Barnes about Jacobs's arrival in Alexandria, Crofts wrote Barnes criticizing the society's decision not to hire a black woman as a freedmen's agent. The RLASS considered sending Rosetta Douglass, daughter of Frederick Douglass, to Alexandria as a teacher, but Wilbur asked them to wait until the conflict with Gladwin and Wells subsided. Crofts expressed her concern: "I know so fully how nearly every thing American is dyed in *"prejudice against color,"* & how it permeates even *the best* of American Anti-Slavery Societies, that I feared lest rejection had been on account of color." Barnes had apparently speculated that Douglass's race would limit her abilities to aid former slaves. Crofts condemned this notion: "I cannot my friend, agree with you in what you say of Miss Wilbur going where no colored woman can go—& doing what no colored woman can do!!" Crofts did not doubt Wilbur's ability, but for her it was a matter of principle: "A *colored* woman should have had the *opportunity* before any one ventured to say, she could not do!!—My views are strong on this subject—& I feel they are the right views. If you send a second teacher, *pray try & find* a suitable colored woman—The New York "friends" have sent the *right* person in Harriet Jacobs."[71] Crofts's letter suggested that Jacobs was more qualified than Wilbur to aid former slaves, further contributing to Wilbur's insecurity over her position in Alexandria.

The Rochester Society never hired another agent, however, and the initial reservations Wilbur held about Jacobs's presence disappeared as their ideas about material aid and the military coincided. Wilbur and Jacobs lived and worked together, developing a consistent policy on freedmen's relief and providing each other with moral support in the face of Gladwin's and Wells's hostility. Although Wilbur resisted the intrusive directions of the New York Quakers, she quickly came around to Jacobs's method of selling clothing to freedpeople. At first Wilbur opposed the idea of selling clothes and informed her patron Emily Howland that she should send contributions directly to her: "After this I mean to distribute myself all the goods that are sent to me. Mrs. Jacobs has given out a great deal within the last few days. Some she gives away & some she sells for a low price. The N.Y. Friends desire her to do so. This morning Mr. G. said that 'no more of the Phil'a things must be given away,' so my operations are confined to what is sent expressly to me."[72] But soon she informed the Rochester Society that she had adopted Mrs. Jacobs's approach: "At first we could not have pursued this method, and indeed I did not like the idea of selling to these people. But after they began to get pay for their work they were willing and able to pay a small price for what was of use to them, and they valued it more for having done so, and I concluded it was best for them to learn the value of things as soon as possible."[73] In fact, Wilbur was overwhelmed with the success of her "business": "I have never taken in so much money in one day, & perhaps never shall again . . . how could I anticipate such an *extensive business?*"[74] Wilbur and Jacobs took control over rooms in the barracks where they conducted their "business," cared for orphans, and taught sewing to freedwomen. While they faced constant harassment from Gladwin, Wilbur found Jacobs's support gave her additional strength in her battle against him.

Together Wilbur and Jacobs fought the army's policies toward former slaves. Jacobs convinced General Slough to let them hire a woman to take care of orphans at the barracks and temporarily halted Dr. Bigelow's plan to place orphans in the pesthouse. Before a visit to Colonel Wells, Wilbur and Jacobs "composed ourselves & agreed not to cry if we could help it" and managed to win some temporary concessions from the provost marshal. Wilbur praised Jacobs "decision of character" in the face of their trials as they tried to prevent Gladwin from taking over every room in the barracks.[75] Part of Gladwin's strategy involved sending impoverished freedpeople to the camp in Arlington so he could rent the remaining rooms. When Wilbur returned home for a summer visit to her family in East Avon, New York, Jacobs informed her that Gladwin sent fresh refugees directly on to Washington, so they would not take up room in the barracks. Lucinda, the freedwoman whom Wilbur and Jacobs hired to take care of orphans, also reported that Gladwin had shipped forty refugees from the barracks to Arlington, managing to separate some families in the process. Jacobs's solution was to cut off all rations to freedpeople in the barracks so they would not be considered dependent on government. Lucinda and other freedpeople agreed with this strategy, as Lucinda stated "'I dont want the rations if they will let me alone.'"[76] Both Wilbur and Jacobs kept hoping that influential Northerners would exert enough pressure to remove Gladwin from his position, but his support from Wells and Slough ensured his place.[77] Discouraged, both Jacobs and Wilbur eventually left Alexandria. Jacobs brought her daughter, Louisa, to Virginia to teach in a school bought and paid for by former slaves, but Jacobs informed Wilbur that she would not return to Alexandria after the summer of 1864.[78] Wilbur moved to Washington, where she boarded in the rooms of the Pennsylvania Freedmen's Relief Association and worked as a visitor for the newly established Freedmen's Bureau.

While Wilbur did not achieve her desire for "control" and "management" of slave refugees, she, the Rochester Ladies' Anti-Slavery Society, and Harriet Jacobs forced the government to confront the moral and economic problems posed by emancipation. What was the government's obligation to destitute freedpeople? How should former slaves be treated? Wilbur and Jacobs offered a radical alternative to the emancipation policies of military officials in Alexandria. Though they responded to pressures for freedpeople's self-support, the presence of abolitionist women throughout the South kept the issue of the care and treatment of former slaves in the nation's view.

These early experiments in freedom revealed tensions that continued to divide the freedmen's aid movement: the problem of dependency and the role of women. The end of the war prompted a debate over the goals and organization of the freedmen's aid movement. As freedmen's aid societies regrouped, they retreated both from their commitment to direct relief and from the women who advocated it. As a result, the new organizations marginalized women's efforts, forcing women to find new ways of influencing freedmen's aid policies.

Chapter 2

The Freedmen's Aid Movement Reorganized

When Julia Wilbur left Alexandria, she wrote Maria G. Porter, treasurer of the Rochester Ladies' Anti-Slavery Society, that there were "so many teachers & missionaries in Alex. that things are getting quite mixed up."[1] As the number of reformers and aid societies working with former slaves increased and diversified, abolitionists and government authorities moved to systematize their efforts at the end of the Civil War, pushing women's ideas to the periphery of the movement. In 1863, the federal government established the American Freedmen's Inquiry Commission (AFIC) to investigate the best way for the government to respond to full-scale emancipation. Soon after, a cohort of abolitionist men moved to unite freedmen's aid societies under a national commission on freedmen's relief, supplementing and advising government efforts.

Male reformers in the AFIC and the new umbrella organization, the American Freedmen's Union Commission, shared a vision of Reconstruction based on free labor principles, and they viewed women as obstacles to this vision. Neither commission saw direct relief as advisable, instead emphasizing wage work, education, and legal and political equality. The AFIC ignored women's recommendations for continued aid to former slaves, while the American Freedmen's Union Commission excluded women from leadership positions in their organization. Abolitionist women faced a choice: work under male leadership or set off on their own. Many abolitionist women chose the latter course, including Sallie Holley and Caroline Putnam.

After touring the South and conducting numerous interviews with freedmen's aid reformers, the American Freedmen's Inquiry Commission, composed of prominent Republican reformers Samuel Gridley Howe, Robert Dale Owen, and James McKaye, recommended the creation of the Bureau of Refugees, Freedmen, and Abandoned Lands, an agency one scholar has called "an early example of Federal participation in public welfare."[2] But the conclusions of the Inquiry Commission did not lead to a clear-cut recommendation for relief to former slaves. Rather, as Eric Foner points out, the Commission's recommendations "reflected the tension between laissez-faire and interventionist approaches to the aftermath of emancipation." The Commission called for a Bureau of Emancipation but also advised that African Americans become self-reliant as quickly as possible.[3] The contradictory elements in the AFIC's proposals reflected the political and gendered divisions of those they interviewed.

The questionnaires distributed by the AFIC reveal Northerners' concern with freedpeople's potential dependence. The letter introducing the questionnaire stated that the Inquiry Commission was interested in placing "the Colored People of the United States in a condition of self-support and self-defense," and asked that the readers share their expertise. Questions included: "Are the colored people generally industrious and self-supporting, or not?" "Do the mulattoes seek public charity in greater or less proportion than whites?" "Do you consider them, upon the whole, as valuable members of the community, or not?" Files show that some respondents had a decidedly negative opinion of freedpeople's ability to support themselves. One gentleman from Pittsfield, Massachusetts, responded that the colored people in his community were not generally industrious and self-supporting, that mulattoes were more likely than whites to seek public charity, and that he did not consider colored people valuable members of the community.[4]

Other respondents, typically those who supported the freedmen's cause, defended freedpeople's industriousness. S. G. Wright of Oberlin, Ohio, wrote that while freedpeople had frequently been treated horribly by military officers, they were not discouraged. In response to the question "If they could receive fair pay, would or would not those able and willing to work earn enough to support the whole?" he wrote, "They would lay up money I am sure." Francis George Shaw, president of the National Freedmen's Relief Association of New York and father of Robert Gould Shaw, fallen commander of the Fifty-Fourth Massachusetts regiment, wrote that blacks were "generally industrious and self-supporting" and were on public support "in less proportion" than whites.[5] Vincent Colyer, the former superintendent of the Department of North Carolina, wrote to the AFIC that former slaves were "peaceable, orderly, cleanly, & industrious." While the men had worked diligently for the army, the "women and children supported themselves with but little aid from the government by washing, ironing, cooking, making pies, cakes &c." Finally, Colyer concluded that former slaves were less likely than poor whites to call on the government for assistance. Poor whites, in his view, wanted "*sixteen* times as much" as the poor blacks.[6]

Most testimony advised that less involvement by Northern aid societies and equality before the law could solve any potential problems of dependency. Samuel Gridley Howe wrote that "the negro does best when left alone, and that we must beware of all attempts to prolong his servitude, even under the pretext of taking care of him."[7] Edward Hooper recommended to the Emancipation League, the predecessor to the AFIC, that "equal laws faithfully administered would enable the negroes to take their place in society, as a laboring class, with a fair prospect of self-support and progress."[8] Both Howe and Hooper believed that Northern benevolence and government aid presented a danger to African Americans. They argued that legal and political equality offered African American free laborers sufficient protection as they worked their way up in American society.

The American Freedmen's Inquiry Commission asked a few prominent women their opinion on government involvement in emancipation, and for the most part women's responses reflected the same concerns as the men, concerns that may have been driven by the questions posed by the Commission. Women simultaneously worried that charity would pauperize former slaves, while they defended freedpeople's industriousness. Lucy Chase commented that the freedpeople were "really becoming educated paupers; the greediest and most persistent beggars that could be imagined. One's moral courage was put to the severest test by going among them. I could not walk from the house to the office without being beset by a clamoring crowd." But Chase also wrote that the freedpeople "were clamorous for work."[9] When asked if freedpeople demonstrated industry, Laura Towne, a teacher at Port Royal, responded, "Yes; [they are] a very industrious people." But when asked if the people had much self-reliance, she answered "Not near as much as white men." Towne also noted one thing, land, that she believed would make the freedpeople independent: "I am very anxious that the land should get into their hands. That, more than anything else, will make them a self-relying and self-respecting people."[10] Towne was not the only one to recognize the importance of land ownership to freedpeople's independence, and the sale and rental of confiscated Confederate lands became part of the first Freedmen's Bureau bill in 1865. But the distribution of confiscated land to freedpeople was undermined by politics and Northern investors. Although reformers recognized that land ownership was the solution to many problems posed by emancipation, few had the financial resources to make land ownership a real possibility for freedpeople.[11]

Mrs. Daniel Breed of Washington, D.C., wife of the superintendent of the city's public schools for African American children, also emphasized the self-reliance of freedpeople. When asked to compare them to impoverished whites, Mrs. Breed rated freedpeople favorably: "I have never known any white people so poor and wretched as these. Yet I think they compare favorably with the poorer classes of white people in respect to morality, religion and general behavior. Those who have come out of slavery and are supporting themselves I believe to be superior to the corresponding class of whites." When asked about begging and vagrancy among blacks, she responded: "I have never known but two instances of beggary by colored people during my residence of 10 years in this city." Finally, Mrs. Breed believed that the former slaves needed no preparations for free labor: "All they want is the work to do and they are ready to do it."[12] Mrs. Breed's testimony emphasized the progress and potential of former slaves, a position which reflected her family's long-standing commitment to black education. While the Commission focused its questions on freedpeople's capacity for work or pauperism, the language of free labor and independence pervaded all areas of the freedmen's aid movement, including education. Breed and other women adopted this language to raise support for former slaves.

But the testimony of women to the AFIC also revealed another, more benevolent, approach to Reconstruction in women's relief work among former slaves. The Ladies' Contraband Relief Society of St. Louis had been laboring for the benefit of freedpeople along the Mississippi River since January 1863, "with the special object of relieving the physical wants of the contrabands." Society members explained their work to the Commission before giving their recommendation. They had given $500 toward a church, a schoolhouse, and a shelter for the contrabands on island No. 10. In addition, the women collected $5,000 in cash for boxes of clothing and supplies. The Contraband Relief Society served a large number of former slaves: "A great many urgent requests come from below, and the need seemed to be greatest in and about Vicksburg. The probability was they would suffer more this winter than last. There were at least 100,000 on the river between St. Louis and Vicksburg who were in suffering condition. These sufferers were mostly women and children whose husbands and fathers had in many cases entered the Union Army." The Society was also involved in sending some of these contrabands to Iowa and other Northern states.[13] The members of the Ladies' Contraband Relief Society focused on the needs of former slaves uprooted by the war.

The report of the Ladies' Contraband Relief Society emphasized that former slaves needed aid: "We have no doubt of the necessity of some provision being made for the care and support of these people, especially the women and children. The condition of the country from which they come has been such, for two years, that when they arrive here they are utterly destitute."[14] Although they were concerned with all refugee freedpeople, the women paid special attention to the needs of freedwomen and children. Early in the freedmen's aid movement, women reformers empathized with the plight of freedwomen and their children, showing a gendered understanding of dependence. Northern white women's interest in the plight of freedwomen and their children would remain a strong theme in women's activism in the movement.[15]

But the humanitarian efforts of the Ladies' Contraband Relief Society were largely disregarded by the male-dominated AFIC. The Inquiry Commission concluded that beyond the "certain number of indigent poor, disabled or improvident, to whom it is custom and duty to extend relief," "the Commission believe that the refugee freedmen need no charitable assistance."[16] The AFIC's conclusions reflected the dominant, and somewhat optimistic, view of reformers in the early years of the freedmen's aid movement:

The sum of our recommendation is this: Offer the freedmen temporary aid and counsel until they become a little accustomed to their new sphere of life; secure them, by law, their just rights of person and property; relieve them, by fair and equal administration of justice, from the depressing influence of disgraceful prejudice; above all, guard them against the virtual restoration of slavery in any form, under any pretext, and then let them take care of themselves.[17]

The AFIC's recommendations demonstrated male reformers' faith in the equalizing potential of the market economy and the legal system. With the establishment of a temporary Freedmen's Bureau, and the implementation of a laissez-faire program for emancipation, the policies of the government diverged from the interests of women working on behalf of former slaves.

While the AFIC concluded that former slaves needed only limited government guardianship, and not relief, women lobbied for a different sort of Freedmen's Bureau. These reformers drew on their experiences in the antislavery movement and on women's involvement in benevolent reform. The Ladies' Contraband Relief Society of St. Louis was one example of this strain of thought in freedmen's aid; another was Josephine Griffing, an Ohio abolitionist, feminist, and freedmen's aid activist. Suffragists hailed Griffing as the originator of the Freedmen's Bureau, "that great national charity," for her lobbying efforts: "Few cared to listen to the details of the necessity, and it was only through Mrs. Griffing's brave and unwearied efforts that the plan was accepted."[18] As described in the *History of Woman Suffrage*, Griffing's "career was ever marked with deeds of kindness and charity to the oppressed of every class."[19] In a letter to William Lloyd Garrison, Griffing articulated her ideas for the Freedmen's Bureau. In Griffing's view, the Freedmen's Bureau would be the basis for a "new & purer system of Politics," which would include the participation of women. Griffing wanted a man to head the Freedmen's Bureau who was "fully committed to give us *women* what we do so much need in the *Gov.*—in *Commissions* to carry forward the work of Relief to the Freedmen which he sees to be *our* work *legitimately*." Griffing saw freedmen's relief as women's work and "of great importance to the Freedmen, Women, and the country."[20] She viewed the

Freedmen's Bureau as an opportunity for women to participate more actively in the political life of the nation. By broadening women's sphere and aiding former slaves, Griffing's plan could benefit both white women and African Americans.

Many others shared Griffing's commitment to women's involvement in Reconstruction, and in the Freedmen's Bureau specifically. Julia Wilbur instructed Anna Barnes to send copies of the Rochester Society's annual reports to all members of the American Freedmen's Inquiry Commission, hoping they would get the important message that women's influence was needed among former slaves.[21] Emma V. Brown, a free black woman who became one of the first teachers in the segregated public school system in Washington, D.C., declared, "I don't think women have ever before had so glorious an opportunity to do something—They have always been such insignificant creatures—so dependent." Acknowledging the importance of women's efforts and the Freedmen's Bureau, she wrote, "Miss Perkins and I have a little Freedmen's Bureau of our own."[22] Laura Towne also believed that women could "do good service to the blacks," hoping to repay the debt that the nation owed former slaves: "I have always longed for some opportunity to make amends to the colored people for what wrongs have been done them by our nation, as far as I can if ever so little; and my whole life seems to have been fitting me for the work of instructing these negroes."[23] While Towne referred specifically to teaching, her message of atonement suggests that she too conceived of material aid to former slaves as justice rather than charity. It was the nation's fault that freedpeople emerged from slavery impoverished and dependent, so it was the nation's responsibility to care for them until they could support themselves. Abolitionist women reminded Americans that dependency was not a racial characteristic, but the result of the nation's exploitation of unfree labor.

In the minds of most Americans, however, the success of emancipation depended upon the immediate self-sufficiency of former slaves. The Educational Commission saw this as the lesson learned at the Sea Islands: "The results of the experiment at Port Royal may be looked upon as entirely successful in demonstrating the capacity of the freedmen for self-support in their condition of freedom."[24] As a result, freedpeople's destitution provoked an intellectual crisis among the members of freedmen's aid societies and offices of the Freedmen's Bureau after the end of the Civil War.[25] Although the laissez-faire approach to emancipation dominated Reconstruction politics and reform, a cadre of women demanded that the government alleviate poverty through direct material aid to freedpeople.

Groups like the Rochester Ladies' Anti-Slavery Society, the Ladies' Contraband Relief Society, and female reformers like Griffing, Brown, and Towne labored against the shifting priorities of the freedmen's aid movement and the nation at large, which denied women any role in making policy. Women faced further marginalization as the freedmen's aid movement reorganized and shifted its focus to education, rather than relief or land ownership, relegating most women to subordinate positions.

At the end of the Civil War, the formation of the American Freedmen's Union Commission (AFUC) weakened women's position within the freedmen's aid movement. One group of abolitionists, led by J. Miller McKim, formed the Freedmen's Commission to oversee and manage the work of secular freedmen's aid societies, such as the New England Freedmen's Aid Society, formerly the Educational Commission, and the National Freedmen's Relief Association of New York. McKim's efforts were part of a larger movement among members of the American Anti-Slavery Society (AASS) to rethink their political goals following emancipation. Some abolitionists chose to retire, others left the AASS in order to devote themselves to assisting freedpeople. These developments upset many abolitionists, who wanted the AASS to continue as the premier advocacy group for former slaves.[26] In addition, McKim's new organization proved less friendly to female leadership than the American Anti-Slavery Society. While some abolitionist women remained affiliated with the AFUC's branch societies, others, such as Sallie Holley and Caroline Putnam, chose to work outside the confines of the organized freedmen's aid movement.

In 1865, McKim, formerly an agent of the Pennsylvania Anti-Slavery Society and founder of the Pennsylvania Freedmen's Relief Association, called for a unified and independent freedmen's aid movement, but his ideas stimulated dissension among abolitionists. Reformers had attempted to unify their movement several times previously. In December 1863, five freedmen's aid societies, including the National Freedmen's Relief Association of New York, the Educational Commission of Boston, the Pennsylvania Relief Association, the Western Freedmen's Aid Commission of Cincinnati, and the Northwestern Freedmen's Aid Commission of Chicago, formed the American Freedmen's Aid Commission. The purpose of this organization was "to aid, more efficiently, in supplying the immediate and pressing physical wants of the Freed people; in providing for them homes and employment; in organizing them into communities; and in furnishing them with instructions as their case demands, to prepare them for the privileges and duties of Christian Freemen."[27] In 1865, leaders such as McKim believed a reunited movement might assist and advise the Freedmen's Bureau. The prospect of a new umbrella movement, however, provoked debate about the nature of the movement itself. What would be its primary purpose? The members of the New England Freedmen's Aid Society (NEFAS), concerned with the effects of centralization on their society, initially opposed the formation of a new umbrella organization. As William Lloyd Garrison, representing the NEFAS, wrote to McKim, "It is not understood how the Commission is called for by any exigencies connected with the Freedmen's cause."[28] Yet McKim and others believed that the freedmen's aid movement needed a single legitimate representative, which might lobby the government and influence Reconstruction policy.

McKim's vision had broad implications for the freedmen's aid movement. In December 1865, the American Freedmen's Aid Union (the successor to the American Freedmen's Aid Commission) joined with the American Union Commission, a Republican organization devoted to aiding Southern white refugees, to create the American Freedmen's Union Commission. With this union, the movement transformed itself from a freedmen's aid movement into a movement for the "people of the south, without distinction of race or color." The AFUC's goals were "the improvement of their [the people of the South] condition upon the basis of industry, education, freedom, and Christian morality."[29] While the original Freedmen's Aid Commission mentioned the physical needs of freedpeople in its plan of action, the new American Freedmen's Union Commission highlighted industry and education, making no mention of destitution or unemployment.[30] The new Commission also demanded centralization, under an all-male executive board, which meant affiliated societies would have less flexibility in policymaking and distribution of money and goods collected for freedpeople.

The members of the New England Society resisted these changes. Already reluctant about their alliance with the AFUC, individual members of the NEFAS, including abolitionist Hannah Stevenson, resigned over the proposed Commission. Before the Civil War, Hannah E. Stevenson (c. 1807–87) had been the personal assistant to Theodore Parker, a radical Unitarian minister and abolitionist.[31] After serving as a Union army nurse in Washington, D.C., she helped found the Educational Commission, later the New England Freedmen's Aid Society. As chair of the Committee on Teachers at the time when the New England Society agreed to affiliate with the new Commission, Stevenson wrote to Ednah Dow Cheney, her successor, that she wanted her name stricken from the society's members because she thought they should devote themselves to freedpeople. Stevenson argued that the New England Society should engage in "resolute, vigorous work for the colored people, & them *only*."[32] Stevenson's comments revealed a wariness of associating with a Commission that was not solely concerned with freedpeople. As an abolitionist, Stevenson felt that the movement's primary goal should be to serve as caretakers of former slaves.

Stevenson's decision also reflected her unstated resentment at the all male leadership of the new commission. The AFUC had no female officers, even though its two largest branch societies, the New York National Freedmen's Relief Association (NFRA) and the New England Society had substantial female membership. The AFUC also relied on the financial support of local freedmen's aid societies, many of which were dominated by women. The officers of the AFUC included the Rev. Lyman Abbott as general secretary, McKim as corresponding secretary, George Cabot Ward as treasurer, and Francis George Shaw as chair of the Executive Committee. The Executive Committee consisted of male members of branch societies.

Eventually women gained leadership roles in local associations. Though the women in the New York branch were initially confined to the Ladies' Committee on Correspondence and Organization, a continuation of the Women's Central Relief Association of the Sanitary Commission, by 1869 two women, Ellen Collins and Josephine Shaw Lowell, managed the entire association.[33] Even so, they did not hold executive positions. In the New England Society, women had always held important offices. In 1866, Ednah Dow Cheney was a member of the Executive Committee, and women sat on the Committees on Teachers, Clothing and Supplies, and Finance. By 1868, the Committee on Correspondence also had a woman member, while seven women served as vice presidents. The New England Society's greater acceptance of women's leadership was a legacy of the antislavery movement. Though the more conservative New York abolitionists were wary of women's public activism, Boston abolitionists had been strong supporters of women's rights. Inspired by William Lloyd Garrison, both the American Anti-Slavery and New England Anti-Slavery Societies had allowed women in leadership positions since 1839.[34]

Abolitionist men, particularly members of the American Anti-Slavery Society, had been strong supporters of women's rights, so the establishment of a male-dominated freedmen's aid commission surprised abolitionist women. Yet the structure of the American Freedmen's Union Commission indicates the transformation in American reform brought about by the Civil War. Abolitionist men entered the war years as political outsiders, whose participation in the antislavery movement, and support for women's rights, unmanned them in the eyes of Northern society. With emancipation, abolitionists gained new political respectability. In addition, they no longer had to abjure the U.S. Constitution and the political process as tainted by slavery. McKim and the male abolitionists who formed the American Freedmen's Union Commission now saw politics, law, and the state, male spheres, as the means to accomplish their goals. As their methods and philosophy became tied to the state and Republican politics, women became a hindrance. Close cooperation with female abolitionists threatened to feminize freedmen's aid, just as abolitionist men wanted to masculinize American reform.[35]

Indeed, abolitionist-feminists perceived the significance of the lack of women among the Commission's leadership. Lucretia Mott wrote her sister, Martha Coffin Wright, that she berated her good friend McKim for excluding women from the AFUC: "I told him it was objected, that woman was ignored in their new organizn., & if it really were a reconstructn. for the nation, she ought not so to be—and it wd. be rather 'a come down' for our anti-slavery women and Quaker women to consent to be thus overlooked." Like male reformers, Mott and other abolitionist-feminists also saw the state as a vehicle for reform following the Civil War. But she believed that the American political system, without the participation of women, retained the same flaws as when the Constitution protected slavery. Without women's equality, the nation could not live up to its democratic promise. Instead of joining the Philadelphia branch of McKim's organization, Mott remained affiliated with the American Anti-Slavery Society as well as the Philadelphia Female Anti-Slavery Society. She continued to participate in the organized women's rights movement, and she joined a Quaker freedmen's aid society, the Friends Association for the Aid and Elevation of the Freedmen. Her postwar allegiance to antislavery and women's rights undoubtedly had to do with the exclusion of women, "one half the Nation," from leadership positions in the AFUC.[36]

Two other prominent abolitionist women also declined to join the new Commission, first remaining affiliated with American Anti-Slavery Society, and, after its dissolution, becoming independent reformers. Sallie Holley (1818–93) and Caroline Putnam (1828–1917) were among the only agents who continued to raise funds to support the American Anti-Slavery Society and its newspaper, the *National Anti-Slavery Standard*, after 1865. When the AASS disbanded, Holley joined Putnam at a freedmen's school in Lottsburg, Virginia, where they remained for the rest of their lives. The independent activism of Holley and Putnam affirmed women's authority in freedmen's aid, as they connected their work for former slaves to their rights as women.

Both women entered freedmen's aid after a career in antislavery and women's rights. Sallie Holley was an abolitionist by birth as the daughter of Myron Holley, a well-known antislavery politician from Rochester, New York. His influence on Sallie extended beyond abolitionism to his individualist liberal religion. His daughter wrote, "He utterly repudiated popular theology. He thought it unscriptural, irrational, and demoralising, and that it deplorably hindered the coming of the kingdom of Heaven upon earth." Sallie Holley would later draw on her own conversion to

Unitarianism to convert her audiences to antislavery principles.[37] Holley met Caroline Putnam at Oberlin College in 1848, where they were both outsiders because of their radical Garrisonian abolitionism. As the elder and more dominant partner in the friendship, Holley influenced Putnam on women's rights and Unitarianism (Putnam had been raised a Presbyterian).[38]

At Oberlin, both women learned the challenges of financial independence. Holley relied on the support of friends, including Gerrit Smith, to help cover the costs of her education. But Oberlin's administrators believed in the value of manual labor, and the female students sewed, washed, ironed, cooked, and cleaned to contribute to their education. Putnam described Holley's scramble to support herself at Oberlin, in which she washed dishes and baked bread, worked as a nanny for one professor's children, sewed buttonholes for another professor, and tutored other students, "getting for such work from three to twelve cents an hour, and paying a dollar a week for board and twelve and a half cents a week for lodging."[39] These experiences stayed with the women for the rest of their lives. They remained single and supported themselves through their work for the American Anti-Slavery Society and at the Lottsburg school, but they also relied on the contributions of benevolent supporters in both positions. Holley and Putnam recognized women's tenuous hold on independence, and viewed the debate over freedpeople's "dependence" in this light.

While at Oberlin, Holley and Putnam began attending antislavery and women's rights meetings. The "momentous, the decisive convention" of their careers was in Litchfield, Ohio, in 1850 at an antislavery meeting organized by Josephine Griffing. At this convention, Holley and Putnam met Abby Kelley Foster who immediately recruited Holley to become an agent of the American Anti-Slavery Society when she graduated in 1851.[40] Shortly after Holley commenced her career as a lecturer, Putnam began traveling with her and selling abolitionist tracts and subscriptions to the *Liberator* and the *National Anti-Slavery Standard*.[41]

Holley reveled in her antislavery work, seeing it as a natural expression of her gender. She wrote Putnam of "the duty of anti-slavery women to keep informed as to the progress and mode of the anti-slavery reform in our nation, to be ready to counteract the pernicious influences of such speeches as Clay's and Webster's on the plastic minds of all our young men and women." In addition to keeping abreast of political developments, Holley believed in women's moral influence on American society and culture and felt called to lecture publicly despite the "stigma" she faced when former friends crossed the street in order to avoid her. By August 1851, Holley calculated that she had delivered 156 antislavery lectures. She regularly lectured to audiences of from 400 to 600 people.[42]

During the Civil War, both Holley and Putnam took some much-needed time off from their careers, but they remained aware that emancipation had changed their mission. Like other Northern women, Holley and Putnam began by collecting clothing to send to former slaves in the South: "I have been begging warm, woollen clothing for the 'contrabands' from these farmers and have had the satisfaction of sending a large box to those destitute ones of God's poor."[43] But in 1865, Holley and Putnam chose to remain agents of the AASS rather than join the freedmen's aid movement. Holley believed that the work of antislavery societies would be needed until African Americans achieved equality and justice: "The American Anti-Slavery Society is the only Society in this broad land, amid thirty-millions of people—that demands unfalteringly, a guaranteed equal liberty, equal justice for the black race! The *only* movement devoted to this highest work of Christian patriotism!" She criticized abolitionists who had joined the freedmen's aid movement rather than remaining in the American Anti-Slavery Society. She asked those who questioned the continued necessity of the AASS, "are you afraid the black people will have *too many* friends, *too much* justice, *too much* liberty?"[44]

When Holley and Putnam reemerged into public life at the end of the Civil War, they did not initially take up teaching, relief work, or any of the usual avenues followed by abolitionist women after emancipation. Instead, Holley believed it her calling to demand justice for former slaves. She wrote to Emily Howland, a Quaker active in freedmen's relief and education, to compare her mission to that of other women who worked with former slaves: "We rejoice in all your good works of patience and loving hope among the Freed people, and I should engage in it myself, only that I believe and our New England Anti-slavery friends assure me, that my *special mission*, is to protest against prejudice of color and work on the conscience of people here in the North, to complete this great work of justice for the colored people everywhere."[45] During the immediate postwar years, Holley repeatedly told Northern audiences that suffrage was necessary to "complete" the emancipation of former slaves.

Like other women in the freedmen's aid movement, Holley worked on the conscience of the North, demanding repentance for the sin of slavery. But she and other members of the American Anti-Slavery Society were hard-pressed to convince the public that a nation that had abolished slavery still needed an antislavery society. In 1870, after the passage of the Fifteenth Amendment granting African American men the right to vote, the AASS disbanded. Holley bitterly opposed the end of the Society's work: "the American Nation is not good enough to be trusted with the care of the black race. The blacks still need their long-tried and faithful friends of the American Anti-Slavery Society, which is a very different individual from the Nation."[46] Writing from the South regarding the possible demise of the *National Anti-Slavery Standard*, Putnam agreed: "I could weep and wail to have THE STANDARD stop now! For it is a shield to us, and its continual appearance does give character to the *cause* of *Justice* to the black man that is felt even in this obscure corner of Virginia."[47] Both women felt that the nation had failed in its duty to former slaves, and they carried on the work of the American Anti-Slavery Society on their own.

Holley and Putnam turned to the most common, traditional, and available option open to women in Reconstruction: teaching in freedmen's schools. But unlike most Yankee schoolmarms, they did so without the direction or guidance of the Freedmen's Commission, the American Missionary Association, or any of the other Northern societies who recruited teachers and sent them to the South. Caroline Putnam moved to Virginia in 1868 to establish a school for freedpeople in Lottsburg. She was encouraged to do this by her friend Emily Howland, who had established a similar school in nearby Heathsville. Holley also supported her decision, reminding her that "Emily wants you to work and teach among her people in Virginia. She thinks you would be an admirable person to go."[48] Putnam named the school in honor of her friend, the Holley School. Holley joined Putnam there in 1869, a move that was "the natural continuation of her anti-slavery work."[49]

As was the case with many teachers, Putnam and Holley became the intermediaries between the Northern public and Southern freedpeople, raising awareness of the situation of former slaves in the South. The *National Anti-Slavery Standard* called Putnam the "Prudence Crandall of Virginia," after the Connecticut schoolteacher who had been driven out of the state for allowing black children to attend her school, and the *Standard* regularly printed her letters to maintain interest in the cause.[50] Putnam kept readers involved by returning in each letter to stories of specific freedpeople, such as Alfarata Blackwell, the twelve-year-old daughter of Glasgow Blackwell, who came to Putnam to learn to read, and Mr. Steptoe Ball, a freedman who prayed for land: "Give us this day some land, where we can stay, without fear of being turned off at any minute, and earn in cheerful contentment our daily bread!"[51] Putnam's letters also contained her assessment of politics and racism in Virginia as well as pleas for donations.

Teachers bore significant responsibility for the students and the freedpeople living in the vicinity of the school.[52] When Alfarata first came to Putnam's school, Putnam and Howland decided she was too thin and Putnam wrote Holley: "Have I said plain enough that Alfarata's wardrobe will be gratefully welcome from the North—any pieces of it you can beg will be needed." Putnam described her other students as "poor, little, bare-foot, thin clad children."[53] Winter made it especially difficult for freedpeople who were already overcoming tremendous obstacles to get their education. Putnam wrote, "I am beginning to feel with the coming frosts that the benevolent helpers of the Freedmen among your readers, cannot be spared an appeal to their sympathies, for more warm clothing to keep these little ones tolerably comfortable in their long walks to the school. Four little girls have come *five miles* (from Cherry Point) to-day, and it is damp and raining, and they must suffer severely with their insufficient wrapping and poor shoes."[54] Putnam gratefully accepted boxes of clothing shipped from Massachusetts, Connecticut, Rhode Island, New York, and Pennsylvania, and made no mention in her letters of dependency among freedpeople. She blamed Southern racism and Northern betrayal for freedpeople's poverty, and she tried to convince her Northern allies of this fact.

Putnam berated Republican politicians and newspapers like the *New York Tribune* for failing to protect freedpeople from the "Rebels" who, she wrote, were "seeking to clutch power again with every advantage given to them by Government to crush out loyalty and murder and despoil the Freedmen and their friends." She strongly believed that it was too soon to allow Virginia back into the Union and described those who supported readmission as "heartless and witless." She feared for the fate of freedpeople's schools if put under the authority of Virginia: "our schools will be broken up, if the State is so admitted, and all this valuable preparation of ground for the education of all who will come be *lost*! Does nobody care? And is there no remedy? How basely we have been betrayed by the *Republicans*! These poor Freedmen!"[55] Her sense of betrayal mirrored freedpeople's, as they had hoped for land from the government and protection from the Freedmen's Bureau.

Like many of their peers, Putnam and Holley believed that freedpeople needed land and economic independence from whites to truly achieve equality. When Putnam informed Steptoe Ball that the Freedmen's Bureau would close, "the look of being forsaken suddenly came on him, that was pitiful to see. *'Who then is going to see justice done us now?'*" With the bureau still in operation, freedpeople could continue to hope that the government would help them to own land, "the great desideratum." Putnam wished that her letters would "move some benevolent heart to engage instantly in this thorough mode of reconstruction, as *Government failed* of its golden opportunity to possess the Freedmen of his well-earned right of 'a spot of ground to stand on as his own.'"[56] Putnam noted that without land or some form of economic independence, freedmen could "never have the real freedom of their *vote*," but would instead be at the mercy of white employers intent on influencing their ballot.[57] Holley also commented on the government's failure: "I think it was dreadfully mean and disgraceful in the United States Government not to give some land to those poor negroes who had worked all their lifetime without wages."[58] She believed that the distribution of land to former slaves was only just—reparation for centuries of work without pay. Both women continually reminded abolitionists and the nation of their duty to former slaves.

Through their work at the Lottsburg school, Putnam and Holley also sustained "the dignity of women," demonstrating women's authority in the sphere of racial justice and benevolent reform.[59] As self-appointed spokespersons for former slaves, they constructed their identity as independent women based on their knowledge of the condition of freedpeople in the South. While their position as independent women was in many ways based on the neediness of former slaves, they reminded the nation that dependency was a reality for both women and former slaves. Unlike the schools established by the American Freedmen's Union Commission and its branch societies, the Holley school was "a free school,—no tuition exacted,—and we have no salary."[60] Thus Holley and Putnam relied on "interested and large-hearted people" to continue their mission. Contributors to the school included Gerrit Smith and his daughter, Elizabeth Smith Miller, Emily Howland, Mrs. Francis George Shaw, Boston abolitionist Sarah H. Southwick, Louisa May Alcott and her mother, Abba Alcott, Miss Ellen Emerson, Ellen Collins, and Senator George F. Hoar.[61] Holley and Putnam held positions of power relative to former slaves, but their economic situation was markedly similar to freedpeople's.

Holley and Putnam deliberately chose independence from the freedmen's aid movement, rejecting women's subordinate position in the organized societies. In doing so, they also ignored the Reconstruction policies advocated by the American Freedmen's Union Commission and their branch societies. They believed that as abolitionist women they had a contribution to make to Reconstruction. Holley and Putnam remained committed to women's rights, but they did not take a stand on woman suffrage during Reconstruction, choosing to support suffrage for African American men and participate in Republican politics in Virginia.[62] They continued to connect their status as women to the rights of African Americans. Putnam ran the school until her death in 1917, when it was placed under the authority of the local white school board.[63]

As antislavery women, working independently of the freedmen's aid movement, Holley and Putnam remained involved in freedmen's schools and Reconstruction far longer than Republican politicians, the government, or the abolitionists and reformers who formed the American Freedmen's Union Commission. In all those years, Holley and Putnam stayed focused on rights and justice for former slaves. They believed that the nation had not yet paid its debt to former slaves, and they criticized the federal government for abandoning freedpeople to the South. Like other antislavery women, they viewed the proposals of the American Freedmen's Inquiry Commission as incomplete without a strong Freedmen's Bureau and the full participation of women.

Abolitionist women also disdained the leadership offered by McKim, Lyman Abbott, Francis George Shaw, and the American Freedmen's Union Commission. Nevertheless, many continued to work in the branch societies of the AFUC as administrators and teachers. Women in branch societies largely embraced the educational mission of the Freedmen's Commission, but they found themselves engaged in a struggle over gender and postwar reform with the male leaders of the Commission.

Chapter 3

Women and the American Freedmen's Union Commission

Though denied executive positions in the American Freedmen's Union Commission (AFUC), many antislavery women worked under its auspices. Before the war's end, these white, middle-class women had formed freedmen's aid societies that made up the core of the AFUC. Rejecting the radical choices of Holley, Putnam, Wilbur, and Jacobs, they remained in the North, a decision that consigned them to a subordinate but still powerful role in the freedmen's aid movement. In assuming the daily work of freedmen's aid societies, including correspondence with teachers and fund raising, branch women had direct contact with Commission leaders and members, allowing them some influence over policy. These women attempted to reshape the AFUC along moral and gendered lines.

Historians view freedmen's aid as an educational crusade, but its mission did not become purely educational without struggle, or without larger implications for the movement as a whole. The American Freedmen's Union Commission abandoned relief in favor of education as part of the transformation of the freedmen's aid movement at the end of the war, linking the male leadership of the AFUC to the Republican party and the national government. But the shift to education also offered a gendered compromise with women in the branch societies. Male and female reformers engaged in arguments over policy and style that contained assumptions about gender roles and sexual difference, even as branch women threw their energies into hiring teachers and overseeing the establishment of freedmen's schools. Though women conceded to many of the liberal policies of the Commission, their continued dedication to women's political culture helped keep the freedmen's aid movement alive in the face of public indifference and the threat of political obsolescence.[1]

Despite the continued need for relief to the destitute, establishing a system of public education in the South became the central aim of the freedmen's aid movement. Education had long been an important component of freedmen's aid, but AFUC leaders increasingly concluded that public education was the foundation of Northern society, and the corner-stone of free labor ideology, a view shared by Radical Republicans and the Freedmen's Bureau. As a result, Republicans included public educa-tion as a necessary prerequisite for the readmission of Southern states to the Union. The AFUC faced problems in implementing a public educa-tion system in the South, however, as they confronted the tenuous com-mitment of Northerners and the intransigence of white Southerners. Ultimately, they relied on the ideal of African American independence to explain their withdrawal from the South.

The New York National Freedmen's Relief Association (NFRA) noted the shift away from direct relief in its Fifth Annual Report: "It will be noticed that our movement, which was at first largely one of physical relief, has passed through that stage of its existence, and is fast becom-ing an education enterprise, pure and simple."[2] The NFRA emphasized the educational aspects of the movement and distanced themselves from charity. They prioritized education because of their faith in freedpeo-ple's economic progress, but also because they viewed direct assistance as morally suspect.

J. Miller McKim, a Garrisonian abolitionist and founder of the Amer-ican Freedmen's Union Commission, described freedmen's education as a matter of national significance. In 1867, he reflected, "What was the freedman's movement? Not a mere benevolent association; nor an alms-giving enterprise; not a great National charity. It was a reconstructive movement. Conceived in philanthropy and the love of justice, it was car-ried on in the interest of civilization and religion, social order and en-during organization."[3] Though he acknowledged the AFUC's ties to the antislavery movement, McKim viewed his organization as part of the political mainstream. He clearly distinguished the Commission's admin-istrative and educational work from "mere" charity, denigrating benevo-lence while highlighting the AFUC's larger contribution to reconstructing the South.

In defining their purpose, the leaders of the American Freedmen's Union Commission also sought to differentiate themselves from their competitors in freedmen's education. The powerful American Mission-ary Association, an evangelical society formed prior to the Civil War, threatened the Commission's status as the umbrella organization of the freedmen's aid movement. The AFUC and the AMA competed for con-trol of schools and struggled over the type of education to be offered in the South.[4] For example, unlike the AMA, the AFUC favored the estab-lishment of a common school system, without formal religious affiliation. In an article published in the *American Freedman*, the AFUC's newspaper, Lyman Abbott and other members of a special committee on religion and education concluded:

It is necessary that we should draw with some precision the lines which separate the work of the ecclesiastical from that of the philanthropic associations, and determine whether acting through denominational agencies we will content ourselves with such parochial schools as they may establish, or whether, assigning to them that more district missionary work which is quite sufficient to absorb all their energies, we will combine in one national and unsectarian organization for the establishment in the Southern states of that common school system which is the glory and safety of our country.[5]

The AFUC leadership hoped this mission would allow it to become a nationally recognized association, working closely with the federal government.

Rather than attaining national importance, the American Freedmen's Union Commission suffered a swift decline. At the beginning of 1867, the AFUC announced its support for the establishment of free schools and equal rights for black and white Southerners: "The proper termination of our charity will come when the Southern States shall have formed governments upon the basis of equal rights, civil and political, and shall have put in actual operation free schools for all."[6] But the AFUC failed to establish a system of public education in the South that included African Americans, and the Commission was the first freedmen's aid society to fold in 1869. Its branch societies also closed, though the New England Freedmen's Aid Society lasted until 1876.

Financial difficulties contributed to the early demise of the AFUC and its subsidiaries. The American Freedmen's Union Commission and other aid societies faced serious problems in raising money for freedmen's schools. Contributions to aid societies declined steadily after 1866. While aid societies had been able to raise almost $400,000 a year during 1865–66, by 1869 secular aid societies could barely raise $100,000 a year.[7] As early as October 24, 1866, Hannah Stevenson, Ednah Dow Cheney, John Parkman, and other members of the New England Society contacted Edward Atkinson regarding the sorry state of their treasury. Hoping to get money from Atkinson, one of their founders, the reformers wrote: "We wish to inform you the financial condition of this society. It is simply this. Our treasury is now $12,500 in debt, of which our Treasurer has advanced $3000 on his own responsibility. Our monthly expenses average at least $4000 per month." The Committee on Teachers threatened to resign unless they could guarantee payment to their teachers, but were reluctant to do so: "We should regret exceedingly to offer our resignation, as the work was never more important, or more interesting, but the situation requires instant action."[8]

Education failed to make freedmen's aid the popular cause Commission leaders envisioned. This unpopularity had two principle sources. First, many Northerners believed that the funding and management of common schools was the responsibility of Southern states. Second, the racial prejudices of Northerners led them to question the advantages of supporting freedmen's schools. Combining their fear of black dependency and disapproval of charity, Northern whites separated themselves from the problems created by the destruction of slavery. They believed that once freed, African Americans should take care of themselves.[9]

Freedmen's aid societies faced an additional drop in revenue when the Freedmen's Bureau closed, a gradual process that began in 1868 and ended in 1872. Aid societies depended on the bureau for most expenses other than teachers' salaries, including the rent of schoolhouses and the transportation of teachers to the South. In 1868, Ednah Dow Cheney of the New England Freedmen's Aid Society expressed her anxiety over the demise of the Freedmen's Bureau: "I suppose we are all safe if the Bureau is continued, but what if it is not? Is there any prospect that the Bureau will not be continued?"[10] Ellen Collins, of the New York National Freedmen's Relief Association, wrote to General Oliver Otis Howard, commissioner of the Freedmen's Bureau, to inquire how much financial assistance her society could expect: "We have sent thus far only fifty teachers, instead of one hundred & twenty of last year, and it will be quite out of our power to do as much as we did then, though with your help we can do much better than now. This is a point of great moment. Please tell us what we can count upon."[11] Collins and Cheney feared that without the aid of the Freedmen's Bureau, their schools might close. Their concerns were also personal, as their identities as reformers depended on the Freedmen's Bureau and black education.

The male leaders of the American Freedmen's Union Commission ended their work before the Freedmen's Bureau, however, believing that the new state constitutions in the South provided for African American schools. The AFUC alerted its supporters to this "effort on our part to secure more universal cooperation in the South," and promised that the current need for contributions was only temporary.[12] But the AFUC's assessment of the political situation in the South was flawed. Teachers working in the South realized that the states did not intend to support freedmen's schools. As late as 1871, Cornelia Hancock wrote to the Friends Association for the Aid and Elevation of the Freedmen, in Philadelphia, that she had "less faith now than last year that the State governments will act conscientiously toward the colored people, in opening schools for them, and therefore cannot hope these schools will be supported by aid other than yours."[13] Hancock predicted a bleak future for universal public education once Northern aid societies and the Freedmen's Bureau withdrew.

As the American Freedmen's Union Commission ran low on funds, and Southern states demurred, the responsibility for schools fell increasingly upon freedpeople themselves. Rather than citing financial or political reasons, reformers justified this shift as part of the urgent need to "teach" freedpeople to be self-reliant. After hearing of self-supporting freedpeople's schools in Texas, Ellen Collins, of the New York Society, wrote to McKim that "It seems to me the point of throwing the burden of this work in part on the colored people, cannot be too much urged."[14] Although aid societies had always required some form of fee from freedpeople when they could afford it, in 1867 Northern societies asked freedpeople to contribute a portion of the teacher's salary and buy their books.[15]

Freedmen's aid societies began preferring normal schools to common schools, seeking to create a class of African American teachers and further promote freedpeople's support of their schools. Normal schools trained "native" (African American) teachers, a necessity given declining interest in the North. Although there was always a steady supply of Northern white women willing to teach in freedmen's schools, aid societies could no longer raise the funds to cover their salaries. African American teachers received less pay, so reformers relied on this discriminatory system to make education more affordable for Southern communities. As the Friends Freedmen's Relief Association of Philadelphia reported to John Alvord, superintendent of schools for the Freedmen's Bureau, "warned by indications of waning interest in Freedmen's affairs," they "endeavored at the principal centres to institute Normal classes that from among the colored people themselves teachers may be supplied." The Friends Association also encouraged "the establishment of Associations among them [the freedpeople] for the purpose of providing means for paying for the education of their children themselves."[16] John Alvord noted that the shift to freedpeople's self-support of schools was both necessary and desirable. He wrote, "some popular plan is needed by which this aid shall be co-operative with the efforts of the freedmen, and which shall gradually teach them to be self-sufficient."[17] Aid societies withdrew out of necessity, but they justified their decision by claiming to advance freedpeople's self-reliance, applying free labor values to their assessment of African American education.

Though the American Freedmen's Union Commission announced that the conclusion of their educational work was "visibly at hand" at the end of 1868, Alvord's reports on schools in indicated otherwise.[18] His report for July 1868 demonstrated that freedpeople were indeed contributing a large share to the support of schools in the South. Of a total of 1,831 schools under control of the Freedmen's Bureau, freedpeople sustained 867 in part and 458 wholly. Freedpeople paid more than $95,860 in tuition in the first six months of 1868. But between July 1867 and July 1868, freedpeople contributed $360,000 toward their schools out of a total of $2,002,523 spent on schools all together, or approximately 18 percent. As much as freedpeople were contributing, they were nowhere near financing a school system on their own.[19]

Although certain communities of freedpeople established and funded their own schools, poverty and the opposition of white Southerners hindered universal public education in the South. Alvord, as superintendent of education for the Freedmen's Bureau, was in a particular position to recognize these problems. He praised freedpeople for founding and supporting their own schools, but Alvord also pleaded with the Northern aid societies to stay involved and published evidence in his reports of white opposition to freedmen's schools and freedpeople's poverty.[20] In Alvord's *Ninth Semi-Annual Report,* E. L. Rice reported from North Carolina that "to suspend or curtail the educational work already commenced would be a public calamity." Edward L. Deane wrote from South Carolina that Southern states refused responsibility for public education: "The whites will not interest themselves in behalf of common schools, and it must for years remain the duty of the northern benevolent societies and individuals to continue the aid they have heretofore so liberally granted to the support of graded and normal schools." From Texas, the state that Ellen Collins had admired for freedpeople's support of schools, Major James McCleery wrote that the States should not have responsibility for black education for another decade. "Make the education of the freedmen for the next ten years a national matter, and at the end of that time they will be able to secure their rights through the respective States in which they live. But now they have but little chance."[21]

But in July 1869, as it ceased operations, the Commission touted its achievements. First, it claimed to have unified the freedmen's aid movement. Second, leaders of the AFUC believed they had established a rudimentary public school system, stating, "the foundations will already have been laid. The skeleton of an educational system will already be there, waiting only to be filled up."[22] Significantly, the AFUC attributed its end not to financial problems or the reconstruction of Southern states, but to "the capacity of the emancipated and enfranchised blacks to take care of themselves."[23]

As the freedmen's aid movement withdrew support for freedmen's schools, societies advised freedpeople to help themselves. In the 1870 report of the Philadelphia Friends Association for the Aid and Elevation of the Freedmen, members informed freedpeople that "the time is not far distant when you must take care of yourselves, and if you do not now as well as then, make the best of everything at your command, much suffering will be your portion." For these reformers, self-help was not only a matter of survival for freedpeople, but a means to gain more support in the North by fighting the stereotype of their dependency: "By leading lives of industry, both for yourselves and for your children, you will gradually obtain the respect of your white brethren, who will feel more obliged to lend you a helping hand than if they saw you idle and dissolute."[24] But reformers failed to challenge the image of freedpeople as "idle and dissolute" and, as a result, to convince the North that continued assistance to freedmen's schools was vital to public education in the South.

The American Freedmen's Union Commission failed to become the "reconstructive movement" of "enduring organization" that McKim envisioned, but women in the movement remained committed to freedmen's aid. They challenged the policies and goals of the AFUC, using the familiar language of abolitionism and women's reform. In doing so, they aroused the disapproval of their male coworkers who sought to distinguished their benevolence from women's work of direct aid and service.

The freedmen's aid movement relied upon an established network of female reformers, explicitly calling upon their womanly empathy. Freedmen's aid societies solicited Northern women, who had been members of antislavery, soldier's aid, or other benevolent societies, to raise money for freedmen's relief. Ellen Collins, a former member of the Executive Committee for the Woman's Central Relief Association of the Sanitary Commission, asked Sanitary Commission branches to continue their labors for freedpeople:

The great strength of the Sanitary Commission lay in the earnest women scattered throughout the land who gave their money & their labor to comfort and bless the poor soldier. That was truly a labor of love. We feel that this new object has not the same hold upon the popular sympathies, and we are doubly anxious to secure your cooperation, that the subject may be earnestly and fully presented to the Aid Societies, and the necessity for prompt & liberal action pressed upon their notice.[25]

Similarly, the Women's Central Branch of the Pennsylvania Freedmen's Relief Association appealed to the "good women" in their state to "do for us what they did for the United States Sanitary and Christian Commissions" and "form sewing circles, and canvass their districts or churches for subscriptions."[26]

Women mobilized to provide both education and material aid to former slaves. As the John A. Andrew Freedmen's Friend Society of Boston reported to Ednah Dow Cheney, they began their work in the winter of 1863–64 when "a young lady who had been working hard for the Sanitary Commission, ever since the war began, proposed to some of her friends, who had allowances at their disposal, that they should join her in subscribing one or two dollars, or at least, half-a-dollar, every month;

hoping before long, to collect enough to send a teacher to the freed-men." They intended to supply their teacher with "books, clothing, &c., &c., for the freedmen under her charge." Hannah Stevenson of the New England Freedmen's Aid Society met with members of the Freed-men's Friend Society and encouraged them in their goal of contributing $300 a year toward the education of former slaves. At the first meeting, thirteen were present, and by 1867 the Society boasted almost eighty members. Miss E. C. Putnam informed Cheney that the society's success was due to the letters they received from their two teachers, Louise Fisher and Harriet Smith: "I have not yet told you how much we have enjoyed the letters from our teachers. The more incidents they relate, the more nearly we are brought to their field of labor."[27] Such letters transported Northern women to the front lines of the freedmen's aid movement and reinforced their sympathy for former slaves.

Women formed freedmen's aid societies after hearing of the condition of former slaves in new black population centers like Washington, D.C., and Alexandria, Virginia. During the war, former slaves fled to cities like Washington, which abolished slavery in 1862. Many freedpeople found employment and lodging in the city, but others ended up in military camps. Lucretia Mott wrote her sister, Martha Coffin Wright, in December 1862: "The Washn. & Alexria. freedmen are now claimg. attentn." and reported that she had been to a meeting of a freedmen's aid society (probably Miller McKim's Philadelphia Port Royal Relief Committee) where she found, "some 30 or 40 sewg. away 2 or 3 machines going—Several boxes have been sent." The Association also prepared to send the Heacock sisters as teachers to Port Royal.[28] Two years later, Mott noted similar efforts: "The Race St. [Quaker Meeting] Sewg. Socy. have made up & forwarded 7000 garments—As many thousd. dollars have been placed at their disposal—Our new Assocn. handed them $1200 last wk—."[29] Similar societies formed all over the country. In 1863, the Rochester Ladies' Anti-Slavery Society turned their attention to "a new field of labor," and the Society reported that they had sent "articles as could be made useful to these people" to their agent Julia Wilbur in Alexandria, and money and clothing to a freedmen's school in Kansas.[30]

While the Philadelphia Quaker freedmen's aid societies and the Rochester Ladies' Anti-Slavery Society remained independent, societies like the New England Freedmen's Aid Society and the Women's Branch of the Pennsylvania Freedmen's Relief Association affiliated with the AFUC. Many women, like Hannah Stevenson, did not go willingly into this association. Stevenson opposed the centralization of the freedmen's aid movement and the new goals of the AFUC, but she also resented the disfranchisement of antislavery women. In a letter to Mr. May, probably Samuel May, Jr., president of the Leicester, Massachusetts, Freedmen's

Aid Society, Stevenson described her reaction to the Commission: "the N. E. Soc. was false to its trusts from branch societies, recklessly gave up its independent individual existence to merge itself as a branch in a 'commission', where four secretaries receive salaries, & where NE is represented by 2 members to New York by 12." The two representatives of the New England Society (probably John Parkman and Wendell Phillips Garrison), she wrote, knew "very little of the work of this society."[31] Stevenson disapproved of paying four male secretaries, rather than using that money for teachers' salaries or textbooks, especially when women's voluntary labor was devalued. Compounding the insult of unequal and all-male representation, she believed that women's expertise had been slighted: "The statements of ladies who for 3 years have been an honor to New England by their great and successful labors for the Freedmen, outweigh, in my mind, the loose remarks of Mr. Abbott."[32] Stevenson, an abolitionist, particularly objected to Lyman Abbott, the new general secretary of the AFUC, and founder of the Union Commission, a man who defined himself in opposition to radicals. As he wrote in his memoirs: "I have been an evolutionist, but not a Darwinian; a Liberal, but not an Agnostic; an Anti-slavery man, but not an Abolitionist; a temperance man, but not a Prohibitionist; an Industrial Democrat, but not a Socialist."[33] Although Stevenson initially resigned in protest, her commitment to her work with the Committee on Teachers brought her back, at least until the end of 1866.

In those months when she did serve on the New England Branch's Committee on Teachers, Stevenson clashed with McKim over the rules for teachers sponsored by AFUC branch societies. On July 6, 1866, McKim wrote Stevenson that he and Octavius B. Frothingham, a Unitarian minister and chairman of the Committee on Teachers for the New York National Freedmen's Relief Association, had examined the instructions to teachers and "adopted most of it, making such modifications as seemed to us expedient."[34] Stevenson had been appointed to draw up these instructions, and she was incensed. On July 16, she informed McKim that the New England Committee on Teachers had unanimously rejected his modifications: "The relations between this comm. & its Teachers is peculiar & delicate & not expressed by the tone of your letter. Phila. approves ours." Stevenson also slyly inquired why McKim had encroached upon the prerogatives of the branch societies, insulting the AFUC in the process: "Why! I had no idea you were Chairman of the comm. in the N. Y. Soc. Till this last communication, Mr. Frothingham we supposed to be so; and we accounted you as one of the Head Centres of the great invisible Amalgamation Commission."[35]

Stevenson used the word amalgamation, a synonym for miscegenation, to protest McKim's decision to ally with Abbott and the Union

Commission. Typically used against abolitionists and Radical Republicans by Democrats seeking to arouse the fears of white voters, Stevenson inverted the racist meaning of the term. She viewed the united Freedmen's Commission as diluting the abolitionist and feminist politics of the New England Society. Stevenson wanted to employ the North's resources, including women's voluntary work, to help former slaves, not ex-Confederates. To Stevenson, amalgamation was not the mixing of white women and African American men, but the combination of radicals and moderates, united to aid both white and black Southerners.

Stevenson objected to the style and the goals of the American Freedmen's Union Commission. In her view, the salaried male secretaries of the Commission did none of the work and stepped in only where they were not wanted, violating the "tone of feeling of this [New England] comm. and its teachers." Though she apologized to McKim for using the "heated term" amalgamation and attacking his "pet union," Stevenson eventually resigned permanently from the New England Freedmen's Aid Society, entrusting the Committee on Teachers to her friend Ednah Dow Cheney.[36] While Stevenson disagreed with almost everything about the American Freedmen's Union Commission, however, she did agree with its focus on education.

But not all women in the freedmen's aid movement viewed education as a sufficient means of aiding former slaves, and these women turned to traditionally gendered methods of invoking sympathy to encourage donations. While men emphasized the necessity of assisting freedpeople to become self-reliant, women stressed the desperate situation of former slaves. As Mary Mann, the wife of Horace Mann, wrote to Edward L. Pierce, she had "spent myself a good deal in trying to beg for the present relief of the immediate misery of nakedness & homelessness & I was quite struck with the fact that the meager details of my niece's letters opened the golden streams so readily." Mann instructed Pierce that he could "aid the work of the new Commission more than you think possible by giving all the romance of the thing."[37]

But because of the pressure for self-support, male reformers no longer felt it was wise to portray freedpeople's "nakedness & homelessness." Judge Hugh L. Bond of the Baltimore Association rejected such dramatic appeals on behalf of freedpeople. He wrote to the Pennsylvania Freedmen's Relief Association that "the great cause, however, of immediate emancipation is in danger from indiscreet friends, and no dread of local distress should cause us to hesitate to point out that danger." The danger to which Bond referred was the practice "of presenting strong pictures of physical distress" in order to raise funds. He stressed that the immediate freedom of 87,000 slaves in Maryland had not led to an increase of crime or pauperism.[38]

The American Freedmen's Union Commission, adhering to Judge Bond's advice, pressured its branch societies to reject traditional forms of benevolence and emphasize independence, a move which cost the AFUC its female base. When Northern societies cut back their material and financial support for relief work, women reformers working with freedpeople in the South protested. Mrs. Martha Canfield of the Memphis Colored Orphan Asylum wrote the Rev. J. M. Walden, head of the Western Freedmen's Aid Commission, to complain when Jacob R. Shipherd refused to fund the asylum's activities after promising Mrs. Canfield their patronage. In defense of her request for funds, Mrs. Canfield stated:

Our asylum was located in a part of the city which was easy of access and the sick and destitute among the freedmen and often refugees came to us for aid, we were never without some of that class in the house. We also endeavored as far as possible to care for the sick in the neighborhood. It was not intended that the asylum do this work, but under the circumstances it could not well do otherwise. . . . Mr. Shipherd knew all this when he asked the Commission to aid us, and if he thought us so extravagant why did he encourage us?[39]

Though the men of the Western Freedmen's Aid Commission proved themselves unsympathetic sponsors, Canfield saw that material aid was still very much needed in the South and she relied on the Commission and other Northern societies for support.

Increasing emphasis on education also discouraged Northern women from working for the relief of destitute freedpeople. For example, in June 1866 the Women's Branch of the Pennsylvania Freedmen's Relief Association announced that "The demand for clothing has now almost ceased" and "it is most earnestly urged upon aid societies and those who have worked zealously to provide for the temporal wants of the colored race, that education is now the great desideratum." The leaders of the Women's Branch hoped that their female constituents would support the shift to education: "Several of the ladies officially associated with the 'Branch,' have gone in company with Dr. Parrish, to visit the schools established by this association in the South. We doubt not that they will return fully inspired, and to help inspire others to work as enthusiastically for education, as all have worked during the winter for relief of physical want."[40] But by January 1867, the leaders of the Women's Branch realized this shift was a mistake. Mary Rose Smith stated that they no longer had enough money or supplies to send to freedpeople because their auxiliary societies had broken up and the sewing circles had stopped meeting. Although many Northern women sponsored teachers or traveled South as teachers themselves, other women clearly preferred aiding freedpeople through the more traditional sewing circle.

Figure 3. Sea Island School No. 1, St. Helena Island, sponsored by the Pennsylvania branch of the American Freedmen's Union Commission, ca. 1865–1870. Courtesy Library of Congress, Prints and Photographs Division, LC-USZ62-107754.

The AFUC's message of education and self-reliance did not arouse the interest of benevolent women in the Pennsylvania Branch.[41]

Yet women in the AFUC employed a variety of strategies to combat declining interest in the North. They recognized that Northern opinion turned on the perception that freedpeople were dependent on whites in part because of their benevolence.[42] Miss Elizabeth P. Breck, a teacher in South Carolina, wrote her sponsors of her fears that just such thinking would cause Northerners to quit their freedmen's aid activities. "I trust the northern people will not become weary and relax their efforts in behalf of the freedmen, with the idea that enough has been done and it is now time for them to take care of themselves."[43] In their messages to the North, Breck and other teachers balanced their own commitment to freedpeople's independence and Northern demands for black self-sufficiency against the real and continuing needs of former slaves.[44]

As women made freedmen's aid their vocation, pleas for money to help freedpeople became increasingly personal. Breck was sponsored by the Northampton, Massachusetts, Freedmen's Aid Society, founded in 1862, with James C. Ward as president, Miss M. A. Cochran as secretary, and William Endicott as treasurer. As secretary, Cochran took on much of the correspondence of the Society, including correspondence with its parent association, the New England Freedmen's Aid Society. In October 1864, Hannah Stevenson of NEFAS and Breck pressed the Northampton Society to come up with sufficient funds to send Breck to Mitchellville, South Carolina. On October 8, Stevenson wrote Breck: "I send you the letter to say that we intend to provide at once for Mitchellville what they need so sorely, ie Teachers and a house for the Teachers to live in. Will Northampton feel able so to increase its action as to undertake to raise the funds for building such a house? The estimated cost is $250, but probably it would be more, say $300." Stevenson asked Breck to consult with Miss Cochran and Mr. Ward as soon as possible because "if not successful at Northampton I must be a beggar elsewhere."[45] But several days later Northampton agreed, and Stevenson wrote: "Three cheers for Northampton!"[46]

Stevenson repeatedly referred to herself as a "beggar," suggesting her appreciation of her own dependence on the continued support of other aid societies. "My only business with the money is to be a bold beggar for the Treasury," she wrote Miss Cochran, and praised the Northampton Society for its benevolence: "Your praise has gone far & wide; Northampton steps at once into the foremost rank of Freedmen's Aids'; and we trust you will see much results from this noble effort as will entirely satisfy the generous givers."[47] Such personal appeals stressing the interdependence of teachers, reformers, freedpeople, and the members of aid societies, remained effective when women served as officials. Stevenson referred to this relationship as the "tone of feeling" between the New England Society and its auxiliaries. When McKim rewrote the rules for teachers, he violated these bonds between women reformers.

Because a teacher's ability to remain in the South depended on her relationship with her branch, teachers used their correspondence to encourage continued support from sponsors. Breck went to teach in Mitchellville, South Carolina, in October 1864. She filled her letters to the Northampton society with local color. Breck alternately described the great need of the freedpeople and her appreciation of the clothes and supplies the Northampton society sent her, and the progress that freedpeople were making. The first strategy appealed to Northampton's humanitarianism, the second to their contribution to the independence of freedpeople. Breck's letters also established her expertise on the needs of former slaves, and she urged the Northampton society to rely on her authority.[48]

Breck's first reports back gave a favorable impression of the self-reliance of freedpeople. "They seem to be an industrious people, doing all in their power to maintain their families," she wrote. This letter emphasized freedpeople's self-support:

There are in this village for the colored 456 houses already completed and 22 now in the process of erection with one third of an acre on each lot. About one half the houses have been built at the expense of the government. The inhabitants are constantly increasing, as we learn by a census recently taken that we have 273 colored people here, all of whom support themselves, with the exception of about 100 infirm ones, whom the government furnish with rations.[49]

As refugees from Georgia poured into the town and another winter approached, however, Breck appealed to Northampton's pity, "The clothing is of far more value than you can conceive, and I could dispose of any amount of it, for there are many needy ones here, and I fear there must be a great deal of suffering among them during the coming winter, as it will be impossible for all to obtain employment."[50] Breck pointed out that specific circumstances such as new refugees and winter weather led to the need for Northern donations of clothing.

Breck's letters continued to blend the themes of self-reliance and dire necessity. She asked the Northampton society to send clothing even though freedpeople were no longer desperate for them: "When they are working so hard, I know you will be glad to do everything in your power to encourage them."[51] Another letter began with religious appeals to Northampton's better natures: "Blessed is he that considereth the poor," and "May the blessings of Heaven descend in copious showers upon those who have so promptly responded to my appeal for aid in behalf of these suffering people." Breck did not stigmatize freedpeople for their poverty, instead blaming unfair labor contracts: "I will say that whatever is contributed toward supplying the physical wants of this people is according to my judgment worthily given, as they are not themselves to blame for their present destitute condition."[52] Breck emphasized her authoritative "judgment" in the face of growing Northern criticism of freedpeople's dependency. She asserted the worthiness of freedpeople and associated the current situation of former slaves with slavery, prejudice, and on-going labor exploitation.

In her last letter, Breck reverted to a style of appeal that had been used in the antislavery movement, highlighting the toll that slavery had taken on women. Antislavery appeals on behalf of enslaved women who were whipped, raped, and separated from their children had been of enormous significance in drawing white women into the antislavery movement. Breck relied on the fact that an appeal on behalf of freedwomen would also arouse her sponsors. She reported her visit to Aunt Maria, a sick and dying freedwoman who lived in a horrible shack: "She had been the mother of many children, and often had her heart been made to bleed as she had seen them tied to a post, while the lash of the slave driver was applied to their backs, and what anguish of mind had she experienced when she bade adieu to some who were sold from her to go into distant states uncertain what would be their fate." If Northampton women did not sympathize with tragic motherhood, perhaps they could identify with Eva, a beautiful quadroon, whose husband,

to whom she was devotedly attached, a handsome young man, with hardly enough African blood in his veins to have been classed with that race, suffered martyrdom in '62 with two of his companions all of whom were hung from the limb of a tree nearly opposite our church for the heinous crime of hurrahing for the yankees. So poignant was the grief of the beautiful Eva that she became almost frantic, and her nervous system received a shock from which she has not yet recovered.[53]

Breck turned Aunt Maria and Eva into stock characters from antislavery literature to encourage an emotional response from Northern women. Her concern that Northerners would end their donations to freedpeople led her to appeal more directly to the sympathies of Northern women.

Breck's description of Aunt Maria and Eva employed a common tactic, as abolitionist women used the idea of sisterhood to promote material aid. Josephine Griffing, for example, believed that freedwomen with dependents deserved relief, especially since most were self-supporting as a result of the loss of male relatives in the war. Griffing wrote that freedwomen had a right to a home and a right to keep their families together, and government and private assistance enabled these rights:

These women, the only guardians of their children, feel it to be hard, and an infringement of the right guaranteed by their late freedom, that they must again be broken up and turned over to the possibilities of becoming wanderers and vagabonds, instead of receiving the little pecuniary aid necessary to bind together the heretofore scattered family relations, which both instinct and society recognize as the first want in society, church, and state.[54]

Griffing expected other white women to respond to the plight of freed-women. Her assessment extended gendered abolitionist arguments regarding the effect of slavery on the black family to advocate aid to African American women and children.

Women in the freedmen's aid movement, many of whom supported themselves through their reform work, empathized with freedwomen's vulnerability in the labor market, but the male leaders of the American Freedmen's Union Commission and the Freedmen's Bureau generally designed their policies around a universal freed *man*. Northerners strongly encouraged freedpeople to marry and to model their family lives on the white, middle-class home life of the North. New laws and bureau regulations enforced the husband's duty to support his wife and children. The Fourteenth and Fifteenth Amendments granted political and civil rights to male citizens, expecting African American men to act as the political representatives of their female relatives. But Northern and Southern whites also viewed freedwomen as workers and believed that they should continue to work in the fields and homes of whites. Most policymakers did not attempt to reconcile the ideal of domesticity with the realities of freedwomen's lives in the plantation South because they had difficulty placing freedwomen within a framework of free labor independence or of womanly dependence.[55]

Male reformers focused on the manhood of former slaves, and the accompanying rights and responsibilities. As Jacob Shipherd wrote to General C. H. Howard, the Freedmen's Bureau's assistant commissioner for the District of Columbia, "How much wiser a charity to help a man become more manly, than barely keep alive the flesh and blood!"[56] Shipherd viewed direct relief as unmanly, but he and other male abolitionists also hoped to establish the rights of freedmen based on their manhood, not their race. McKim wrote to William Lloyd Garrison that "We can do more for the freedmen in the name of manhood than of that of color or caste."[57] The *Pennsylvania Freedmen's Bulletin* stated, "Our sympathy in behalf of the freedmen is not because they are black, not because they are negroes, but because they are MEN, whose interests have been neglected, whose rights have been outraged, and whose manhood has been almost crushed out of them."[58] The use of "manhood" may have been intended to represent all freedpeople, but it clearly did not. The political strategies of abolitionist men excluded both black and white women.

The gender battles in the freedmen's aid movement were not confined to clashes over the relationship of branch societies to the AFUC or the most effective basis for appeals to the North. Men explicitly criticized women's efforts, privileging masculine, efficient, objective reform, and berating those reformers who rejected their standards. Such attacks on women dated back to the Civil War, when the male leadership of the Sanitary Commission attempted to subvert the influence and power of their female peers. As Nettie Sanford wrote to Annie Wittenmeyer, the Sanitary Commissioners' efforts were "a movement against you and woman's right to dispense alms."[59]

After the end of the war, women in the freedmen's aid movement experienced such criticism. Josephine Griffing, an agent of the National Freedmen's Relief Association of the District of Columbia, was attacked for her advocacy of greater relief and her efforts at keeping freedpeople's destitution in the public view. John Murray Forbes, a businessman involved in the Port Royal Experiment, belittled women reformers and Griffing in particular in a letter to Edward Atkinson, Boston cotton manufacturer and founder of the Educational Commission. Forbes initially wrote of the poverty of Washington freedpeople and the great need for charity: "as to the Freedmen, they are absolutely dying here of cold and starvation. I have poured out all the balance of my charity fund in one channel and still have to do more, but the demand is so urgent that no private purse can begin to reach it." But he later amended his assessment of the situation, writing, "Gov't are giving blankets and rations and fuel, so I use Endicott's check sparingly—hope Mr. Channing will get back to oversee the charitable Mrs. Griffin [sic]. Women with misery around them see a little too much through the *heart*."[60] Thus Forbes dismissed Griffing's efforts, and called for male supervision to transform her sympathies into rational, efficient benevolent work.

"Manly" reformers also accused Griffing of manufacturing images of poverty that damaged the reputation of the freedpeople and the freedmen's aid movement. Her appeals were no longer appropriate to a movement that wanted to reject benevolence and promote the self-reliance of freedpeople. In a letter to Jacob R. Shipherd, agent of the AFUC in Washington, J. Miller McKim complained of an appeal by Griffing that presented the District as "a scene of half naked women and children—attached to and living in stables, garrets, and cellars, as well as thousands of shanties. There is much more suffering now than there was last year." In a sarcastic analysis he wrote that if what Griffing wrote were true, the AFUC should be "denounced for maintaining teachers and others in Washington which have either no eyes to see or no hearts to feel the distress." General Howard "should be impeached for the gross dereliction of duty," and Congress "should be called upon to abate a nuisance so well calculated to make democracy, freedom, and emancipation a stench on the nostrils of all people." McKim, Shipherd, and others made sure that the rhetoric of freedmen's aid was dominated by masculine images of self-reliance and independence, not half-naked women and children.[61]

These criticisms of Griffing's style reflected the tension between the male leadership and the female base of the freedmen's aid movement, which had been in many respects a feminine crusade. Women comprised the majority of members, especially as teachers and in branch societies, and they mobilized to help impoverished former slaves.[62] Teachers like Elizabeth Breck constantly appealed to their parent societies for greater aid for the poor. One correspondent in Washington wrote to the New England Freedmen's Aid Society that "sewing schools and schools for reading, writing and spelling are excellent in their time and place; but fingers blue with cold can hardly manage a needle with dexterity and eyes sunken and vacant with hunger might not be able to see the words in a spelling book."[63] Laetitia Campbell wrote to her sponsor, Mrs. Mary K. Wead, of the poverty, hunger, and sickness she witnessed: "I could never have supposed that human beings could live as these people do. We daily see sights that draw tears from our eyes, and make our hearts bleed when we feel how utterly powerless we are to do anything to relieve them."[64] Hannah Stevenson instructed the teachers sponsored by the New England Society and its auxiliaries to have a maternal relationship to their students. She wrote Elizabeth Breck that "we should send with you another Teacher, to live together & assist you in the Teaching in School & motherly care of the Freed people."[65] But the male leaders of the American Freedmen's Union Commission had little interest in becoming mothers to former slaves.

Most organized freedmen's aid activity had ended by 1870; the educational efforts that survived did so thanks to the work of women, who continued to send teachers to the South. The society with the most active women, the New England Freedmen's Aid Society (NEFAS), lasted the longest of any branch of the American Freedmen's Union Commission, until 1876. In these final years, the women of the New England Society advocated Northern intervention in the South and expressed their ongoing commitment to freedmen's education, refusing to follow the AFUC and other branch societies. Though women reformers felt pressure from male reformers who urged freedpeople's independence, they continued to push for aid to freedmen's schools.

Ednah Dow Cheney (1824–1904), a Boston transcendentalist and philanthropist, was the central figure in the NEFAS as a member of the Executive Committee and secretary of the Committee on Teachers (after Hannah Stevenson resigned). She also organized an annual festival for teachers returning from the South for the summer. Cheney's interest in education began before the Civil War, when she helped found a school of design for women, similar to one in Philadelphia, which trained women in skills that would make them self-supporting in the new industrial economy.[66] In addition to her work in the freedmen's aid movement, she also participated in the women's club movement and joined an organization devoted to liberal religion, the Free Religious Association.

Cheney's commitment to women's political culture shaped her experience in the freedmen's aid movement. The New England Woman's Club and the Free Religious Association were both founded in 1868, the same year the American Freedmen's Union Commission began its rapid withdrawal from freedmen's education. As Cheney wrote of the Woman's Club, "it was a true child of the times, and evidently filled a want felt by many." The "want" Cheney referred to was women's need to participate in the public sphere. The remedy was a strong association of women formed to fulfill a social mission: "No young woman is satisfied to live without a purpose, and a woman in the loneliest town on the prairie does not feel isolated when she can go weekly or monthly to her club, or once in two years to the General Federation, and gather strength and comfort and intellectual help by meeting with other women."[67] In articles written for the *Index*, the journal of the Free Religious Association, Cheney argued that Free Religion's recognition of the primacy of individual conscience and women's rights gave women "freedom and the full opportunity for self-development." But her support for women's rights also acknowledged women's "nature" or "sphere" as "the tenderer sex."[68] Cheney remained committed to women's benevolence in a culture of reform that was increasingly hostile to it. She and other women in New England Freedmen's Aid Society sustained freedmen's education by relying on the gendered activism of women.

In many ways, the New England Society's policies toward freedpeople mirrored those of the American Freedmen's Union Commission. Though initially concentrating their efforts on material relief and advocating the "perpetuity" of the Freedmen's Bureau, in 1865 the society left off all relief efforts in favor of education.[69] Their support for education came with a caveat; in September 1865 the society voted to charge fees for the freedmen's schools. As head of the Committee on Teachers, Cheney suggested that freedpeople contribute to the aid and support of schools wherever possible. When Lyman Abbott of the AFUC urged that no new schools be set up, "except where cooperation can be secured," the NEFAS agreed.[70]

The NEFAS diverged from the AFUC, however, in continuing to appeal for direct aid to freedmen's schools. An appeal in 1866 pleaded with readers to persevere in their work for freedmen: "Do not on any account, we beseech you, think of giving up your organizations. Never was the need greater! Never were there opportunities so great as now. Will not all consider their obligations, their duties, their interests in this matter, and act accordingly! . . . The cause of the freedman cannot wait!"[71] The NEFAS continued these humanitarian appeals in hopes of fighting the growing lack of interest of the North.

The New England Freedmen's Aid Society pushed its constituents to fund freedmen's schools until the Southern states assumed their legal responsibilities. Like reformers in the American Freedmen's Union Commission, they wanted the people of the South to contribute more to the support of schools: "We are especially desirous during the coming year of stimulating the people of the South themselves to new efforts in the support of schools."[72] But, unlike the AFUC, which saw its work as nearly complete, they also told their Northern audience that the freedpeople still needed help: "We feel that we have a right to ask the confidence of the public for another year, and to entreat them to hold on to the work while the need is still so great."[73]

The reformers of the New England Society criticized the American Freedmen's Union Commission for prematurely ending its work. In response to the AFUC's farewell address, the *Freedmen's Record*, organ of the NEFAS, stated: "We cannot agree with what it says about its mission being accomplished." When the AFUC applauded freedpeople's self-sustaining educational efforts, the NEFAS reaffirmed its commitment to public education: "The limit of our work will not be reached until the rights of the negro are fully acknowledged by law, and a public school system is established in all the states in which we have labored, to which he is freely admitted."[74] The NEFAS's continued commitment to sustaining Northern interest in their cause, through dramatic appeals which proclaimed the necessity for aid to freedmen's schools, allowed it to hang on longer than most other aid societies.

But in a short time, the New England Society grew frustrated, echoing the earlier sentiments of the American Freedmen's Union Commission that education should be the responsibility of the Southern states and the freedpeople. In November 1869, the NEFAS announced that they would cease a large portion of their work at the end of the current school year: "The establishment of a public school system at the South, both for blacks and whites, has now become so far an accepted idea by the State governments and people of the South, that we ought to resign our guardianship, declare our wards of age, and trust them to carry out this great principle themselves."[75] The NEFAS trusted that the vote would allow freedpeople to secure public education for their children. Members also denied that financial insolvency contributed to their decision. If they gave up their work for public education in the South, it would only be because of their success: "We have never given up our schools from despair of support for them, but because we felt that we should gradually prepare for the time when the South should resume the control of her own educational affairs . . . should our work therefore cease, it will not be because we have failed but because we have succeeded." In her memoirs, Cheney recalled that the work of the New England Society ended when the South had established a public school system.[76] By 1873, the NEFAS claims were remarkably similar to those of the AFUC a few years earlier.

Women played a part in the New England Society's surrender of freedmen's schools. Because women were doing the daily work of the society, they were central to the changes in the NEFAS's policies. In 1869, Cheney wrote of the importance of freedpeople supporting the schools: "It seems to us that the time has nearly come when the people can and ought to support and manage the schools themselves."[77] At the annual meeting of the society in 1870, Cheney and Lucretia Crocker reported that the policy of the NEFAS had come to reflect "the necessity of the society going on teaching the freedmen until they were able to do without its aid; and to gradually withdraw that aid as they came to stand on their own two feet. This was the way to make them manly and self-reliant."[78] Women in the NEFAS had adopted male reformers' rhetoric of independence.

But while the NEFAS joined the mainstream, its members remained the most active advocates for former slaves. The NEFAS encouraged its branch societies, each of which supported a teacher, to turn their support toward teachers for normal schools. In 1870, Ellen Collins and Josephine Shaw Lowell of the New York National Freedmen's Relief Association turned over all their normal schools to the NEFAS, as the two could no longer run them. In response, the NEFAS reported plans to assist these schools as long as possible:

Everything depends on the support the Branch societies & the general public are willing to continue to us. We have always said and still say that we do not think the Normal schools can be self-supporting or ought to be given up for some years more, & we shall endeavor to have them all supported. For this reason we have tried to give the teachers of our Normal schools to our strongest societies who will be most likely to continue their aid.[79]

The NEFAS offered as much support as they could to the New York Society's schools: "In adopting your Normal Schools we mean to make the same effort to keep them up that we do our old ones, but we shall be somewhat dependent on the interest of the Branch societies in this matter, & your schools will have the disadvantage of a less strong hold upon their affections, perhaps."[80] The NEFAS relied on an established community of women to back their schools. Like Cheney, these women were dedicated to education as a basis for independence and equal rights both for African Americans and white women, and they drew on a shared history of antislavery and women's rights activism. After Lowell and Collins retired, the New England Society was the sole remaining branch of the AFUC calling for aid to freedmen's schools.

Yet the group's increasing emphasis on self-supporting schools was doomed to failure because of freedpeople's poverty. Miss Kelley, a teacher in Gloucester, Virginia, found freedpeople were unable to contribute their share of her salary: "The people are so poor, she fears they will not be able to raise all they have proposed—She will be very glad if the Society will assist in paying her salary. . . . Has supplied most of her scholars with books for which they cannot pay yet. She has to be responsible for them."[81] J. E. Lazenby, a teacher for the New York society, wrote "at the urgent request of the colored people to know if we will not give some assistance in keeping up the school until April or May, when they hope to receive aid from the County."[82] Although the Committee on Teachers sometimes came through with funds for these schools, its official policy was otherwise: "Voted, that this Committee will in no case make up any deficiency in the amount pledged by the people towards the support of the schools, but will withdraw the teacher if the agreement is not carried out to her satisfaction."[83] This policy shows a clear lack of appreciation for the poverty of Southern blacks and an overly strict adherence to a policy of self-reliance. Such rules also negatively effected the careers and economic independence of female teachers. Although the middle- and upper-class women of the New England Society held a strong commitment to freedpeople, their policies were not free from the influence of paternalism, racism, or free labor principles.

The pride and joy of the NEFAS was the Cheney Educational Association, formed by the freedpeople of Cheraw, South Carolina, which successfully supported a school independent of Northern or state assistance. As the NEFAS instituted its policy of self-support, the people of Cheraw took steps to keep up their school. In September 1869, Mr. Shrewsbury, the teacher at Cheraw, reported that the people had agreed to pay a "tax" of 25 cents per month for each scholar. One month later, he reported that the parents were contributing $10 a month and as the schools grew, this sum would increase to $15 a month. In April 1871 Shrewsbury reported that the people had raised $105 for teachers' salaries and that their educational association had paid for all school expenses, including new desks.[84] The constitution of the educational association at Cheraw demonstrates freedpeople's commitment to education and mutual aid. Their constitution recognized "the paramount importance of education and the grave responsibility resting upon us to secure its advantages in the fullest sense to our children, that they may become useful citizens and ornaments to society." The constitution bound the community together in support of their schools: "its object shall be the fostering and encouragement of Education in our midst and the advancement and material interest and welfare of our people; the erection of a building for school and other purposes . . . and binding upon us such as the support of schools and the purchase of suitable text books and other matters incident to Educational work."[85] Though this community's commitment to education was admirable, their strong financial support of the Cheraw school was only necessary because of the withdrawal of the NEFAS and the lack of state funds. The promotion of self-sustaining freedmen's schools by the AFUC reinforced the laissez-faire attitude of the state and federal governments toward public education in the South, contributing to the emergence of separate and unequal schools.[86]

The American Freedmen's Union Commission proclaimed its success when Southern states endorsed public education and the U.S. Constitution guaranteed the rights of African American men. In fact, their strategies were only partly successful. State support for African American schools proved illusory, and Southern blacks depended on Northern philanthropists, including the American Missionary Association, to aid their schools for years to come. Male reformers' emphasis on equal rights under the law and free labor ignored the poverty and inequality that continued to govern the lives of many former slaves, especially freedwomen and children.

Though the New England Freedmen's Aid Society followed the same trajectory as the American Freedmen's Union Commission, turning from common schools to normal schools and urging freedpeople's self-reliance, the NEFAS continued its involvement in freedmen's schools longer than any other branch society of the AFUC. This was due to the efforts of Ednah Dow Cheney, Hannah Stevenson, Lucretia Crocker and others. These women kept up correspondence with teachers and branch societies and endeavored to keep teachers funded as long as possible. Their long record of aid reveals a strong commitment to freedmen's aid and education. In her biography of Lucretia Crocker, Cheney herself highlighted the importance of women to the New England Society. Cheney noted Crocker's strong devotion to the freedmen's cause: "she worked and hoped for the freedmen's society as long as it could possibly be kept alive."[87]

Struggling to keep their schools alive, women accommodated the politics of the AFUC in order to retain their prominent positions in the movement. Nevertheless, Cheney and other women maintained their independence in the face of male leaders. Many, like Cheney, chose to return to women's reform, in the club movement, the women's rights movement, or the WCTU, to achieve their goals. Though they could not avoid contact with the Commission, other female reformers also struggled to assert women's vision for the freedmen's aid movement. In the work of these agents, visitors, and teachers, the radicalism of women's proposals for Reconstruction can truly be seen. These women continued to argue for federal intervention, relief, and land reform, while seeking political rights and economic independence for themselves and former slaves. African American women in particular exposed the sexual and racial biases imbedded in the policies of the freedmen's aid movement.

Chapter 4

Mothers of the Race: Black Women in the Freedmen's Aid Movement

In 1862, Elizabeth Keckley (c. 1820–1907), former slave and dressmaker to Mary Todd Lincoln, formed the Contraband Relief Association (CRA) to "do something for the benefit of the suffering blacks," refugees to Washington, D.C., from Maryland and Virginia. Keckley described freed-people as "my own race," yet she also distinguished herself from them by identifying the members of the CRA as "well-to-do colored people."[1] Keckley's society was one of many African American freedmen's aid organizations established independently of (and often competing with) the American Freedmen's Union Commission and its branches. Black women involved in the freedmen's aid movement, like Keckley, Frances Ellen Watkins Harper, Charlotte Forten, and Rebecca Primus established themselves as representatives, teachers, and advisors to former slaves. But by joining the freedmen's aid movement, these women also con-fronted their conflicted relationship to former slaves. Free black women struggled to recognize their connection to emancipated slaves without discarding their financial, educational, and cultural differences from freedpeople. African American women overcame this contradiction by using both their race and their class to justify their authority in the move-ment. Some women even presented themselves as mothers to the race, an idea that both acknowledged their bond with former slaves and asserted a gendered authority over those same freedpeople.[2]

Occupying a middle ground between freedpeople and northern whites, African American women became effective advocates for former slaves.[3] Though women in the freedmen's aid movement shared common goals, African American women expressed a distinct vision, emphasizing racial pride, self-help, leadership, and the close connections between slave and free. Both black and white women wanted to aid former slaves, while ex-panding their own political influence. Together, they criticized laissez-faire Reconstruction policy, and advocated radical measures like land reform, universal suffrage, and intervention. Yet African American women also challenged white perceptions of race, equal rights, free labor, and dependency, drawing on their personal investment in the outcome of Reconstruction.[4]

Northern blacks saw emancipation as an opportunity to demonstrate their equality with whites and they immediately formed their own freedmen's aid organizations in response to new conditions. As Richard H. Cain, African Methodist Episcopal clergyman and later congressman from South Carolina, stated, "We know how to serve others, but have not learned how to serve ourselves. We have always been directed by others in all the affairs of life; they have furnished the thoughts while we have been passive instruments, acting as we were acted upon, mere automatons." Cain viewed freedmen's aid as the means through which African Americans could elevate freedpeople and prove themselves as citizens and leaders. He lamented the scarcity of "Negro gentlemen" in the developing movement and called upon educated, middle-class blacks to become involved:

Negro gentlemen and ladies must become teachers, among them by example as well as precept, teach them that though they be black, they are as good as any other class whose skin is whiter than theirs; teach them that their complexions may differ but man is man for all that. Finally: colored men in the North have got to come to this doctrine, that black men must think for themselves—act for themselves, and thus help our white friends to elevate us by a proper recognition of our manhood.[5]

Although Cain included free black women in his appeal, his gendered language linked racial pride to masculinity. Indeed, for Cain, freedom and independence were masculine traits. Women might participate in subordinate and traditional positions as teachers, bestowers of Christian benevolence, and transmitters of values.[6]

Many Northern blacks took up Cain's call for independent aid societies and the consequent assertion of black manhood. The African Civilization Society (ACS), established in the 1850s by the emigrationist Henry Highland Garnet, remodeled itself into a freedmen's aid association during the Civil War.[7] One correspondent to the *Christian Recorder*, the newspaper of the African Methodist Episcopal Church, applauded the African Civilization Society for being an all-black freedmen's aid organization:

It is truly refreshing to see a combination of colored gentlemen looking after the affairs of their people, and especially sending colored ladies and gentlemen to teach those persons who are surrendered into this new condition of life. There has not been such a step taken by any society formed by the colored people in this country before. All have contented themselves with raising moneys and collecting clothes to be placed at the disposal of others.

The author, Junius, praised the independence of the ACS and its male officers. He concluded that all African Americans should participate in similar efforts: "It is time that we should do our own thinking and acting, for our own best interest. We should enter heartily into this good work and form auxiliary societies all over the country; collect means and send teachers into every part of the South where we can get access."[8]

Like Cain, Junius connected freedom to manhood. He emphasized the leadership of "colored gentlemen," underscoring both the class and gender components of male authority. Junius presumed that the welfare of former slaves depended on the wisdom and guidance of such men. He also tied this leadership to the future of the entire race, acknowledging Northern blacks' interest in emancipation. But in order to insure the recognition of black manhood, Cain, Junius, and the ACS consigned women to an inferior position. While some women, including Mrs. Sarah Tilmon, an employment agent who worked with Josephine Griffing and the Freedmen's Bureau, achieved status in the organization, most women were teachers, a position that did not challenge middle-class gender roles.[9]

Not all Northern blacks supported the freedmen's aid movement; those who favored integration and equal rights were particularly skeptical of a group like the African Civilization Society that emphasized manhood, racial pride, and separatism.[10] At one meeting of the ACS in Washington, D.C., George T. Downing and Charles Lenox Remond charged Cain and the ACS with "being the tools of colonizationists." Downing and Remond questioned the separatist strategy of the ACS, including the wisdom of black churches and schools.[11] Frederick Douglass, the most prominent advocate of integration, told white reformers that he felt the freedmen's aid movement was too paternalistic and encouraged the dependence of former slaves. Although Douglass felt that freedmen's aid societies might be needed in the immediate postwar years, he thought that any charity would "be an injury to the colored race—They will serve to keep up the very prejudices, which it is so desirable to banish from the country." Instead, Douglass believed, reformers should be working for justice and equality: "My mission for the present is to ask equal citizenship in the state and equal fellowship for the Negro in the church. Equal rights in the street cars and equal admission in the state schools . . . this is what we count and must not lose sight of in all our schemes of benevolence with special reference to the Negro."[12]

Yet the question of civil rights created further divisions in the movement. African American men united in support of the Fifteenth Amendment, alienating women activists. Frederick Douglass, Robert Purvis, and others favored woman suffrage, but argued that Reconstruction was the "negro's hour" and that passage of universal male suffrage should assume priority. Rather than join their abolitionist allies, Elizabeth Cady Stanton and Susan B. Anthony refused to endorse the Fifteenth Amendment, and broke away from the American Equal Rights Association to found a society that would be committed solely to the issue of woman suffrage: the National Woman Suffrage Association.

African American women in the North felt this split most painfully, and they turned away from suffrage to freedmen's aid, where they could assert their unique authority. As Roslyn Terborg-Penn points out, black women were "torn between identifying with racial priorities or with gender priorities."[13] Though most supported the Fifteenth Amendment, free African American women wanted the vote for themselves, as well as proper recognition of their womanhood. Emphasizing their essential role in the transition to freedom, middle-class black women viewed the freedmen's aid movement as an opportunity to both uplift former slaves and advance women's public stature.

For example, the writer Frances Ellen Watkins Harper (1825–1911) embraced the Fifteenth Amendment while also supporting freedmen's aid and women's rights. Harper began her career in the antislavery movement and achieved fame for her abolitionist poetry. She married in 1860, but her husband died during the war. While this loss enabled her to continue her career, it also reinforced her need for an income. During Reconstruction, Harper committed herself to "lasting service for the race," a service based on gender, class, and her identification with former slaves.[14] Harper's mission was often overtly paternalistic; as an educated, middle- class woman, she saw freedmen's aid as "a field for civilizing work." Nevertheless, she linked her future to former slaves: "Still I am standing with my race on the threshold of a new era, and though some be far past me in the learning of the schools, yet to-day, with my limited and fragmentary knowledge, I may help the race forward a little."[15] Harper toured the South after the Civil War, promoting both education and civil rights. She traveled to "every Southern state in the Union, save two," holding meetings for former slaves. Harper relied on funds raised at her speeches to support herself, but she often spoke for no payment, as she hoped to convince as many people as possible.[16]

Harper mapped out a specific role for both freedwomen and elite women in the freedmen's aid movement, challenging the masculine vision of the African Civilization Society. By Harper's own account, she sought freedwomen out specifically in her travels: "Part of my lectures are given privately to women, and for them I never make any charge or take any collection. . . . I am going to talk with them about their daughters and about things connected with the welfare of the race. Now is the time for our women to begin to try to lift up their heads and plant the roots of progress under the hearthstone."[17] Harper identified the progress of African Americans with the progress of women, and she longed for other women to join her: "Oh, if some more of our young women would only consecrate their lives to the work of upbuilding the race!"[18] Harper believed that the efforts of women, in both the private and public sphere, were essential to the advancement of blacks in American society. As mothers and wives, women provided the civilizing guidance of morality and religion. Harper wanted to extend African American women's moral influence from individual homes through the entire nation.[19]

In addition, Harper pushed white feminists to expand their definition of women's rights to include such concerns as freedmen's aid and black civil rights. At the founding meeting of the American Equal Rights Association in 1866, Harper proclaimed that "justice is not fulfilled so long as woman is unequal before the law." But she admonished the other participants that "we are all bound up together in one great bundle of humanity, and society cannot trample on the weakest and feeblest of its members without receiving the curse in its own soul."[20] She chided suffragists for putting their faith in the ballot and for thinking the vote would "cure all the ills of life," a message aimed also at black men. Instead, Harper urged white women to be "good" and aid others less fortunate than themselves: "While there exists a brutal element in society which tramples upon the feeble and treads down the weak, I tell you that if there is any class of people who need to be lifted out of their airy nothings and selfishness, it is the white women of America."[21] Although she joined the American Equal Rights Association with the belief that it would unite issues of race, sex, and class, Harper also contributed to its breakdown, criticizing activists, like Stanton and Anthony, who placed their own interests ahead of former slaves.[22]

Harper also analyzed white women's "nothings and selfishness" in *Iola Leroy; or, Shadows Uplifted*, her 1892 novel about Reconstruction. The educated daughter of a white planter and his slave, Iola Leroy does not discover her racial identity or slave status until her father's death. Harper created a character who passes for white in order to illustrate the racial dilemma of many light-skinned African Americans. Before the end of the Civil War, however, Iola Leroy bridges both racial and class divisions, announcing her intention "to cast my lot with the freed people as a helper, teacher, and friend."[23] She marries an African American doctor and they move to North Carolina, where Leroy informs her neighbors that she is "going to teach in the Sunday-school, help in the church, hold mothers' meetings to help these boys and girls grow up to be good men and women." As in her lectures to freedwomen, Harper linked motherhood and racial progress. She also presented Leroy as a model for all women. By contrast, Harper criticized white women for perpetuating racism rather that uniting around gendered values such as morality and benevolence. One character calls white women "the aristocratic element of our country," seeing them as the torchbearers of racial prejudice. Throughout the novel, white women befriend the title character thinking she is white, only to reject her when they discover she is African American.[24]

Many others also viewed middle-class black women as integral to the work of Reconstruction. Mrs. Amanda Turpin wrote in the *Christian Recorder* that "female influence" was especially important in the new field of labor presented by emancipation: "the influential female is called to perform a great portion of the work; therefore, let us rally to a post of duty, and help to burst open the dark prison doors of ignorance, that the light of intelligence, mental and moral improvement, may break forth and shine into the minds of our once down-trodden and oppressed, but now freed race."[25] Like Harper, Turpin believed women should provide moral and intellectual leadership, uplifting former slaves by expanding their role as mothers.

Yet reformers also advocated the leadership of educated African American women because of their assumptions about race, class, and gender. William J. Wilson advised the American Freedmen's Inquiry Commission to recruit middle-class black women as role models for freedwomen:

There is a class among us possessed of intelligence, personal habits & moral tone far above what is generally estimated; First class housekeepers. Now, I am satisfied, if Matrons, Teachers, & etc. could frequently be selected from this class of our colored women, indeed if it could become quite general, these Freedwomen would as a consequence beget a confidence in themselves to speedily improve their habits. But more than this, by the example & the precept, would women of this class inspire their own sex & race to habits of cleanliness, industry & virtue.[26]

Wilson not only defined womanhood in terms of domesticity and morality, he also favored middle-class women because of their presumed superiority in these areas. He believed middle-class women could teach former slaves to perform their domestic and maternal duties responsibly. Though he limited women's activism to traditional gender roles, he acknowledged the importance of women to freedmen's aid.

During Reconstruction, Wilson, Turpin, and Harper pioneered a new place for black women in the nation as a whole—as "race women," social and cultural leaders for former slaves. In an acknowledgment of women's influence, the *Christian Recorder* identified Frances Ellen Watkins Harper as a modern-day Deborah, an Old Testament judge, who proclaimed "the law of God and the gospel of liberty."[27] Significantly, Deborah was also a mother to Israel. Assuming the role of mother and judge, and preaching God's law over man-made laws like the Constitution,

Harper's postwar lectures instructed former slaves in freedom and reminded white Americans of their complicity in the sins of slavery. Harper addressed both black and white audiences, assuming a leadership role among African Americans and a mediating position between whites and blacks.

Accepting the call of Harper and Turpin, African American women became teachers to influence both Southern blacks and Northern whites. Charlotte Forten (1837–1914) jumped at the chance to teach freedpeople in South Carolina. For a self-supporting single woman like Forten, teaching in the South offered a reliable salary, a mild climate, and a chance to do something noble and worthwhile.[28] Forten's desire to become a freedmen's teacher grew from her personal and familial connections to the antislavery movement. But, as scholars suggest, Forten's complex identity also shaped her career during the Civil War. Though a free woman from a once prosperous Philadelphia merchant family, she and her father had constant financial troubles. She associated with both black and white reformers, but felt most comfortable in the small circles of her extended family and friends. She expressed herself best in writing and never became a prominent abolitionist lecturer, as Harper did.[29] Instead, sponsored by J. Miller McKim's Port Royal Relief Association of Philadelphia, Forten taught on St. Helena Island with Laura Towne and Ellen Murray from October 1862 to May 1864. There, Forten discovered her power to influence Northern perceptions of emancipation.

The only African American woman teaching on the Sea Islands at the time, Forten mediated between white Union soldiers, "Gideon's Band," and the majority of the population of the Sea Islands, former slaves and African American soldiers. Forten viewed freedpeople as culturally very different from herself, and she remarked on their wonderful singing and amusing dress and speech. But the Northern whites on St. Helena and in neighboring areas sought her counsel in their dealings with former slaves.[30] Edward L. Pierce, Col. Thomas Wentworth Higginson, and Gen. Rufus Saxton all found themselves in deep and intense conversations with Forten on emancipation, black army units, education, and literature. Passing judgment on which superintendents were antislavery and which were "strongly prejudiced," she aided the former and chided the latter.[31]

When Forten published "Life on the Sea Islands" in the *Atlantic Monthly* in 1864, she merely expanded her audience of Northern whites. Forten's first article, published in May, although highly evocative of local color, had two principle messages. First, she related the tremendous obstacles that slavery had placed in freedpeople's path to independence. And second, she described the extraordinary progress of former slaves in a brief time. Forten noted that in the "quarters," former slaves lived in "miserable

huts, with nothing comfortable or home-like about them." Visible rem-
nants of slavery existed everywhere, from the scars on the limbs of "Old
Bess," to parents who had lost their children to slave traders or to
death.[32] Forten doubted that "the haughty Anglo-Saxon race, after centuries of such an experience as these people have had, would be very
much superior to them."[33] Instead, Forten found it remarkable that freedpeople were so eager to learn and so willing to sacrifice for an education.
She concluded: "Daily the long-oppressed people of these islands are demonstrating their capacity for improvement in learning and labor. What
they have accomplished in one short year exceeds our utmost expectations."[34] Forten felt pride that "mine own people" had accomplished
and survived so much and committed herself to standing by their side
in future struggles.[35] In her emphasis on progress, Forten's message was
similar to other abolitionists in the freedmen's aid movement. Unlike
white abolitionists, however, Forten identified herself with former slaves.

While Forten was a well-known abolitionist, whose views were published in national journals, African American teachers without such
connections also served as important mediators between the North and
former slaves. Sponsored by the integrated Hartford, Connecticut, Freedmen's Aid Society and the Baltimore Association for the Moral and Educational Improvement of the Colored People, a branch of the American
Freedmen's Union Commission, Rebecca Primus (1836–1932) journeyed
to Royal Oak, Maryland, in 1865 to teach former slaves. Eventually, after
two years of hard work and fund raising, she and the freedpeople of
Royal Oak built their own school, later called the Primus Institute in her
honor. In comparison to former slaves, Primus was well off; her family
owned their own home and were members of the Talcott Street Congregational Church in Hartford. Her father worked as a clerk in a grocery
store, her mother was a seamstress. Before she went to the South, Primus
taught in the Talcott Street Church's Sunday school.[36] As much separated
Primus from former slaves as united them. Her letters demonstrate the
way Northern blacks negotiated freedom and their relationship to former slaves.

As Farah Jasmine Griffin argues, Primus became increasingly politi-
cized through her work with freedpeople.[37] Like other teachers, Rebecca
Primus wrote letters from Royal Oak to raise funds for freedpeople, trying to connect Southern blacks and their Northern benefactors, both
black and white. Primus emphasized the hard work of freedpeople and
continuing oppression by Southern whites. In April 1866, she reported
that freedpeople were plowing and planting, and "soon I expect everything will be looking very thrifty about here." Freedmen found ready
employment in the area even though the whites did "not pay sufficient
wages."[38] In addition, blacks in Royal Oak confronted the threat of

violence: "There are some lawless fellows in these towns and there is nothing too bad for them to do to a colored person. I trust something like justice will be given to the black man one of these days, for they are persecuted almost as badly now as in the days of slavery."[39] By exposing the true character of black life in the postwar South, Primus reminded her friends and colleagues of the factors undermining industry and thrift. Like Forten, however, Primus stressed progress: "they are industrious and hopeful of the future, their interest in the school is unabated & many of them deny themselves in order to sustain it."[40] Rather than accommodating white views of black dependency, Primus stressed the self-reliance of former slaves.

Despite her advocacy for freedpeople, Primus and the Royal Oak residents were mutually aware of their differences. When Primus visited black families in the area, they entertained her lavishly and she always described the meals in detail for her family: "I find they are so neatly & comfortably situated & they are so desirous to have visit them, it will not do to slight any. My food Thurs. consisted of cabbage & bacon, Fried chicken, sweet potatoes, apple-sauce, bread, biscuits, ginger, pear, & peach preserves which were very nice, and a cup of tea."[41] Primus recognized the generosity, hard work, and pride that went into the meal, but she also acknowledged that the families understood her as someone "other": "they don't know me, at least they do not quite understand my ways etc. They seem to labor under the false impression that I'm an uncommon personage—that there's no one like me, but what should lead them to think this is beyond my comprehension."[42] African Americans in Royal Oak viewed Primus as a foreigner, but they also embraced her as teacher and ally.

Although Primus praised the hospitality of families in Royal Oak, she did criticize Southern blacks, particularly their religion and dress. In Hartford, Primus belonged to a Congregational Church, and in the South she occasionally attended either an Episcopalian or a Presbyterian Church. She chose denominations that furthered the social aspirations of her family and resembled the Yankee churches with which she was familiar. She commented on Southern blacks' tendency toward revivals, conversions, and subsequent lapses: "the southerners are so emotional & fond of excitement that it's nothing more than could hardly be expected from them."[43] Her plain manner of dress mirrored her sedate approach toward religion and she mocked the fancy clothes preferred by freedwomen: "I see a number of the blacks attired in their new spring hats, bonnets, & dresses some in the latest styles. I judge, & oh! such looks some presented! Some of these people make themselves appear so much more ridiculous than they really are."[44] But Primus tempered her mockery with understanding, for she realized that freedpeople's clothing was a statement. Former slaves asserted their freedom by dressing well. Their new status was reflected in their outward appearance, where it would be visible to whites.[45]

While Primus judged former slaves, her letters contain many more comments on racism and the struggle for equality. Primus's radicalization was both personal and professional. After a conflict with the local postmaster, Primus had her mail directed elsewhere, offending him and his wife. Refusing to accept subordination, Primus noted, "These white people want all the respect shown them by the col'd. people. I give what I rec. & no more."[46] She also described discrimination against black teachers by freedmen's aid societies, a problem mentioned by Charlotte Forten as well. After the resignation of two white teachers in Baltimore, Primus wrote disapprovingly that "instead of putting competent col'd. teachers in their places, they have got some new white ones."[47] She felt it was her right and duty to educate former slaves, and she refused to remain silent when faced with the frustrating and downright discriminatory policies of aid societies.

While Forten and Primus were able to present their views to the North in their own voices, the opinions of other African American women were filtered through white reformers. White women often wrote glowing reports of free black women's work with freedpeople, but these reports reveal more about white women's goals for Reconstruction than African American women's perspective. Black women appear in white women's writings as voices of authenticity, as examples of women's important place in the work of Reconstruction and as proof of freedpeople's needs. While Frances E. W. Harper and other women were "modern day Deborahs" to the black community, their partnership with white women frequently obscured their vision for Reconstruction.

For example, the famous antislavery lecturer Sojourner Truth (c.1799—1883) worked with freedpeople in Washington, D.C., after the Civil War, but since Truth was illiterate, she relied on others to relate her story for her. Frances Titus, a white friend of Truth's from Battle Creek, Michigan, compiled Truth's *Book of Life*, published as an addition to Truth's narrative in 1878. As Nell Irvin Painter points out, the *Book of Life* presents "a fractured portrait," featuring both Truth and Titus, thus making it difficult to differentiate between their views.[48] In describing her efforts for former slaves, Truth/Titus portrayed Truth as concerned with typical Northern and middle-class values such as "industry and virtue": "Sojourner spent more than a year at Arlington Heights, instructing the women in domestic duties, and doing much to promote the general welfare. She especially deprecated their filthy habits and strove to inspire them with a love of neatness and order."[49] But Truth escaped

Titus's shadow by reprinting letters, such as her official appointment by the National Freedmen's Relief Association of New York, that confirmed her important place in the freedmen's aid movement. The president of the association, Francis George Shaw, recommended Truth "to the favor and confidence of the officers of the government, and of all persons who take an interest in relieving the condition of the freedmen, or in promoting their intellectual, moral, and religious instruction."[50] She further illustrated her connections to political power and important reformers by printing letters from O. O. Howard, commissioner of the Freedmen's Bureau, assistant commissioner John Eaton, and a description of her 1864 interview with President Lincoln.

Though Truth proudly published letters showing her close ties to the government and white reformers, she also criticized white efforts on behalf of former slaves. As a Northerner, Truth was not immune to the Protestant culture that emphasized hard work as a means to get ahead, and she interpreted her own life through this lens. During Reconstruction, Truth devoted significant energy to her work as an employment agent for the Freedmen's Bureau, bringing freedpeople from Washington, D.C., to jobs in Rochester in the winter of 1867. Truth contributed to freedpeople's economic independence while securing her own with a salary from the Freedmen's Bureau. But the *Book of Life* also faults the project of assisting freedpeople to migrate to the North as an inefficient and costly method of relieving destitution.[51] Disillusioned by her work as an employment agent, Truth criticized the government's overwhelming focus on finding freedpeople remunerative employment.[52] For Truth, slaves' "years of uncompensated services" deserved payment from the government in the form of a land grant in the west.[53]

Rather than appeal as a former slave, an abolitionist, or a women's rights activist, Truth recreated herself as the adopted mother of her race in order to argue for government action.[54] Truth's identity as a mother to her people grew from two experiences. As a slave, she had been cruelly separated from her children. But she had also attained freedom, a measure of economic independence, and celebrity. Truth used these two aspects of her identity to become an ideal spokesperson for freedwomen and children, "the future nation." She lobbied the government to provide former slaves with land, schools, and material assistance. Truth's interest in freedpeople and in women's rights intersected. She realized that as a woman and a mother, she could not secure the necessary justice for her nation of children: "She regretted now, as ever, that women had no political rights under government; for she knew that could the voice of maternity be heard in the advocacy of this measure [land ownership], the welfare, not only of the present generation, but of future ones, would be assured."[55] Truth stressed the importance of women's voice in Reconstruction policy, but she also acknowledged the limitations placed on women due to their exclusion from political power.

As Titus threatened to mute Truth's voice, so too did Truth's alliance with abolitionist-feminist Josephine Griffing serve to hide Truth's goals for Reconstruction. Truth and Griffing had known each other since the 1850s. They were coworkers in the antislavery and women's rights movements and, when they met again in Washington, D.C., in 1864, they embarked on a mutual mission to find freedpeople jobs and homes in the North. Their correspondence suggests that the two were close enough so that Truth stayed in Griffing's home when she was in Washington. As Griffing wrote Truth in Rochester in 1869, "We miss you much, still feel glad that you went when you did—as it has been so very cold in the building and no new stove or any repairs."[56] Although Truth and Griffing shared a commitment to freedpeople's migration to the North, their attitude toward the poverty of freedpeople differed. Nell Irvin Painter and Carleton Mabee suggest that Truth, like many Americans, cast freedpeople's poverty in terms of "moral deficiency" and fought to liberate freedpeople from their "dependence" on the government.[57] Griffing's approach differed markedly—she stressed the "rights of the poor" and justice for freedpeople, which in her definition included government and private assistance.[58]

Despite these differences, Griffing depended on Truth's renown as a black woman and former slave to get her message across to the National Freedmen's Relief Association (NFRA) of Washington, D.C., to Rochester friends, and to the freedpeople. According to Griffing, Truth "understood" freedpeople, and could draw "them out on subjects they seldom converse upon with others." Thus when Griffing referred to Truth, she could claim to speak with even more authority.[59] In her 1866 report to the NFRA, Griffing related an anecdote about Truth to illustrate the special hardships faced by freedwomen, a story that might have been told differently by Truth. Truth had approached a freedwoman waiting to receive rations. Truth reportedly said to the woman: "Why don't you go to work and get out of the Government poor-house? See how old and how strong I am, *because* I work." The woman explained to Truth that as she had labored without pay as a slave and her children had all been sold away from her, she did not have the "heart" to work. Ironically, this woman assumed that Truth had always "been your *own*" and had not experienced the same troubles, when in fact the opposite was true.[60] While Truth continued to believe in the inherent value of work, even when she was separated from her children, this freedwoman claimed she would not work until she had found her children.

Rather than use Truth as an example of how hard work could benefit former slaves, Griffing pointed to the injustice of denying people who had labored for the nation's profit, without remuneration, adequate support. Griffing reported that "*there is a great distress*, and alarm is felt among the old and infirm, that after giving their labor and strength to slavery, they are at last to die of hunger" because of the government's policy of ending rations. Deflecting possible criticism, Griffing reported that she had "endeavored faithfully and discriminately to carry out the policy of assisting those only who were unable by their own efforts to procure the necessaries of life."[61] Griffing also appealed to the readers' sympathy for a mother who had lost all her children to slavery.

Although Truth may not have approved of Griffing's support for government rations, both felt that the nation owed former slaves for their labor. They also shared a belief that the "voice of maternity" in Reconstruction policy would insure the welfare of freedpeople. In addition, Truth and Griffing knew firsthand the struggle independent women faced to support themselves and their families. Both Truth and Griffing were fighting a comparable battle for adequate compensation for their labors among freedpeople and Griffing prodded her readers on Truth's behalf: "We hope her rare efforts will be duly appreciated and generously sustained."[62] Despite Truth's years of hard work, financial independence was beyond her reach. Though Truth may not have explicitly questioned free labor ideology, she ultimately advocated land reform as a basis for freedpeople's independence rather than wage labor.

Seeking to avoid the sexism of some societies like Cain's African Civilization Society, the discriminatory employment practices of white societies, and the dominance of white abolitionists, some black women formed their own organizations. As mentioned earlier, Elizabeth Keckley established the Contraband Relief Association in 1862. Because of her relatively lucrative profession, as dressmaker to Mary Todd Lincoln, she had the means to engage in this kind of work. Keckley's connections to Mrs. Lincoln and white politicians helped her raise money, and she also had a base of support among the growing middle-class black community in Washington.[63]

Although a former slave, Keckley saw herself as a "well-to-do" career woman. Born in Virginia, Keckley claimed to be the daughter of her owner, and indeed her light skin caused her problems. Keckley's owners abused her severely, but she also confronted the "base designs" of a white man in the neighborhood. She wrote tersely, "Suffice it to say, that he persecuted me for four years, and I—I—became a mother."[64] Her owners moved west to St. Louis, where Keckley undoubtedly heard of the case of *Dred Scott v. Sandford*, which originated in that city and was making its way toward the Supreme Court. Scott, a former slave, sued his owner for the freedom of his family, charging that the time spent traveling through Wisconsin legally ended their bondage. Keckley reassured her owner that she would not pursue the same method of attaining freedom as Dred Scott, stating, "I will only be free by such means as the laws of the country provide."[65] In 1855, she purchased freedom for herself and her son, taking up residence in Washington, D.C., and working as an elite seamstress first for Mrs. Jefferson Davis, and then Mrs. Lincoln. Her business allowed her to employ others and at the same time gave her access to the most powerful politicians in the country.

While separating herself from other former slaves, Keckley simultaneously highlighted her experience with slavery. In her autobiography, *Behind the Scenes; or, Thirty Years a Slave, and Four Years in the White House*, she informed the reader that she was "raised in a hardy school—had been taught to rely upon myself, and to prepare myself to render assistance to others." The one thing she gained from slavery was the "important lesson of self-reliance."[66] Though Keckley rejected the presumption of black dependence, she did acknowledge that not all African Americans shared her self-reliance. During the war, she encountered former slaves who had learned the same lessons, but for others, she judged, "dependence had become a part of their second nature, and independence brought with it the cares and vexations of poverty."[67] Her emphasis on environment, particularly the experience of slavery, distinguished Keckley's views on the subject. Keckley was deeply proud of her independence, but when she returned to visit her former owners, well-dressed, with contacts among famous politicians, she rebuked them for having failed to educate her as child.[68] In other words, she decried dependency but blamed white slaveholders for its prevalence among freedpeople.

Throughout her memoir, Keckley held up free African Americans as models of both independence and charity. Her catalogue of contributors to the Contraband Relief Society listed people of high status, accomplishment, and success. The Reverend Mr. Grimes, his wife, and Mrs. John Sella Martin started a branch of the Contraband Relief Society in Boston, which, Keckley explained, "sent us over eighty large boxes of goods, contributed exclusively by the colored people of Boston." Other contributors included Henry Highland Garnet, the black waiters at the Metropolitan Hotel, and Frederick Douglass.[69] By giving such examples, Keckley asserted African American equality, and hinted at their superiority.

Keckley explicitly criticized Northern whites for failing to respond to the needs of former slaves. She wrote that "the mute appeals for help too often were answered by cold neglect. . . . the great masses of the North learned to look upon your helplessness with indifference—learned to speak of you as an idle, dependent race. Reason should have prompted kinder thought. Charity is ever kind."[70] Such a laissez-faire approach to Reconstruction, Keckley argued, betrayed former slaves after their sudden emancipation. Keckley especially condemned the Northern view of blacks as "idle," since whites had long depended on the labor of slaves for their prosperity. In denial about their debt, whites left the work of uplifting freedpeople to the free African Americans of the Contraband Relief Society. Whatever success was achieved by former slaves, then, was accomplished despite the neglect of whites and the hardships of slavery. Keckley believed that freedpeople soon would be entirely self-reliant, and she pointed visitors to Washington to the Freedmen's Village, a freedmen's camp in Arlington, for evidence of "prosperity and happiness."[71]

Keckley also exploded conventional depictions of black dependence, describing white women as almost entirely dependent upon her. After Keckley moved with her owners to St. Louis, the family relied on her sewing skills to survive: "With my needle I kept bread in the mouths of seventeen persons for two years and five months . . . working so hard that others might live in comparative comfort."[72] In the White House, Keckley established herself as the chief advisor and confidant to Mrs. Lincoln, the daughter of Kentucky slave owners, and she was the first person Mrs. Lincoln sent for after her husband's assassination. In severe debt, Mrs. Lincoln planned to raise funds by selling the beautiful clothes that Keckley had sewn for her. When this scheme failed, the only people who sympathized with Mrs. Lincoln's financial plight were African Americans, "who intend to take up collections in their churches for the benefit of Mrs. Lincoln," though she ultimately refused their assistance.[73] In contrast to Mrs. Lincoln's dependency, Keckley portrayed herself and other self-reliant African Americans as the true heirs of President Lincoln. Finally, Keckley's success also surprised her former owners, as white Southerners believed that slaves could not survive without the protection and care of their masters. As her former mistress, Mrs. Ann Garland, pointed out to Keckley, "you get along in the world better than we who enjoyed every educational advantage in childhood."[74] Keckley reversed the white view of black dependency, showing white women as helpless without the black women who sustained their households and their wardrobes.[75]

Fittingly, Keckley maintained her independence throughout her life. Though the publication of her autobiography resulted in scandal that threatened Keckley's reputation, she later taught dressmaking at Wilberforce University. Before her death, Keckley moved back to Washington, D.C., and took up residence in the Home for Destitute Colored Women and Children, an organization partially founded by the Contraband Relief Society. In contributing to the welfare of her race, Keckley also provided for her future. At the same time, she implicitly and explicitly criticized whites for their flawed interpretation of both race and charity.

Keckley and other African American women in the freedmen's aid movement challenged white definitions of dependency, rights, and justice. As self-identified "mothers" and role models, they nurtured and instructed former slaves while acting as intermediaries between Southern blacks and Northern whites.[76] In proclaiming their status as mothers to the race, however, African American women also reaffirmed their superiority to former slaves and emphasized their educational and cultural differences. But this class-based approach to freedmen's relief was combined with a close identification with former slaves. Realizing that Reconstruction would shape the lives of all African Americans, regardless of their condition before the war, Northern black women sought to influence the aftermath of emancipation, struggling for equal partnership and authority with black men and white women in the freedmen's aid movement.

Chapter 5

The Freedmen's Bureau and Material Aid

Like African American women, white abolitionist-feminists rebutted notions of black idleness and dependency in order to convince Reconstruction policymakers to grant greater material aid to former slaves. In Washington, D.C., abolitionist-feminists sought work as agents of the Freedmen's Bureau, responsible for visiting freedpeople in their homes and distributing rations and fuel. Though female agents endorsed the ideal of independence, they also publicized the extreme poverty of former slaves and requested government and Northern assistance. They resolved this paradox by expanding the definition of the deserving poor to include women with children, the families of Union soldiers, the elderly, and the sick.[1] Demanding an enduring institution to alleviate the poverty of the most needy freedpeople, these abolitionist-feminists envisioned a radical Freedmen's Bureau, far different from the temporary agency promoted by Republican politicians, the military, and the American Freedmen's Union Commission.

In 1865, few Americans supported a permanent agency to assist former slaves. The American Freedmen's Inquiry Commission recommended only a temporary guardianship, and most Northern whites hoped former slaves would immediately enter into the free workforce and become self-supporting wage laborers. In his autobiography, General O. O. Howard, commissioner of the Freedmen's Bureau, explained the tenuous political situation of his agency. He wrote, "From the start I felt sure that the relief offered by the Bureau to the refugees and freedmen through the different channels, being abnormal to our system of Government, would be but temporary." Howard's distaste for federal intervention framed the life of the Freedmen's Bureau. In his view, the bureau was a political anomaly, not fully supported by even its Republican friends.[2]

By contrast, white female reformers, including Julia Wilbur and Josephine Griffing, valued the Freedmen's Bureau as an agency through which they could protect freedpeople and influence government policy. The activism of these women presaged the maternalism of reformers in the Progressive era, who expanded women's sphere into public policy and social welfare by arguing on behalf of poor women and children.[3] As they argued for greater aid to former slaves, however, they also generated a backlash. While Wilbur did not face the same antagonism she had in Alexandria in 1863, Griffing found that her presence as a distributor of relief stimulated charges of dependency against freedpeople and hostility toward women reformers.

Abolitionist-feminists embraced the idea of a government agency devoted to aiding and protecting former slaves. The first woman and one of the first civilians hired by the Freedmen's Bureau, Josephine Griffing (1814–72), believed that the new agency had the potential to link freedmen's relief and women's political power.[4] In 1846, Abby Kelley Foster converted Griffing to Garrisonian abolitionism and Griffing became an agent for the Western Anti-Slavery Society in Ohio, soon participating in the woman's rights movement as well. During the Civil War, Griffing acted as the western agent for the Women's National Loyal League, an organization founded by Elizabeth Cady Stanton and Susan B. Anthony to petition the government to abolish slavery. Viewing the federal government as crucial to the success of emancipation, in 1864 she left her husband, Charles Stockman Spooner Griffing, in Ohio, and moved with her daughters to Washington, D.C., to work as the agent of the National Freedmen's Relief Association of the District of Columbia. As the NFRA agent, she lobbied the North and the government on behalf of former slaves.[5]

Requesting the appointment of women as freedmen's agents, she petitioned Congress to allow Northern and Western women to "share more fully in the responsibility and labor, so remarkably laid upon the Government and the men of the North, in the care and education of these freedmen." Griffing expressed special interest in freedwomen and children and asked that Northern and Western women be commissioned "to look after, and secure the general welfare of these women and children of the freedmen" as their "wants and necessities are fully understood by your memorialists."[6] Like many early feminists, Griffing appealed to gender conventions to justify women's expanded role in the public sphere. But Griffing's radical request also indicated her interest in an unprecedented partnership between women activists and the federal government.

Griffing also pressed for the establishment of the Freedmen's Bureau, hoping abolitionist women might guide the government's efforts on behalf of former slaves through this agency. In a May 1865 letter to O. O. Howard she described her commitment: "Perhaps no person has felt more interest in the creation and the character of this Bureau than I have. I see the necessity for it now more than ever before."[7] To show their appreciation for Griffing's political activism, Republican leaders encouraged Howard to give her an official position in the agency. He appointed her assistant to the assistant commissioner for the District of Columbia, in June 1865.

Julia Wilbur also viewed the creation of the Freedmen's Bureau as an opportunity for women to exert greater influence over material aid to former slaves. In March 1864, Wilbur corresponded with Anna Barnes about the destitution in Washington, D.C. "About a month ago I did feel as if I might do more good somewhere else perhaps. That in W. people were suffering more than they were here," she wrote.[8] This poverty, Wilbur's problems in Alexandria, and the establishment of the Freedmen's Bureau all encouraged her to transfer to Washington. At the beginning of 1865, she moved her belongings to 207 I Street, where she boarded in the Pennsylvania Freedmen's Relief Association building. Although the Freedmen's Bureau did not pay Wilbur directly until 1867, upon her arrival she was appointed agent in charge of the district "west of 18th street, and the whole of Georgetown." She and her sister Eliza Hartwell visited freedpeople in this area, distributed clothing, and gave out "tickets" for soup, wood, and blankets.[9]

Despite her negative experiences with army officials in Alexandria, Wilbur and the Rochester Ladies' Anti-Slavery Society counted on the military staff of the Freedmen's Bureau to crush the "rebels against Freedom."[10] "I hope and believe Gen. Howard is equal to the task he has assumed," Wilbur told her readers. "Since the Freedmen's Bureau went into operation, many wrongs have been remedied."[11] A visit to Richmond, Virginia, shortly after the end of the war, further convinced Wilbur of the potential of the Freedmen's Bureau for good. Forty soldiers guarded the almshouse of that city, she reported, and some "were rough, ignorant, and prejudiced; they took to negro driving naturally. Such men should never be out where they can wield any power over others, especially the weak and helpless." In this context, Wilbur believed, "a woman's presence was greatly needed," as the soldiers stood over freedwomen with a whip "and in several instances women were beaten and otherwise abused."[12] Previous to her arrival, small children were hired out, or apprenticed, but she requested that children be kept at the almshouse, where they could be cared for by their mothers and taught by a Philadelphia teacher. After Colonel Brown, the Freedmen's Bureau superintendent, arrived, he told Wilbur he would return the apprenticed children to their mothers. Wilbur was confident of Brown's abilities: "I felt that he could be trusted with the interests of the Freedpeople, and then, and not till then, did I feel at liberty to leave Richmond."[13] By linking Colonel Brown's mission to the efforts of female agents, Wilbur feminized both the military and the Freedmen's Bureau.

In Washington, Wilbur and Griffing found fertile ground for the work

Figure 4. Julia Wilbur (undated). Courtesy Haverford College Library, Quaker Collection, Julia Wilbur Papers, Collection 1158.

they planned with the Freedmen's Bureau. The Civil War prompted a large migration of former slaves into the city, as they sought freedom, safety, and work behind Union lines. The black population of Washington increased by 223 percent between 1860 and 1870, from 10,983 to 35,455 African Americans.[14] In her 1865 report, Wilbur calculated that there were between "twenty-five and thirty thousand colored persons in Washington and Georgetown, and a large share of these are lately freed slaves."[15] Freedpeople in the District needed shelter, food, and other assistance. As Wilbur reported, "It is very bad for the poor who live in the shanties & old homes. There are several soup houses here now, & Government has distributed blankets & wood. I forgot whether I wrote you in my last of the terrible amount of suffering here?"[16] The contraction of the federal government at the end of the war contributed to freedpeople's problems. As the army disbanded, many black soldiers lost their means of support, and "by degrees, both men and women were thrown out of employment."[17] Wilbur predicted that women with small children, the elderly, and the disabled, "will be subjects for Northern benevolence for some time to come."[18]

In this situation, Wilbur believed that female agents were desperately needed. Across the river in Alexandria, the number of schools and teachers had increased, but only one woman remained "who gives exclusive attention to the wants of the poor."[19] The Rochester Ladies' Anti- Slavery Society (RLASS) applauded Wilbur's new status, viewing her presence as a necessary supplement to the labor of the Freedmen's Bureau: "there is a pressing need of Agents, self-sacrificing earnest workers, who are heartily interested in the work all over the South."[20] The RLASS also vowed to care for and educate former slaves "until they shall be sufficiently enlightened and qualified to provide for themselves."[21]

Though their language emphasized freedpeople's subordinate status, female agents struggled to refine a notion of the deserving poor that allowed them to describe the horrific conditions in Washington and surrounding areas without blaming former slaves or implicating themselves in freedpeople's poverty. To obtain the donations that allowed former slaves to survive, groups like the RLASS needed to stimulate their members' sympathies while allaying fears of pauperization. Thus Wilbur claimed that she distributed goods to freedpeople "without lessening their self-respect, or diminishing their self-reliance."[22]

As advocates for former slaves, the RLASS, Wilbur, and Griffing also rejected the strict dichotomy between independence and dependence to point out freedpeople's real destitution. In a controversial appeal published in antislavery and Republican newspapers throughout the North, Griffing described the condition of "twenty thousand" freedpeople who had migrated to the city during the war. "A host of miserable women, with large families of children, besides old, crippled, blind and sick persons" sought refuge in the District, according to Griffing, many of whom lived in "shanties, garrets, cellars, and stables" and were without wood, beds, blankets, food, and clothing. Griffing stated, "mothers and sons and wives and children, of soldiers still in Government service as Regular U.S. troops, are suffering for the necessaries of life."[23] In "A Plea for Humanity," Griffing again outlined her concern for "old men, invalids, and babes" and "wives and mothers of men in Government service." After giving examples of specific cases, Griffing pointed out that "These cases might be multiplied. Their name is legion." She called upon the friends of humanity "to aid now" and that "in succoring these victims of a nation's sin ye are succoring Christ."[24] Griffing stressed the nation's responsibility for the condition of former slaves. She emphasized that many of the refugees were relatives of Union soldiers, adapting arguments for military pensions to freedmen's relief. Griffing also focused her appeals on women, children, the elderly, and the sick.[25]

Such dramatic appeals for impoverished freedpeople were partly a function of agents' ambition and economic insecurity. Wilbur's livelihood depended on her employment as a freedmen's agent, employment which rested on freedpeople's need for her aid. The Rochester Society paid for Wilbur's room and board and gave her a small salary. In asking for donations, Wilbur pleaded both for herself and for freedpeople: "I do not feel that my work in Washington is quite done. I think I can be of service to the Freedpeople there for another year at least; and I have learned with grateful satisfaction, that your Society, trusting in the continued kindness of its friends, will probably be enabled to sustain an Agent in Washington through another winter at least."[26] Though Wilbur secured her own independence through freedmen's relief, her identity as benefactor of former slaves combined her desire for economic and political agency with her desire to alleviate the extreme poverty of freedpeople.

As an independent woman with three daughters, Griffing felt similar economic pressures, and for this reason it is unsurprising that she highlighted the gendered aspects of dependency. Describing the plight of single mothers, Griffing wrote, "Women who go out to service put their little ones in bed or cover them with rags on the floor, and go in search of five or ten cents' worth of work to buy a stick of wood and a loaf of bread."[27] The Freedmen's Bureau wanted freedwomen to be self-supporting, and Griffing generally concurred with this view, but she also believed that women needed special assistance. Often the sole care givers to their children, freedwomen also faced low wages, high rents, scarce housing, and the high cost of fuel. On January 5, 1866, Griffing visited the homes of three women who exemplified freedwomen's plight. Sarah Lucas was a widow, sick from exposure and wet feet; both she and her two children needed clothing and her children had no shoes. Lucas also had no wood and, according to Griffing, her shanty was unfit for habitation. Susan Perry had a sick baby and also cared for her dead sister's two children. Griffing reported that she needed bread and wood. Perry could not work because "her children kept her from going out for work." Adeline Washington, a widow with one child, could not walk, and lived in a horrible shanty. When Griffing went to visit her, "she had just got up from a pile of rags on the floor; no bed, no pillow, no chair, no table, no dishes." Washington's child was wearing thin clothes and both had almost frozen the previous day from want of wood.[28] Griffing relied on common ideals of motherhood and domesticity to argue for greater relief.

Wilbur extended Griffing's gendered analysis to make a legal argument for freedmen's relief. By explaining how racism and slavery contributed to freedpeople's poverty, she argued that material aid was reimbursement for damages inflicted by whites. In Petersburg, Virginia, where local authorities disbursed relief, Wilbur learned that "many whites received rations who neither needed or deserved them," while "the colored people who applied for them were treated so badly, that a very small number went for them at all." She demanded equal treatment for dependents of all races, arguing, "Favors have been lavishly bestowed upon white rebels, but all the colored people ask is simple justice."[29] Wilbur concluded that the federal government was "obliged" to care for destitute freedpeople until the South expressed its willingness "to do its duty toward these people."[30]

More importantly, Wilbur believed that the entire nation shared liability for the damage done to the neediest former slaves. While Wilbur argued that most freedpeople were self-sufficient, she also noted that "many of the Freedpeople must, from the nature of the case, be dependent upon the Government or upon the community where they live," including those whom "Slavery has rendered helpless or incompetent."[31] Wilbur argued that slavery had injured certain populations of freedpeople, making them unable to live up to free labor ideals. She underscored the problems of the aged and sick to draw attention to the nation's duty to former slaves. In arguing for a home for dependent freedpeople, Wilbur wrote, "Many of these persons became helpless and dependent through the hardships and abuses of slavery; and it seems quite right that they should continue to receive, as they have done since the first of their being free, the special care of the Government which so long upheld a system calculated to make its victims helpless and dependent." She believed that such an asylum would be "a perpetual rebuke to the atrocities of the past."[32]

The recognition of this injured class allowed Wilbur to respond directly to those who labeled freedpeople idle, criticizing them for their ignorance and lack of sympathy: "It is slander upon these people to say they depend upon Associations for clothing, and upon Government for food. . . . They expect to help themselves, and they try to do so, too."[33] In July 1865, Wilbur proclaimed, "Only two hundred and twenty paupers out of a population of twenty-five thousand!" The following year, Wilbur calculated that at most there were fifteen hundred receiving rations at any one time. In addition, she argued, most of this relief did not come directly from the government, but from the "Contraband Fund," or the deduction taken from the wages of black men employed by the government during the war.[34]

Wilbur believed that policymakers ignored evidence of freedpeople's self-reliance and degraded the poorest among them by forcing them to prove their destitution to receive rations, fuel, and clothing. "I often thought that the poor in many instances, earned the full value of the clothes they received in the efforts required to obtain them," Wilbur wrote. She rejected the notion of indolent freedpeople living happily off the state, noting, "I state these things to show my Northern friends who think the Freedpeople are merely idle, passive recipients of the benefactions of Government, that it is not always easy and pleasant to receive charity, or to be dependent on others for the absolute necessaries of life."[35] Wilbur argued that the government humiliated freedpeople already demeaned by society's racism. She stressed that only extreme poverty forced freedpeople to turn to the government for assistance.

Demanding greater aid to impoverished freedpeople, Wilbur and Griffing also asserted women's particular interest in the welfare of former slaves. After obtaining official positions in the Freedmen's Bureau, abolitionist-feminists demanded a further reconstruction of women's political status. They argued that enfranchising women was a necessary counterpart to federal intervention in emancipation, as female voters would support just and equitable policies toward former slaves.

Female agents of the Freedmen's Bureau were at the vanguard of a larger community of women working in the federal bureaucracy and seeking to shape U.S. government policies. The Treasury Department began hiring female clerks in 1861, and other offices saw the wisdom of employing women at reduced wages to handle the growing workload of wartime administration. By 1870 there were 958 female employees in government offices.[36] This transformation cheered abolitionist-feminists not only because it allowed women greater independence, but because it positioned them to push the government to be an instrument of reform, fulfilling the promise of the Reconstruction Amendments and the Freedmen's Bureau acts. Abolitionist-feminists in the Freedmen's Bureau lobbied Congress both for freedmen's relief and women's suffrage. Indeed, they connected freedmen's aid to women's rights, arguing that the welfare of former slaves depended on women's political participation.

As an employee of the Freedmen's Bureau and a member of the National Woman Suffrage Association, Griffing saw women's rights leading to justice for former slaves. As she stated in one speech, the perfection of American "political, educational, social, and labor interests" could only be achieved through the "equal intermingling of *both* halves of humanity." Griffing pointed to "the corrupt, inconsistent, one-sided, and inadequate legislation of the country, whose salvation, she contended, lay in its speedy recognition and admission of the counterpoising moral element of the woman nature," a statement which must have alluded to Reconstruction policy.[37] Griffing viewed the failures of Reconstruction through the lens of women's suffrage, writing to Elizabeth Cady Stanton that "I see the want of regulation in national affairs, that can never be accomplished, while Govmt. is administered on the *male* basis of representation."[38]

Abolitionist-feminists understood freedmen's aid as a way to exert the moral influence of women in government and national policy while working for women's suffrage. *The Revolution*, the paper founded by Elizabeth Cady Stanton and Susan B. Anthony, published accounts of Griffing's freedmen's aid activities in Washington. One correspondent reported approvingly that as a "lover of justice and equal rights," Griffing "saw the necessity of a bureau in the government, where the rights of the poor might be redressed."[39] Lucretia Mott also sent Griffing money and offered her support for Griffing's work, writing "Thy labors I know are blessed."[40]

Though the Rochester Ladies' Anti-Slavery Society did not actively support the women's suffrage movement, members shared a commitment to a broad definition of women's rights. They believed women performed a necessary and valuable service to the nation by working in the Reconstruction South. More radical than her sponsors, Wilbur actively pursued suffrage for both women and African Americans. After black men received the vote in Washington, D.C., Wilbur "rejoiced that I had lived to see so much progress," but she also felt "a little jealous—the least bit humiliated" when the men voting demonstrated that they did not know how to read. "No earthquake followed these proceedings, and I presume no convulsion of nature would have occurred, had white *women* and black *women* increased that line of voters," Wilbur told the RLASS, and she increased her suffrage agitation.[41] In 1869, she and six other white and black women registered to vote with the board of election in Washington, D.C., as part of a National Woman Suffrage Association campaign to assert women's right to vote under the Fourteenth Amendment. As the women proclaimed, they were "entitled to the franchise."[42]

Like Griffing, Wilbur saw women's rights and the rights of African Americans as inseparable.

Yet Wilbur did not view suffrage as the exclusive means of assuring black freedom or women's equality. Politicians and male abolitionists assumed the vote would give freedpeople the independence and power to protect and uplift themselves. Wilbur agreed, viewing Northern charity as a substitute, necessary "until a more liberal city government recognizes the Freedpeople as a part of its poor, and makes provisions for them accordingly. And now that colored men have a voice in the government we trust that before long this will be brought about."[43] But Wilbur also believed that suffrage was not enough: "*politics* are both intricate and uncertain. In view of all that has passed, I know we have no reason to be discouraged. But it seems a long time to wait for the consummation of our hope—a hope that freedom from persecution will sometime be enjoyed by the colored race."[44] Since even political rights could not necessarily overcome prejudice or discrimination, Wilbur and the RLASS advocated continued federal intervention and the involvement of Northern women.

The presence of women, their demands for equality, and their gendered understanding of poverty and dependence aroused the hostility of men in the Freedmen's Bureau and the freedmen's aid movement. Though Griffing gained her desired "commission," her appointment to the Freedmen's Bureau and her appeals on behalf of freedpeople aggravated the American Freedmen's Union Commission, particularly Jacob R. Shepherd, the Commission's secretary in Washington. In July 1865, Shepherd wrote a Freedmen's Bureau official of his own vision for the Freedmen's Bureau, which emphasized the wisdom of "a charity to help a man become more manly!"[45] Associating freedom with free labor and masculine self-reliance, Shepherd took exception to Griffing's focus on the dependent population of former slaves. In October, he explained the danger of Griffing's appeal to General Howard: "Mrs. Griffing is simply irrepressible: & yet she must be repressed, so far as you and I have to do with her, or else we must bear the odium of her folly. She still represents the '20,000 utterly destitute' as needing *outright support* from Northern charity." Shepherd disparaged Griffing's call for "outright support." He also informed Howard that Griffing was politically unsound and presented her as a foolish woman, whose sympathetic appeals for freedpeople were a danger to his vision of "manly" charity: "Located as she is, & endorsed by the head of the Bureau, she sends her appeal everywhere to the glee of the copperheads, who want no better reading to confirm their 'I told you so!' but to the sore annoyance of all sensible men." Shepherd urged Howard to get rid of Griffing: "Mrs. Griffing is hopelessly unfit for the responsible position she fills, & cannot be too permanently separated from it."[46]

Griffing's appeals threatened Shipherd and other freedmen's aid leaders by challenging the efficacy of their policies. Shipherd claimed to have guaranteed freedpeople's manly self-sufficiency and he believed Griffing's representations of destitution provided fuel for Democrats and other political opponents of emancipation. But her position as a woman "endorsed by the head of the Bureau" proved just as dangerous to the male leadership of Shipherd's commission because she was connected to both the state and the female base of the freedmen's aid movement. In reaction, Shipherd repeatedly denigrated Griffing's abilities as a woman, comparing her to "sensible men." In calling for her "repression," Shipherd urged Howard to return Griffing to her appropriate sphere. In his view, the Freedmen's Bureau was no place for a woman, especially one that refused to accept male authority.

Shortly thereafter, Howard revoked Griffing's appointment and the Freedmen's Bureau issued a press release dissociating itself from Griffing and her appeals: "This Bureau has not received any funds from Mrs. Griffing and does not assume responsibility of the collections she is making. The number of actual dependents upon the Gov't for support, through this Bureau in Washington, varies between three and four hundred."[47] S. N. Clark explained to Mr. E. Carpenter of Colchester, Connecticut, that Griffing was no longer connected to the bureau: "That connection has ceased. She has no authority to solicit funds for the Freedmen's Bureau and no official information to sustain her statements of the suffering among the Freedmen."[48] Clark's strong disavowal of Griffing resulted from her statements regarding the freedpeople of Washington; he hurried to reassure the public that the bureau was not supporting a large number of dependent former slaves. His denial that Griffing had "authority" or "official information" also assuaged the fears of those who worried that Freedmen's Bureau policy was being dictated by a woman.

Griffing's demands for material relief for freedpeople clashed with the Freedmen's Bureau's commitment to free labor and independence, even after her dismissal. Following her discharge, Griffing continued her association with the Freedmen's Bureau. The National Freedmen's Relief Association of Washington kept her on as their agent, but Griffing also acted as a visitor for the bureau and the bureau financially supported her employment agency and industrial school. Her eldest daughter, Emma, remained a paid employee of the bureau.[49] However, the Freedmen's Bureau attempted to limit Griffing's relief activities. Bureau agents who disagreed with her view of relief reported that she exaggerated cases of destitution and recommended freedpeople to the bureau for aid who did not really need it.

Many of the differences between Griffing and men in the freedmen's aid movement resulted from the ascendance of masculine attitudes toward charity, which were accelerated by the Civil War and emancipation. Griffing's methods drew on women's political culture, offering moral appeals on behalf of suffering freedpeople and relying on networks of sympathetic women. The Freedmen's Bureau, working in conjunction with the male leadership of the American Freedmen's Union Commission and other aid societies, believed that free labor and equal rights would be enough to insure a successful transition to freedom. While Griffing's definition of the worthy poor was expansive and included women with children, General Howard and other bureau agents expected freedmen, women, and children to be self-supporting.[50]

In essence, gendered understandings of charity and dependency pitted Griffing against the men of the Freedmen's Bureau. Bureau agents saw Griffing's pleas for material aid, even for poor women and children, as counterproductive. Like Shipherd, agents W. F. Spurgin and Capt. Will Coulter blamed Griffing and other like-minded reformers for what they perceived as the dependent behavior of freedpeople. Spurgin, the local superintendent of the Freedmen's Bureau in the District, believed Griffing was one of those individuals who "seemingly actuated by the best of motives visit among the colored people with a view of ascertaining cases of distress." Spurgin insisted that women drew the category of the deserving poor so broadly as to make no distinction at all: "They bend ear to their complaints, make no discrimination between those able to work and those unable and advise them to apply to the Freedmen's Bureau for assistance. Some of these should be assisted, others should not." In other words, he believed Griffing was advising freedpeople to apply for aid they did not need. Spurgin viewed these tactics as delaying freedpeople's self-reliance: "Work can be obtained for every man, woman, and child in the District. . . . They must sooner or later learn to depend upon themselves nothing can make them independent and respectable more quickly."[51] Like other Bureau agents, Spurgin believed that former slaves had earned only the right to work for wages and freedom from their forced dependence on masters.[52]

Spurgin adamantly denied Griffing's portrayal of freedpeople, but he also revealed his own assumptions about African American dependency. Spurgin argued that freedpeople wanted and even expected support from the state:

I am deeply impressed with the opinion that persons able to work, white and colored, should be forced to do so and as this Bureau is held responsible for the colored people, I have the honor to recommend that all charitable associations and individuals working for their good be made to understand this point. This would lessen the dissatisfaction among the freedmen and do away with the idea prevalent among them that the Government is always to be responsible for their support.[53]

Like Shipherd, Spurgin believed Griffing's descriptions of "the great destitution and starvation of the freedmen of the District" to be "basic fabrications." Adapting Wilbur's charge of "slander" against freedpeople to his own purposes, Spurgin argued that Griffing's methods reflected poorly on former slaves and the government: "These reports are a libel upon the freedmen themselves, upon the citizens of the District, and upon the Government which has provided and still continues to provide all the assistance necessary for the relief of the destitute colored poor of the district."[54] In Spurgin's hands, the discourse of idleness became a powerful weapon that could be used against both freedpeople and the female agents who demonstrated the inadequacies of the masculine approach.

Capt. Will Coulter also disapproved of Griffing's style of freedmen's aid, leading him to repeat Shipherd's call for removal two years after her official discharge. Like Spurgin, Coulter complained that Griffing exaggerated freedpeople's poverty, implying that she did not investigate before giving assistance. In response, Griffing began to include the following statement when she recommended freedpeople to receive clothing or rations: "I certify on honor that the above named cases are absolutely destitute."[55] Coulter was also frustrated by her resistance to his commands. In November 1867, he finally accused Griffing of illegally obtaining government transportation for freedpeople. He submitted a report given to him by Major Vandenburgh which supported his view: "*Mrs. Griffing* has tried and nearly succeeded in *fraudulently* obtaining transportation issued to *Ann Brooks* for *Mary Ann Sims* who was debarred from its benefits and had been refused in *Mrs. G.'s* presence. I think this is a deliberate attempt on the part of *Mrs. G* to defraud the *Gov't.*" Coulter called for her dismissal and announced his inability to work with such "insubordinate and unreliable agents."[56] Nothing came of these charges, and Griffing remained an employment agent of the Freedmen's Bureau and a representative of the National Freedmen's Relief Association of Washington.

Female agents struggled to keep the Freedmen's Bureau focused on direct assistance even as its leaders shifted the bureau's focus to education. General Howard never wanted the Freedmen's Bureau to be a relief agency, but the needs of the freedpeople forced it to provide rations, fuel, housing, and other forms of aid to freedpeople and refugees. At every opportunity, however, Howard cut the supply of rations and turned the bureau's efforts in other directions. By 1867, Howard viewed education as the best kind of aid, and he wanted it to be the primary mission

of his agency. As he recalled in his *Autobiography,* "While we were laboring hard to reduce the number of freedmen's courts, hospitals, asylums,
and eleemosynary features generally, we extended the school operations."[57] Howard claimed that he felt comfortable ending all the operations of the bureau, except for education and pension distribution, in
1868. He wrote, "Matters in all respects touching Bureau operations
during the year gave assurance that at the end of the term fixed by law,
July 16, 1868, I could lay down my heavy burden of responsibility with
good hope of the future if not with positive satisfaction."[58] Like J. Miller
McKim of the American Freedmen's Union Commission, Howard maintained that the Freedmen's Bureau had largely met its goals by laying the
framework for a system of public education in the South.

Both Wilbur and Griffing argued for continued relief to former slaves,
battling declining Northern support as well as the demise of the Freedmen's Bureau. Wilbur pointed out that individuals and societies discon-
tinued their contributions, or gave solely to educational efforts. She
noted, "Many persons express surprise that help is still needed in Washington, since so much has been done for the Freedpeople there."[59] The
Rochester Ladies' Anti-Slavery Society voiced their dismay that "in any
Christian community, there should fail to be a cordial interest and ready
help in the work," but concluded that "Slavery, though as we trust, prac-
tically dead, still exhales a poison over our land, making hearts which
are warm in sympathy towards the white race, cold and indifferent to the
welfare of the black."[60] Although many believed it was time for the Freedmen's Bureau to end its work, Wilbur disagreed. She commented, "Now
if the whites behave so badly with the Freedmen's Bureau in operation,
we can easily imagine what the situation of the freedpeople would be
were the protection of the Bureau withdrawn."[61] Wilbur expressed her
wish to continue her work in aiding destitute freedpeople, though the
funds of the RLASS were "exhausted." In 1869, after losing her RLASS
and Freedmen's Bureau salaries, Wilbur sought employment in the
Patent Office, where she worked until her death in 1895. In her career in
the Patent Office, Wilbur continued to link women's rights to the federal
government.[62]

Griffing fought the termination of the Freedmen's Bureau's relief
work by appealing directly to General Howard's Christian sympathies. In
1869, Griffing wrote to Howard that "there still remains a duty to be performed in feeding and clothing the worn-out Slaves not properly belong-
ing to the Hospital or Poorhouse, and who are in this District Wards of
the Gov't."[63] Like Wilbur, Griffing continued to emphasize the specific
needs of the sick and the elderly. As she wrote, "I take the liberty of
appealing to you in behalf of the old & feeble (only)." On November 22,
1870, forty-nine aged freedpeople had "applied for 'just a little,' as they

had no fire and I could only supply a few of those absolutely sick in their shanties & homes. For this purpose alone the Sec. let me have two cords for this week now all gone and thinks he may let me have a small amount next week for the aged who are sick." Older freedpeople also needed more than wood. Necessity demanded that they be taken care of and Griffing felt strongly that it was her responsibility, General Howard's, and the government's: "At this moment a dozen old women and men, standing waiting at my door—some of them actually shaking with ague— asking for clothes, wood and shoes & stockings. I am in distress on their account, as from years of working among them their wants have become my wants. How shall we provide for them?"[64] By using the word "we," Griffing suggested that Howard and the government had a continuing obligation to freedpeople.

Griffing's desperation also flowed from her personal stake in freedmen's relief. Like Julia Wilbur, Griffing relied on her career as a freedmen's agent for survival. As she begged Howard to continue assistance to needy freedpeople, she also appealed on behalf of her own position in the Freedmen's Bureau. After the bureau discharged her along with most of its other agents in August 1868, Griffing asked to be reinstated to her duties under the Educational Division, one of the only remaining divisions of the bureau. She did this not only because she believed the freedpeople still required her services, but also because of her personal financial need. Griffing described her financial situation to Howard in a letter written in September 1868: "I have no home whatever outside of this city—having put my house and village lot into Freedmen's work in 1865–6 as I deemed it my duty to do—and having loaned Mr. Williams, Freedman from Florida six hundred dollars, in January last—which has not been paid because of the seizure of his cotton, and the constant raid upon him by the rebels (and this was all my ready means)." Griffing stated that it was now difficult to support her daughters: "I am now greatly embarrassed to pay the board and necessary expenses of three without remunerative employment."[65] Several months later she appealed to Howard to buy the house in which she had lived for the past four years for $5,000. Griffing offered to repay him $1,000 after six months and then $1,000 annually plus interest. She wrote, "I need not say to you that with my three daughters I need a home." But Griffing also wanted to continue her work in Washington, seeing her well-being and the needs of freedpeople as interrelated: "I feel that I am called to work in this District— and shall be greatly strengthened by your encouragement in this matter."[66]

Howard did not lend her money, but Griffing remained in the District, supporting herself and her children as a freedmen's agent until her death in 1872. When the Freedmen's Bureau ended all its work but education and the distribution of pensions, Griffing recreated herself as the bureau's inadequate replacement: "So far as a humble individual can be, I am substituting to these a freedman's (relief) bureau; sanitary commission; church sewing society, to aid the poor; orphan asylum; old people's home; hospital and alms-house for the sick and the blind; minister-at-large, to visit the sick, console the dying and bury the dead."[67] But Griffing also believed that private charity alone could not help freed-people. In 1871, she appealed to the city of Washington for money: "the want of food is so great among at least a thousand of these, not one of whom is able to labor for support, that it is impossible to provide the absolute relief they must have, by further contributions from the chari-table and the humane."[68] Until the end of her life, Griffing viewed gov-ernment assistance as the only solution to the poverty of freedpeople in Washington.

Other women also lobbied the government on behalf of former slaves, though their pleas were ignored. In 1870, Rachel Wilson Moore Town-send (c. 1799–1877), a Philadelphia Quaker minister, spent a great deal of time with impoverished and ill freedpeople in Washington. Townsend noted that her appeals fell on deaf ears when she asked Congress for an appropriation for "the colored poor": "I talked to Senators about it. They replied they never noticed these people, and, what is more, they answered that they came to Washington to look after their own busi-ness, and not to take care of Washington niggers or any other niggers." Parker Pillsbury, a male abolitionist but also a women's rights activist, added to her testimony: "If Senator Sumner and the rest of them there in Washington cared no more for these people before the Fifteenth Amendment was ratified than Mrs. Townsend shows, what will they do for them now?"[69]

Women's appeals for aid to freedpeople continued to provoke criti-cism as the political climate grew increasingly hostile to federal inter-vention. Horace Greeley, editor of the *New York Tribune*, critic of Radical Reconstruction, and future presidential candidate, wrote Griffing: "In my judgment you and others who wish to befriend the Blacks crowded into Washington do them a great injury. Had they been told years ago, 'you must find work; go out and seek it,' they would have been spared much misery. They are an easy worthless race, taking no thought for the mor-row, and liking to lean on those who befriended them. Your course aggravates their weaknesses, when you should raise their ambition and stimulate them to self-reliance."[70] Greeley's opposition to Griffing's meth-ods revealed his belief in the natural dependence of African Americans, but his opinion also reflects his faith in American society to provide equal opportunity for all. Griffing's experiences during Reconstruction, including her work with former slaves, her fight for women's suffrage, and her struggle to support herself and her daughters, made her question the equalizing potential of free labor ideology.

In the face of personal attacks that threatened their livelihood, Griffing and Wilbur vehemently challenged the government's free labor policies. They argued that women should be officially commissioned to provide aid to freedpeople. As agents of both freedmen's relief societies and the Freedmen's Bureau, they lobbied the government to continue material assistance to former slaves through the bureau. Arguing that the deserving poor included the relatives of Union soldiers, as well as widows, single mothers, children, the ill, the elderly, and others who had been permanently damaged by slavery, Griffing and Wilbur pressured General Howard to meet the nation's obligations to former slaves. In their view, close cooperation between abolitionist-feminists and the Freedmen's Bureau offered the best protection of freedpeople's rights.

Though historians frequently, and often correctly, comment on the racism, paternalism, and other limitations of women reformers, female agents' advocacy of ongoing federal intervention was truly radical at a time when Americans distrusted the expansion of federal power and disapproved of a national charity for former slaves. Abolitionist-feminists did not merely use freedpeople to further their own power, they argued for a different approach to freedmen's relief, one that complicated and sometimes transcended the debate over black dependency, acknowledging the nation's obligation to former slaves.[71] Women also demonstrated their radicalism through their proposals for land reform, which would allow the nation to pay its debt to former slaves while furthering African American independence.

Chapter 6

Land Schemes

As all observers in the South noted, freedpeople desired to own land above all else. In 1869, Caroline Putnam reported that "The strong wailing cry of this afflicted people is '*Land*! O! for a spot to stand on!' and surely there must be some way devised for their relief."[1] Primarily agricultural laborers, former slaves viewed farm ownership as the best means of establishing their economic security and their independence from whites. Land also represented the ultimate solution to the perceived problem of black dependency for many Northerners. American political thought had long prized yeoman farming as the economic ideal, from Jeffersonian and Jacksonian Democrats through the Republican Party. When land confiscation and redistribution proved politically impossible, Northern policymakers disagreed over how best to facilitate African American property ownership. Most Republicans hoped that wage labor could provide African Americans with enough savings to purchase land, but this expectation proved unreasonable for most freedpeople. When Reconstruction failed to establish former slaves as property owners, female reformers began their own experiments in land reform.[2]

Three women endeavored to establish freedpeople as landowners: Emily Howland in Virginia, Cornelia Hancock in South Carolina, and Sojourner Truth in Kansas. While Howland and Hancock purchased land to sell and rent to former slaves, Truth solicited signatures for a petition to Congress and gave speeches promoting the allotment of land in the West to Southern blacks. Influenced in varying degrees by antislavery idealism, feminist commitment, a gendered version of free labor ideology, and a specifically northern brand of paternalism, Howland, Hancock, and Truth attempted to bring freedpeople their "great desideratum."[3] Though constrained by the ideological limitations of their own beliefs, they made a serious attempt to finally resolve the debate over black dependency. These women rejected the guidance of government and Northern aid societies and undertook to solve the primary problems of emancipation in the South: exploitative labor and race relations, and freedpeople's right to the land.

These women were probably aware of previous attempts at land reform: Fanny Wright's plantation Nashoba, Gerrit Smith's settlement at North Elba, and the Port Royal Experiment. In 1825, Wright, "the red harlot of infidelity," whose public career as a free thinker and advocate of women's rights made her a social outcast, bought land in Tennessee with inherited money and funds she raised from investors. Wright hoped to encourage manumission; she urged slave owners to allow their slaves to purchase their liberty as laborers at Nashoba, an undertaking that she estimated would take about five years. While the slaves worked toward their emancipation, Wright argued that they would be educated and learn the "value of industry." After successfully purchasing their freedom, the former slaves would continue to labor in a cooperative setting, for the good of the community. But Wright could not convince Southerners to go along with her plan, and by 1828 the experiment had ended.[4]

In 1846, wealthy abolitionist Gerrit Smith offered 120,000 acres of land in northern New York state to African Americans at no cost. Intended to help poor blacks become self-reliant landowners, Smith also designed his proposal to combat racist notions of black dependency and to secure the vote for thousands of black property owners in the state. In 1849, John Brown, who became famous for his raid on Harper's Ferry, moved to North Elba and made the black settlement his home. Like Nashoba, Smith's plan was unsuccessful. He succeeded only in encouraging Brown and approximately one hundred blacks to move there, and settlers contended with poor land, the cold climate, and white land speculators.[5]

In establishing African Americans as property owners, the Port Royal Experiment had also failed miserably. Much of the land was bought up by Northern investors or returned to its former owners. Some former slaves could afford to purchase land at Port Royal only with the aid of Northern whites. Edward Hooper, for example, asked his father for $600 to buy a plantation for his "man Harry," who would repay him gradually.[6] After the war, the problem grew worse. Although Congress initially gave the Freedmen's Bureau authority over confiscated Confederate land, and charged the agency with renting and selling the land to freedpeople, President Andrew Johnson's policy of restoration frustrated this aspect of the bureau's mission. Most Republicans viewed confiscation as politically untenable and were unwilling to fight the president on this issue. In 1866, Congress passed the Southern Homestead Act, another attempt to establish former slaves as yeomen farmers. Few freedpeople could afford to buy even the inferior land made available by the bill, however, and the act ultimately failed in its purpose. Many Southern blacks remained plantation laborers.[7]

Though the government's weak attempts proved disappointing, Nashoba and North Elba suggested an alternative that combined free labor ideology and antislavery reform. Though both experiments had failed, their example of direct intervention by Northern philanthropists retained its potential. Rather than freedpeople progressing gradually from wage laborer to property holder, philanthropists could underwrite black land ownership and thus speed the economic independence of former slaves. But buying land for freedpeople was an expensive proposition, one which few reformers could afford to see through.

The land experiment of Emily Howland (1827–1929) was inspired by her Orthodox Quaker abolitionism and funded by her family's wealth. Her father, Slocum Howland, made his fortune as a merchant and landowner in Sherwood, New York. He frequently attended meetings of the American Anti-Slavery Society and his home was a stop on the Underground Railroad. Emily Howland attended a school run by Susanna Marriott, an active Garrisonian, and heard numerous antislavery speakers when she was growing up.[8] And, from 1857 to 1859, Howland taught at Myrtilla Miner's school for free black girls in Washington, D.C., which Howland later described as "one of the places in the Capital to be visited," which through "spite and pro-slavery prejudice it lived and throve." Miner supported the school by begging money from Congress, encouraging visits from reporters, and with contributions from Northern benevolence, especially Philadelphia Quakers.[9] Howland's interest in education, particularly for white women and African Americans, remained one of the driving concerns of her life.

Howland traced her interest in education, antislavery, and women's rights to her Quaker roots in upstate New York. Howland's maternal grandfather, Joseph Tallcott, had a lifelong interest in the "education and training of children" and, in the Orthodox Quaker community surrounding Scipio Monthly Meeting, "interest in the subject of education never wavered."[10] Howland took to heart the Quaker counsel regarding slaves: "whether there is any object of beneficence more deserving of attention, than that of training up the youth of this injured part of the human family, in such virtues, principles and habits, as may render them useful and respectable members of the community." She was proud that Friends figured in "every field of work for humanity and for the growth of justice and truth in the earth."[11] In addition, Howland also credited the Quakers with placing "woman beside man in the church."[12] Howland consciously chose not to marry, and wrote that she took "the position of single woman voluntarily."[13] Following Reconstruction, her feminism drew her to the women's rights movement, and she became the president of her local suffrage society.[14]

Howland's land scheme also grew out of her experiences as a freedmen's aid reformer in Washington, D.C., and Northern Virginia. In 1863,

Howland returned to the Washington area to teach and distribute relief in freedmen's camps. Howland received intermittent support from Northern societies, but like other abolitionist women, she resisted the drive for centralization in freedmen's aid. She preferred to work autonomously, and she disapproved of the ways the umbrella Freedmen's Commission spent its money.[15] In February 1863, Francis George Shaw encouraged Howland to affiliate with the National Freedmen's Relief Association of

Figure 5. Emily Howland (1864). Courtesy Friends Historical Library, Swarthmore College.

New York. "We are endeavoring to induce our friends at the North to send their contributions through our Association," he wrote, "because being in correspondence with all parts of the country we can the better judge where is the most urgent want & thus send the needed supplies if in our power."[16] But Howland felt that she could best determine who was destitute and what was needed since she was working on the front lines. She told her father not to contribute to aid societies but to send money directly to her: "I can use it to a good purpose far more directly than if it were put into the treasury of a society."[17] When she did receive assistance from Northern associations it generally came from Quaker organizations in Philadelphia and New York City. Most of Howland's work for freedpeople was funded by her father.[18]

Despite Howland's willingness to distribute charity to former slaves, she complained about freedpeople's "dependence" on government and northern support. Her descriptions of camp life decried the moral effect of material relief on impoverished former slaves. Howland wrote that new refugees would arrive at the camps almost daily and at times the new arrivals could number as many as six hundred. The impoverished refugees often brought no clothing or other belongings.[19] Although the government tried to provide employment for freedpeople and encouraged them to plant food, the camps were not a conducive atmosphere for any type of industry due to poor living conditions, disease, the heavy population turnover, and the large population of children and the elderly. Reformers described these factors, with harsh judgment, as the "idleness and depravities of camp life."[20] In freedmen's camps, the need for relief seemed never-ending. Howland concluded, "it is perfectly useless to attempt to supply the wants of these importunate miserables. I shall stop the attempt to do it very soon. The best thing to do for them is to instruct and elevate them, out of their rags and beggary."[21] Rather than distribute clothing and food, Howland preferred to help the freedpeople in more lasting ways: "I have brought some garden seeds & potatoes to give out, this is the kind of almsgiving I like."[22] Thus Howland embraced the value of hard work, economic independence, and the free labor criticism of outright charity for former slaves.

Their experiences in freedmen's camps led some female reformers to hold racist notions of black "idleness." Howland's friend Sallie wrote from Camp Todd that she would only aid those who were self-reliant: "I have made up my mind to help these people who help themselves and those who can't I'll report to the Bureau." Sallie also remarked on the "shiftless" freedpeople at Fort Runyan where Howland had worked previously: "I told them to wash up water was cheap and they could mend. I tell thee those people are lazy & extravagant. After all thee gave them last winter if they had taken care they would not be so destitute now. They send their children to school about one day a week." Sallie much preferred the freedpeople at Camp Todd and Mason's Island; she liked all of them except one family, who were, she thought, "worthless & improvident & ungrateful."[23] Sallie criticized what she perceived as freedpeople's dependent and thankless behavior in freedmen's camps. She approved of cleanliness, hard work, and thrift, characteristics that reflected her free labor priorities.

But Howland expressed more sympathy than criticism. She believed that government indifference and white racism were former slaves' greatest obstacles. In 1866, Howland wrote about how difficult it was to witness such suffering and be able to do so little about it: "It is painful to think of some thousand of people around you half famished." Hunger was one of many problems; winter was the most difficult time for the freedpeople because of the cold and the price of fuel. "I dread the cold weather for them," she wrote, "I do not see where the wood is to come from to warm these little patched up houses about the thickness of pasteboard." Howland stated that older people had the most difficult time providing for themselves: "Nearly every day several poor old stiffened aunts and uncles appear at my door for meal, often hobble along several miles. The same ones do not come frequently so I know that they only come as a last resource."[24] Howland knew that freedpeople used white

Figure 6. Freedpeople entering a refugee camp, *Harper's Weekly,* January 31, 1863 (drawn by A. R. Waup). Courtesy Library of Congress, Prints and Photographs Division, LC-USZ62-088812.

benevolence only in extreme circumstances. Her assessments reflect a gendered approach to freedmen's relief that implicitly criticized the efforts of male reformers and the Freedmen's Bureau.

Howland and her friends supplemented the work of the Freedmen's Bureau by offering immediate relief to sick, widowed, elderly, and simply impoverished former slaves. In 1865, Howland sent Anna Searing, a friend from home and a teacher in the District, ten dollars for what Searing described as "needs that cannot be reached in any other way than by an immediate bestowal of charity." As a bureaucratic agency, accountable to the public, the Freedmen's Bureau could not act quickly enough to provide emergency clothes, food, or fuel. Searing offered the example of "a widow near us whose whole family were sick with the small pox and she had lately recovered from sickness and unable to go to service even after her children had been conveyed to the Hospital. We presented her case to the Bureau but it was some time before they acted and meanwhile the family must not suffer for food and fuel."[25] Because of their private and often personal funding, Howland and her friends had the flexibility to be generous. Lizzie Bailey reported that Dorcas Holland, an aged freedwoman from Freedmen's Village, a camp specifically for elderly freedpeople, came to her complaining that she was suffering for food. Bailey reported that she was going to investigate the case as Holland was poorly dressed and very thin: "If I find she is really suffering as she said I shall take some of my own money and get them something right away until you can send me some for now it is very hard times for them they can get no work and the weather continues very cold so that they really need some assistance now, the clothing you have will be very acceptable."[26] Like Bailey and Howland, many female reformers gladly gave their own money when government and Northern assistance was not forthcoming. Their parallel efforts constituted a women's version of the Freedmen's Bureau.

While donating money and clothing for freedpeople's relief, Howland also pursued her interest in education. Howland helped establish schools by finding Northern support for teachers, aiding in the purchase of buildings, and acting as a go-between for freedpeople and the bureau. She encouraged her friend, the Reverend Mr. J. R. Johnson, to teach at several schools in northern Virginia and convinced the Philadelphia Friends to pay him a salary of twenty dollars a month.[27] Mr. J. P. Read of Falls Church, Virginia, wrote Howland to obtain support for his daughter's Sabbath school. Read and his daughter kept up the school of sixty students, but they had been doing so without pay:

The colored people here have never called on the Government for any thing and are industrious and well behaved set as can be found in any community it appears to be their misfortune that my daughter started a Sabbath school among them (now one year since) as it appears to cut them off from all the Charitable Societies. I have made a number of applications but have not been able to get anything towards sustaining a school among them one says apply to the government another say you do not come under our society another say we cannot do anything as your daughter does not belong to any Christian church and yet another say you are a baptist you had better apply to that denomination.

Though Read had difficulty acquiring financial assistance from competing secular and religious freedmen's aid associations, Howland offered him ten dollars per month. Read's financial obstacles were gone, but the Civil War further disrupted his school. In 1864, rebels murdered him for educating African Americans.[28]

Howland quickly decided that freedpeople needed to become landowners to achieve independence and protect their schools and homes. With the aid of her father, Howland bought land at Heathsville in Northumberland County, Virginia, in 1866. She selected freedpeople to settle on the land and pay rent until they could afford to purchase it from her. Howland reported to Sallie Holley that she had "colonized there 'Uncle Moses' and two other families." She hoped to establish a "prosperous colony" with "none to molest," and stated that "it is my purpose that they ultimately become possessors of their homes." Howland described these settlers as her "proteges," suggesting that she perceived even elderly men as her pupils.[29] She also used the word "colony" twice, implying a certain imperialism. But Howland's experiment was far more radical than previous proposals for colonization, which had advocated the settlement of African Americans in Africa or the Caribbean. Instead, Howland established independent black land owners among former Confederates.

Howland viewed education as a crucial component of her experiment, and she started a school in Heathsville immediately. By early 1867, she had sixty students at her school, with an average of thirty attending every day. Howland also taught a Sunday School with attendance reaching one hundred scholars. Like the American Freedmen's Union Commission, Howland encouraged whites to attend her school. Unlike the AFUC, she succeeded, though she constantly referred to the hostility she faced from local whites. As one bureau agent reported after visiting her school: "The work in Heathsville is progressing very favorably under the auspices of Miss. H. and she has accomplished one thing so far I know is without precedent, viz. She has induced several poor white children to enter the school and study and recite side by side with the colored children."[30]

Howland's work became a model for what could be achieved by women's private, independent charity. Freedmen's teacher Caroline Putnam praised Howland's work at Heathsville and urged other women to follow in her footsteps: "Why should hers be, so far as I know, the solitary case of one young woman, single-handed and alone, without society or support outside of the gifts her own character prompted, working like leaven this widespread influence that is felt up as far as Westmoreland County." Putnam criticized a Carolina teacher who could not run her household for less than $80 a month, since Howland calculated that hers cost one-tenth of that. Putnam asked "are there not enough women to be found in the North, willing to try it for a year? And make their old gowns do that time at least?"[31]

Howland's accomplishments at Heathsville turned on three intercon-nected factors: her institutional independence, her wealth, and Heaths-ville freedpeople. As a teacher for a northern aid society, she would have been dependent on shaky financial support and policies formulated by others. At Heathsville, she could apply her own reconstruction policy. Howland was able to run her household for $2 a week because she clearly had other financial resources on which to draw. In addition, she relied on the support of Heathsville freedpeople, who due to Howland's phil-anthropy were probably more prosperous than freedpeople in other communities. Though Howland successfully promoted her agenda, her independence was limited by her sex. Howland had made the deliberate decision to remain single, but she was still bound by family ties. In 1870, her parents grew ill and they called their unmarried daughter home to care for them.

Howland returned to the North permanently, but she continued to support and visit the Heathsville community. As she reflected on her experiment in 1871, Howland expressed satisfaction that her project brought justice to Heathsville: "Since coming here & learning the frauds & extortions practiced on the people I see it has been a great benefit to them for land to be owned in their midst held for them to buy at fair price & sure title. It has been a check on the whole oppressing class to know there was a refuge. I wish at least one farm was owned for such a purpose in every Co. It would be a great check of the wicked wills of the old slaveocracy, who let no whit of a chance escape to oppress them."[32] Because Howland saw economic independence and political and civil equality as connected, she viewed land ownership as the only way to pre-vent the continued exploitation of black labor in the South.

Emily Howland's father, Slocum Howland, also assisted other land pur-chasing ventures, such as that of Cornelia Hancock (1840–1927), a New Jersey Quaker. As with so many women, the Civil War brought Han-cock into a public career, allowing her to shape important national pol-icy. In 1863, Hancock began her career of public service by traveling with her brother-in-law, Dr. Henry T. Child of Philadelphia, to Gettys-burg to nurse the wounded. She continued to volunteer as a nurse for the Army of the Potomac until the end of the war. Hancock's first contact with former slaves came that winter when she worked in a "contraband" hospital in Washington, D.C., for three months. Like Emily Howland, Julia Wilbur, Hannah Stevenson, and other women in the freedmen's aid movement, Hancock never married, choosing instead to make a life's work of reform. Hancock worked as a freedmen's teacher in South Carolina for ten years, from 1866 to 1876. After Reconstruction, she turned her interests to the urban poor, helping found both the Society for Organizing Charity and the Children's Aid Society in Philadelphia. Hancock's experience in the freedmen's aid movement undoubtedly shaped her career in charity organization, as her philosophy remained "to help people help themselves."[33] Thus Hancock represented a human bridge between the poverty debates of Reconstruction and the Progressive era.

Hancock met Emily Howland in Washington, D.C., when the former worked in the freedmen's camps and the latter at the contraband hospital. Hancock reported that Howland was "all about," commenting further, "I like her very much."[34] Although Hancock's primary concern at this point in her career was for Union soldiers, her short stay in Washington helped her formulate her vision of Reconstruction. Witnessing the mistreatment of African Americans and their impoverished condition, Hancock decided to launch her own scheme to aid and uplift freedpeople through land ownership.

When Hancock first arrived in Washington in 1863, she appealed to friends and relatives for donations, simultaneously portraying freedpeople's poverty and dependency. As she wrote her mother and sister, "I shall depict our wants in true but ardent words, hoping to affect you to some action. Here are gathered the sick from the contraband camps in the northern part of Washington. If I were to describe this hospital it would not be believed." The hospital witnessed at least one birth per day and between forty and fifty new arrivals every day. Hancock explained, "They have nothing that anyone in the North would call clothing."[35] If they had no clothes on hand, Hancock advised her female relatives to "call an especial meeting and send some. If you could see the hordes of people in need, I do not think you would delay."[36] To her young nephew, she wrote: "Thee need to feel very glad thee was not born a contraband for lots of them have nothing to wear but a little thin frock and not a very warm house to sleep in."[37] Concern for the welfare of former slaves was tempered by her frustration with what she saw as freedpeople's dependence on whites and the government: "they bother me to know what the 'govrnor' (government) is going to do with them. Such ignorance no where reigns as among contrabands. They will hang on to a white person as their only hope." Hancock, with other Northern reformers, saw freedpeople as remaining virtual slaves, requiring the guidance and aid of whites.[38]

Yet Hancock also criticized military authorities and former abolition-ists for inadequately supporting freedpeople. She reported that a system of "second hand slavery" existed in the freedmen's camps, where the army employed blacks but frequently reneged on paying them for their labor. Hancock wrote her brother that "nothing for the permanent advancement of these people can be effected until the whole matter is removed from the military authority and vested in a separate bureau whose *sole object* is the protection and elevation of these people."[39] She told her mother that the Philadelphia Freedmen's Relief Society sent nothing to freedpeople in Washington, and asked her brother: "where are the people who have been professing such strong abolition proclivity for the last thirty years?—certainly not in Washington laboring with these people whom they have been clamoring to have freed. They are freed now or at least many of them, and herd together in filthy huts, half clothed. And, what is worse than all, guarded over by persons who have not the proper sympathy for them."[40]

Hancock argued for a well-funded and aggressive Freedmen's Bureau. Echoing Josephine Griffing, she envisioned a separate bureau solely ded-icated to protecting freedpeople. Hancock also believed that the men leading the bureau should have "living souls in them large enough to realize that a contraband is a breathing human being capable of being developed if not so now." The officers should be "good energetic, anti-slavery persons," men or women. Hancock emphasized the importance of this bureau to the future of the nation: "I feel this is the duty of every individual to urge upon every senator and congressman that this step must be taken." Hancock accepted that men would run the bureau, but her emphasis on "anti-slavery persons" and "every individual" suggests she believed in women's full participation.[41]

Hancock favored a centralized private movement to supplement the bureau, but the organization that emerged, the American Freedmen's Union Commission, failed to inspire her, perhaps because of its male leadership and modest program. In January 1864, she wrote that "A national Sanitary Commission for the Relief of Colored Persons of this class would save lives and a great deal of suffering."[42] Yet Hancock never joined the AFUC or any of its branches. When she went to South Car-olina to teach freedpeople in 1866, she was sponsored by the Philadel-phia Friends Association for the Aid and Elevation of the Freedmen.

Like most reformers, Hancock believed in education, though her argu-ments contained a typical note of condescension. In her reports to the Friends Association, Hancock stressed the importance of education: "It seemed to me, in my observations, that by far the most permanent good that is being done for the South, are the schools; they are of course but a drop in the vast ocean of ignorance."[43] She also emphasized the progress and accomplishments of her pupils who attended regularly despite the demands of field labor, and she urged the Philadelphia Quakers to continue their contributions: "I hope that from what I have written you may conclude that the way you have chosen to aid the South is a permanent good that can never be effaced by any politician or intriguer, and that you may be encouraged to give of your abundance, that the good work may go on."[44] Hancock further alerted her readers to the problems still evident in black education in the South—one teacher had been driven from town, while another was only protected because she was related to a bureau officer. Indeed, she stressed, former slaves still needed Northern assistance.[45]

Like Howland, Hancock saw education as one pillar of freedmen's independence; another was "possession of land," the freedpeople's "chief anxiety."[46] Hancock attacked the rapid evolution of a tenant farming system in South Carolina. In early 1870, planters offered freedpeople a two-year contract, giving them temporary control of land that needed to be cleared. Hancock remarked that this "invariably proves a good bargain for the planter, and a poor one for the colored man," as freedpeople "live two years in a place until the land becomes productive, when the planter takes possession again." She lamented the failure of the government to give freedpeople access to confiscated land: "Had that been done, by this time thrifty little farms would have been the result." Though the government seemed in no hurry to aid freedpeople in becoming landowners, Hancock still held out hope that liberal legislation might grant freedpeople access to the Jeffersonian vision of America.[47]

In the meantime, Hancock took matters upon herself. She asked Slocum Howland for financial assistance in buying a plantation on Cat Island. Hancock expressed the same motivations as Emily Howland: without help from friends, it was almost impossible for freedpeople to purchase land without getting cheated. Hancock wrote, "When I can sell this to them and give them a good title it will be the first land disposed of to col. people in this parish I believe, and it is a scandalous shame the promises that have been made to them if they would clear up ground &c. Some have paid hundreds of dollars and got no title."[48] Only when abolitionists bought and sold the land could these frauds end.

Hancock's plan combined altruism with practicality, providing for herself and former slaves. Hancock told Howland that she wanted to demonstrate two things on Cat Island: "that women & colored persons are capable of managing for themselves."[49] To insure the success of her land venture, Hancock planned to pay freedpeople to clear the plantation of wood: "They need ready money to live upon until they raise something upon the land. Wood is profitable and I want the land cleared. I want to get 500 cords cut this year and all say a profit of one dollar per cord can surely be made."[50] Thus, Hancock informed Howland, both she and former slaves could earn a steady income, while enabling freedpeople to purchase the land and begin a cash crop.

Hancock's plan to prove the independence of women and African Americans failed on a number of levels. Hancock had to scramble for a living on Cat Island. As she wrote Howland in 1875, she hoped to stay in South Carolina for another year, but she wanted "some assurance from somebody that I shall neither starve nor be obliged to beg next year."[51] One problem Hancock faced in her venture was that the freedpeople preferred to buy land from the government, probably because they held more faith in a government that had freed them than in the white people they were acquainted with. Even after she convinced freedpeople of her good intentions, Hancock expressed disappointment with her land scheme, concluding "it has failed entirely to accomplish the meaning of the purchase (viz. the settling of the colored people)." Hancock pointed to freedpeople's poverty as the explanation, writing, "I can assert that it will never be of use to col[ore]d. people they never have enough money ahead to buy anything."[52]

Hancock expressed the frustration that many reformers felt. Facing Northern indifference, a depressed Southern economy, and freedpeople's descent into debt peonage, she returned to Philadelphia in 1876 to search for remunerative employment. But her bitterness over the failed experiment also affected her view of former slaves. In 1875, Hancock wrote to Howland, "The colored people are full of uns, uncivilized, uncultivated, &c. &c."[53] After spending almost ten years in the South, Hancock's commitment to former slaves faltered. Rather than continue to struggle side by side with former slaves, Hancock abandoned her radical experiment a year later.

Despite the obstacles to African American property ownership, the land issue enabled reformers to challenge the fears of pauperization and idleness that permeated Northern society.[54] In 1870 and 1871, Sojourner Truth traveled throughout the Northeast giving speeches and collecting signatures on a petition to Congress, which proposed land allotment as the solution to the large number of "dependent" freedpeople in the nation's capital. Truth and the petitioners stated, "we believe that the freed colored people in and about Washington, dependent upon the government for support, would be greatly benefitted and might become useful citizens by being placed in a position to support themselves." They proposed that the government "set apart for them a portion of the public land in the West."[55] As Nell Irvin Painter and Carleton Mabee suggest, Truth viewed unemployed freedpeople as morally suspect, delinquent vagabonds. But while Truth claimed land would enable freedpeople "to become independent through their own exertions," her message also advocated the radical measure of land reform.[56]

In her *Narrative* and *Book of Life*, Truth introduced her petition to Congress by describing freedpeople as "sinned against as well as sinning." She detailed the crimes perpetrated upon former slaves, especially in the nation's capital.[57] Slavery continued in the District of Columbia until 1862. As Truth observed the public buildings in Washington, symbols of national power, she noted, "*We helped* to pay this cost. We have been a source of wealth to this republic. Our labor supplied the country with cotton, until villages and cities dotted the enterprising North for its manufacture, and furnished employment and support for a multitude, thereby becoming a revenue to the government."[58] Both the North and South had profited from slave labor, so Truth concluded that former slaves deserved a share of its "dividends." "Who can deny the logic of her reasoning?" asked Truth's amanuensis, who included a quote from abolitionist Parker Pillsbury to sustain Truth's argument: "our nation will yet be obliged to pay sigh for sigh, groan for groan, and dollar for dollar, to this wronged and outraged race."[59] Truth believed the nation could pay its debt by giving some of the unoccupied lands in the West to blacks, much as it had to Indians and railroads.

Truth's speeches promoting land allotment appealed to Northerners' aversion to charity for former slaves, while reminding her audience of the nation's debt to freedpeople. Journalists, seeking to use Truth for their own purposes, often missed this. When Truth said, "True statesmanship demands that government give them lands in the West, thus paying a little of that great debt we owe this long oppressed people," a Northampton, Massachusetts, newspaper reported that Truth criticized the government for giving charity to freedpeople rather than "putting them in the way of sustaining themselves."[60] But Truth's argument for land distribution always depended on both the desire for black independence and her belief in the nation's obligations. On Long Island, Truth described the destitute and dependent condition of former slaves, and then she "spoke of the white people, and their holding human beings in bondage, and asked how it would be with them when summoned before the bar of Judgment to answer for their deeds upon earth."[61] White Americans, North and South, were responsible for former slaves, and Truth called upon her audiences to make amends for slavery, and facilitate freedpeople's independence, by giving them land.

Truth's focus on land ownership grew from her own struggle for economic independence. In 1860, she purchased a home in Battle Creek, Michigan, but she labored to hold on to it, lecturing and selling her photographs and narrative. Despite her hard work, Truth did not prosper, making her vulnerable to the same dependency that freedpeople

Figure 7. Sojourner Truth (ca. 1864). Courtesy Library of Congress, Prints and Photographs Division, LC-USZ62-119343.

faced. As a result, she connected both African American and women's rights to economic equality. At one postwar women's rights convention, she argued that "I have a right to have just as much as a man," and she informed the men and women in the audience, "What we want is a little money." But like other women reformers, Truth did not view independence and dependence as absolutes, and she asked her listeners to "help us now until we get it."[62] Truth stressed that without aid neither African Americans nor women could attain the free labor ideal of property ownership.

As Nell Painter notes, Truth's plan was ultimately unsuccessful. She journeyed to Kansas in December 1870, but no specific plan for settlement came of this trip. Politicians remained uninterested and her petition was ignored. Audiences undoubtedly came away from Truth's lectures sustained in their views of the dangers of government support for freedpeople. But former slaves did not lose their desire for land, and, in 1879, many freedpeople left the South in an "exodus" to Kansas, fulfilling Truth's vision.[63] During Reconstruction, Truth's radical call to the nation to pay its debt to freedpeople served as a reminder of Reconstruction's failures to transform the lives of former slaves.

As Eric Foner points out, land confiscation and redistribution were at the "outer limits" of Radical Republicanism during Reconstruction. Only a few Radicals, most notably Thaddeus Stevens, consistently and publicly supported confiscation. Though all Republicans acknowledged that land ownership represented the ultimate ideal of economic independence, they did not support violating Southern property rights to facilitate this independence. Republican politicians also contended with the ideological limitations of free labor, which stressed the model of the self-made man, and the political opposition of their constituencies.[64]

Women in the freedmen's aid movement went beyond voicing their support for land distribution to former slaves, to implementing programs of land ownership in the South and advocating such endeavors elsewhere. These women intended to resolve the dilemma of black "dependency" and the continued poverty and exploitation of former slaves by establishing former slaves as landowners. Despite Howland's success, Hancock's proposal to sell land to former slaves, like the Southern Homestead Act, failed when freedpeople could not earn the money to buy land. Sojourner Truth shared many of the same free labor values and paternalistic assumptions as Howland and Hancock, but she framed the distribution of land as part of the nation's debt to former slaves. Without government backing, however, women's efforts to establish freedpeople as landowners were limited, confined to what private monies could fund.

Women's struggle for economic and political independence was tied to that of former slaves. Howland asserted her independence from the freedmen's aid movement by controlling the process of Reconstruction in one part of Virginia. As a woman, however, her family obligations placed limits on her work in Heathsville. Cornelia Hancock relied on financial support from Philadelphia Quakers and the Howland family for her economic and educational endeavors on Cat Island. But economic problems in the South made it difficult, if not impossible, for African Americans or women to prove they were capable of managing for themselves. Sojourner Truth supported herself by lecturing for the distribution of land to former slaves. Though she managed to make a meager living from her speeches, she failed to translate her power as a speaker into the transformation of northern consciousness. As employment agents, women also confronted the limits of free labor ideology to provide economic independence for women or African Americans.

Chapter 7

Female Employment Agents and African American Migration to the North

Though women like Josephine Griffing, Emily Howland, and Sojourner Truth presented an alternative to the Reconstruction plan advocated by the Freedmen's Bureau, they nevertheless assumed that former slaves would work for their bread. The bureau hired women as employment agents (also known as intelligence agents in the nineteenth century), making them crucial figures in the slaves' transition to wage labor. As Freedmen's Bureau agent Waity Harris reported to the Rhode Island Association for Freedmen, "One of the most important branches of our work so considered by Gen. Howard is to encourage and incite these people to leave Washington and go where good homes and competent wages can be procured for them, for we still have a large class of unemployed colored people among us."[1] But female agents often promoted an agenda that clashed with the employment policies of the Freedmen's Bureau. While the Freedmen's Bureau urged, and sometimes coerced, freedpeople to migrate to plantations in the South and Southwest, women favored migration to Northern states, including Michigan, Ohio, New York, Rhode Island, Connecticut, and Massachusetts.[2] The Freedmen's Bureau championed self-support as an end in itself, but abolitionist women believed that free labor should also include other freedoms, such as education and legal and political rights. Josephine Griffing and other abolitionist women pushed Northern migration "as a measure of justice and economy." Griffing herself believed that life in the North offered "compensating labor, and protection of law and humanity."[3]

Approximately nine thousand freedpeople accepted Freedmen's Bureau transportation to the North during Reconstruction, and female employment agents significantly contributed to this endeavor.[4] Historians estimate that Josephine Griffing and Sojourner Truth aided the Northern migration of five to seven thousand freedpeople.[5] Abolitionist women created a network of employment agencies and personal connections, which, supplemented by Freedmen's Bureau transportation, facilitated the migration of freedmen, women, and children.

As in their relief efforts, female agents were especially interested in assisting freedwomen. Anna Lowell, of the Howard Industrial School for Colored Women and Girls in Cambridge, Massachusetts, believed freedwomen would benefit both economically and morally from the training and placement she provided. She wrote, "Instead of living in poverty and dependence they are all supporting themselves by honest labor, and their children will be even more benefitted than they . . . it is the best and only thing to be done to save them from evils which can only be realized and appreciated by those who have been familiar with it."[6] Lowell viewed Northern homes as a haven from the sexual and labor exploitation freedwomen faced under slavery. In addition, abolitionist-feminists viewed paid work as potentially liberating, especially for women. As employment agents, they offered freedpeople a route to independence that they themselves had followed. But white abolitionist women held an idealistic view of life in the North. Despite abolitionist women's hopes, Northern migration often created more problems for freedpeople than solutions.

The Freedmen's Bureau's migration policy responded to the dramatic increase in the black population of Washington, D.C., during and after the Civil War.[7] Following Appomattox, thousands of African American soldiers returned to the private sector, leaving former slaves facing high unemployment and a housing crisis. The National Freedmen's Relief Association of Washington reported that the "destitution and suffering" exceeded anything they had previously experienced.[8] In order to decrease the number of freedpeople, particularly unemployed freedpeople, in the city, the Freedmen's Bureau actively encouraged former slaves to emigrate between 1866 and 1868. Commissioner O. O. Howard's goals were "the relief of the Government from the support of those who are dependent upon it" and "the amelioration of the condition of those who are so dependent."[9] The reality of black poverty in the nation's capital was a political embarrassment for Howard. Decreasing the number of freedpeople dependent on government and private charity, and relocating former slaves to areas offering employment seemed an attractive solution.

In 1866, General Howard's brother, C. H. Howard, the assistant commissioner for the District of Columbia, more explicitly articulated the motives of the Freedmen's Bureau: "it is highly desirable to diminish the number of unemployed freedpeople in the district as much and as speedily as possible."[10] The Freedmen's Bureau accordingly invested in migration, paying for freedpeople's travel expenses to Northern or Southern destinations, "where labor is in demand, and where it is needed," in order to ease the burden on the city and the bureau.[11] In addition, the bureau paid the rent of intelligence agencies, hired white and black employment agents, and paid Griffing, Truth, and other agents to escort freedpeople to the North.

General Howard's desire to distance the agency from any association with charity fueled these migration policies. From the beginning of his tenure at the Freedmen's Bureau, Howard vowed that the government would not support freedpeople "in idleness."[12] Paid migration was a transitional form of assistance, conceived to force Washington freedpeople to abandon government rations in favor of private wage labor. In 1866, Assistant Commissioner Howard announced that freedwomen who declined government transportation would not receive material aid: "It is important also, as you well know, to have the Women provided for before Winter. None who refuse to go (without good reason) will receive any aid from the government here. Please keep record of any such."[13] While women agents were bound by the Freedmen's Bureau's instructions, they vigorously protested unjust policies. Josephine Griffing opposed any coercive tactics to encourage freedpeople to migrate, viewing such measures as "an infringement of their right to live in society." In a report to the National Freedmen's Relief Association, she stated her concern that the bureau's imperatives would separate freedwomen from their families: "These women, the only guardians of their children, feel it to be hard, and an infringement of the right guaranteed by their late freedom, that they must again be broken up."[14] While Griffing remained a strong defender of migration, she was unwilling to force freedpeople to leave Washington, especially if emigration would divide families.

Designed to address the concerns of free labor advocates, the Freedmen's Bureau's migration policies nonetheless faced political problems in the North. Though some Northerners actively sought former slaves as employees, others wholeheartedly opposed black migration. Oliver St. John, who ran an intelligence agency in Brooklyn, New York, listed the benefits as well as possible objections to black migration to the North. He agreed with Howard that migration promised freedpeople not only housing and work, but the much vaunted independence from government care: "Thus put to lucrative and useful work, they will be saved from demoralizing influences which are postured by idleness and want." St. John also feared that the inevitable black poverty would tax local relief agencies and provide fuel for the political enemies of African Americans and the bureau, "by exploiting the prejudices of the lower classes and by perverting such uncomfortable facts of delinquency, theft or drunkenness as will probably occur among such large masses." He suggested that former slaves "will fail to meet the expectations of the Northern people."[15] The experiences of other employment agents validated St. John's concerns. Waity Harris encountered hostility when she took five girls to Lima, New York. She reported that she "met with a very cordial reception from those interested in my work; but there was another class, who did not seem to feel very well pleased at the idea of these people coming among them and one of the number took upon himself to make some demonstrations."[16] Northern resistance was also influenced by the fear of black dependency. After receiving a complaint from Mrs. Black of Cleveland, C. H. Howard inquired "whether any freedpeople have been sent to Cleveland by Mrs. Griffing . . . for whom employment had not been provided previous to their going."[17] Northerners worried that blacks would offer competition to white labor, or alternatively, become dependent on public support in their communities.[18]

Laura Haviland, another agent who brought freedpeople to the North, discussed Northern fears in her memoir. In 1866, Haviland escorted fifteen orphans and forty laborers to Cleveland. Several months later, Burton Kent, the county superintendent of the poor, wrote her, "Many persons transported by you last year have become a county charge, and it has become an intolerable burden to the tax-payers. Any person bringing a child or indigent person into this county without being legally indentured, shall be prosecuted to the full extent of the law." In part, Kent and other Northern officials simply wanted to reduce their relief rolls, a common goal for local authorities. Though Kent probably opposed the distribution of charity to all outsiders, racial assumptions also shaped his threat, for he viewed black migrants as especially prone to pauperism. Haviland immediately went to the county poorhouse only to find that "no colored child had been there, and of the fifty-one inmates but three were colored; and only one man (Mr. Morris Brown) who came with me the previous summer had been received. He was discharged in a short time." She attributed Kent's letter to racial prejudice and questioned whether Morris Brown's short stay had really been "an intolerable burden to the taxpayers."[19]

While Northern states did not necessarily provide freedpeople with the "protection of law and humanity," Griffing and other women continued to assist migration, believing that the North offered freedpeople greater liberty and opportunity. Though women with official positions escorted large groups of freedpeople to the North, teachers and relief workers also facilitated the migration of individuals. Emily Howland tried to place a married couple with her "Cousin Mary" as early as 1863, though Mary "could not have the man." In 1866, Howland informed her father that she was coming North with a young girl: "I shall bring a little girl, if I do not get a home for her in Philadelphia, Sarah Boyer to whom I wrote on her behalf has found two homes for my choice, if I get none before."[20] Like other freedgirls who migrated to the North, she would live with a Northern family, work as a domestic servant to pay for her room and board, and attend school. Although Howland never engaged in employment efforts to the extent that Griffing, Truth, and Harris did, she continued to write home of "girls" she was sending or bringing to the North. As she informed one relative, "I do it for the good of the girls, not specially interested in supplying the community with help."[21]

Women's success in finding freedpeople jobs and homes in the North relied on contact with Northern communities, the efforts of family and friends, and the aid of abolitionists and reformers. Howland counted on relatives and friends to help her find homes for freedgirls, while other women sought the assistance of prominent abolitionists. Mrs. L. M. E. Ricks, a loyal white refugee from Louisiana who billed herself "the Freedmen's friend," visited Lucretia Mott on her way through Philadelphia. Mott reported to her daughter that Mrs. Ricks had taken "2 or 300 out West—some to Michigan—& used all her means, of course." Ricks' visit to Philadelphia gained her at least $35 in contributions and Mott's praise for her wonderful "energy" and "incessant talk." Mott viewed the "distribution" of freedpeople to the West as a positive response to the poverty of freedpeople in Washington and noted that "good accots. come of nearly all Mrs. Ricks has taken." Mott's freedmen's aid society, the Friends Association for the Aid and Elevation of the Freedmen, also raised $150 for Frances Dana Gage "for the same purpose."[22] Since 1862, Gage had lectured to raise money for the relief and education of former slaves, but, like many abolitionist-feminists, she focused on issues of black labor and migration following the Civil War.[23]

To solicit funds, Gage joined forces with Josephine Griffing in emphasizing the moral and economic benefits of freedpeople's employment in the North. She published a newspaper article describing her encounter with the "noble, untiring" Griffing in a New York train station, "surrounded by sixty of the colored people, with whom she was journeying on to Providence, R.I." Griffing informed Gage that the government paid "no incidental expenses." Since Griffing's arrival in New York with sixty freedpeople, she paid a drayman "to take their little boxes and traps across the city," they waited four hours to see the president of the railroad, and the freedpeople "had to have bread and bread costs money." Gage's description stressed not only Griffing's desperate need for funds but also Griffing's mastery of the situation, reinforcing women's important role in freedmen's aid. The article then artfully appealed to both women's benevolence and their concern that African Americans, now freed from slavery, would become idle and dissolute. Griffing thanked Gage and her friends for their contributions, stating, "Tell your ladies to persevere. Every dollar they spend in providing homes for these people, where they can labor independently, thus being useful to themselves and employers, is worth ten dealt to them as paupers."[24] Gage and Griffing formulated their appeals to garner the sympathy and charity of Northern women.

Despite support from abolitionists, problems beset female agents. Isaac and Amy Post assisted Griffing and Sojourner Truth in Rochester, New York, yet the two women faced significant impediments in that city. Griffing initially appealed to the Posts to send material aid to impoverished freedpeople in Washington: "Work is so exceedingly scarce & living so high, that you can see that 30,000 of these people here must suffer."[25] Truth then asked Mrs. Post if she could find "some good places for women that have children," thus identifying freedwomen and children as the primary objects of their benevolence.[26] After advertising in the Rochester *Democrat* and the Rochester *Express*, Truth received numerous requests for domestic servants, farmhands, and "a young girl not above eleven or twelve years old to assist in taking care of young children."[27] While Griffing and Truth successfully placed a number of freedpeople with Rochester employers, they also confronted the social, economic, and political pressures that surrounded African American migration. Rumors abounded in Rochester that General Howard opposed Truth's work. In addition, three thousand employers requested freedpeople, and many grew disgruntled when their demands could not be met. Griffing wrote of freedpeople's reluctance to make the journey to Rochester: "We are moving Heaven and Earth, to speak figuratively, to inspire the people to go. But all the causes that you remember to have existed last year, Sojourner, are still keeping them here." Southern employment agents spread rumors of "the *climate* and *character* of the North," but freedpeople's family ties also contributed to their unwillingness to leave Washington. Griffing and Truth had difficulty finding homes for entire families because most Northern employers did not want children under twelve years of age. "As though Black Babes were 12 yrs old when they were born," Griffing commented.[28]

As agents contended with the conflicting desires of Northerners and freedpeople, both enemies and friends of the Freedmen's Bureau remarked on the similarity between bureau-sponsored migration and the slave trade. President Andrew Johnson, a political opponent of the Freedmen's Bureau, once referred to assisted migration as the bureau's "traffic in negroes."[29] Abolitionists who supported the Freedmen's Bureau also criticized the system for exploiting African Americans. Julia Wilbur, agent of the Rochester Ladies' Anti-Slavery Society, noted that freedpeople were suspicious of the employment agents' motives: "The colored people believe that agents get $5 a head for each one they send away, and that the first month's wages is withheld to pay this $5 and other expenses." Freedpeople also heard reports of abuse from Northern employers. Wilbur continued, "Persons come back and tell of these things, and in some instances complain of ill treatment from those who hired them. Such reports deter any from going away. They think they may as well stay where they are as go elsewhere and be cheated out of their earnings. When we all learn to treat colored people kindly and justly, there will be less difficulty in inducing them to go North."[30] Freedmen's Bureau records lend support to Wilbur's account. Freedpeople who went to the North with the help of Griffing and the bureau often felt robbed by their Northern employers. To give one example, in May 1870, General Howard's assistant wrote Griffing regarding the complaint of Susan Wilson, whom Griffing had transported to New York. Wilson's employer, Mr. Vanderville, paid for her transportation but then deducted it from her wages. Wilson wanted Griffing to reimburse her.[31] How well did Griffing and other agents screen their prospective employers? Did they seize any opportunity to send a freedperson to the North? In the North, as in the South, freedpeople entered a free labor system that was not truly free. Instead, removed from familiar surroundings, freedpeople were at the mercy of their new employers.

Women's status as paid agents caused further controversy over African American migration to the North. Women pursued salaried positions for two principal reasons; they wanted to aid former slaves and secure their own financial independence.[32] But since the Freedmen's Bureau did not cover all the expenses its agents incurred, Griffing and other women often supplemented their bureau salaries by charging employers for their services. One advertisement for Griffing's agency noted such a fee: "We exhort everyone in want of farm hands or household service to write to Mrs. Griffing, No. 394 N. Capitol St., Washington City, inclosing two postage stamps. It would be better still to inclose $5 at once, and ask her to send such help as you need. Our women are overworked, our farms not half tilled for want of help."[33]

Not all reformers approved of this fee. Critics equated agents' charges with a new kind of slave trade. For example, Julia Wilbur advised Sojourner Truth that her fees would encourage rumors that she was "speculating." Truth, knowing that her livelihood depended on this income, defended her commission: "the people come and are willing to pay what I ask 5 cts. or 1 dollar for the sake of having help and they think it is no more than right for me to have it for they feel pleased of the idea of me trying to get them a place to earn for themselves."[34] Truth and other paid female agents asserted their economic interests, adapting free labor ideology to their own ends. While Wilbur also believed women's reform activities should be compensated, she remained uneasy with the larger meaning of agents' fees in the context of emancipation.

Employment agents were, in some cases, entrepreneurs, who built institutions that combined charitable functions with personal profit. Mrs. Sarah A. Tilmon, "a lady (colored) of great energy, intelligence, industry, and Christian prudence," worked with the African Civilization Society and the Freedmen's Bureau as an employment agent.[35] As an agent, she embodied the ACS pledge of black self-reliance. "Mme. Tilmon's Intelligence Office," located at 104 E. Thirteenth Street, advertised "First class Cooks, Chamber maids, Waitresses, Seamstresses, Nurses, and Laundresses." During 1867, she reported that in one month, seventy-six freedpeople had passed through her office, including adults and children. She placed freedpeople in positions and homes in Providence, Hartford, New York, Boston, Newark, Farmington, Flushing, and Albany.[36] Tilmon also served as matron of the African Civilization Society's Home for Freedchildren and Others.

Tilmon's enterprise troubled other freedmen's aid reformers working in New York City. Ellen Collins of the New York National Freedmen's Relief Association reported that children in Tilmon's charge were "begging that they were poorly fed and kept in a room without sufficient ventilation." Collins's accusations primarily grew from her disapproval of the Freedmen's Bureau's migration policy; she preferred that the state, through her organization, apply its energy and resources to sending teachers to the South.[37] Yet like Wilbur, Collins also expressed discomfort with Tilmon's open entrepreneurship. Female agents achieved financial independence through the sale of African American labor, an alarming echo of the slave trade. But Tilmon's openness regarding this commercial transaction also contradicted the traditional understanding of women's reform as voluntary and self-sacrificing. As African American agents, both Tilmon and Truth exposed the self-interested aspects of freedmen's aid, intensifying white women's anxieties about their role in Reconstruction. As a successful black businesswoman, especially one with an official relationship with the Freedmen's Bureau, Tilmon challenged the very purpose and philosophy of the NFRA's white reformers, whose endeavor depended on the image of dependent and uneducated African Americans.

These concerns did not undermine Tilmon's work or her relationship with the Freedmen's Bureau. Tilmon refuted the charges, inviting C. H. Howard to inspect her rooms and the refectory at any time. Tilmon also informed Howard she did not know Collins, and asked him to inform her "of the whereabouts of this Ellen Collins."[38] Tilmon worked with white agents such as Josephine Griffing, but the office (and interests) of the N.Y. National Association, run by Francis George Shaw and other prominent white New Yorkers, though physically located at 76 John Street in New York City, was far removed from Mrs. Tilmon's Intelligence Agency.

Such accusations often came from other female agents, who competed for prominence and funding even as they struggled to influence the politics of freedmen's relief. Mrs. Ricks, the employment agent who visited the Motts in Philadelphia, blamed "some enemy of mine" for the allegation that she was selling transportation. Following the charge, the Freedmen's Bureau removed her from her position as agent, a devastating blow. Ricks wrote to protest her innocence: "I have never sold, nor would I sell any transportation I have labored hard and in good faith for the Freedpeople for more than twenty months, and now I am myself as destitute almost as they are." Ricks felt hurt by the charge on both a personal and financial level, and she informed C. H. Howard that she would always associate the Freedmen's Bureau with this "unjust accusation": "the words you said Gen. Howard will ring in my ears as long as I live. Gen. Howard, I am a poor woman and I am an honest woman."[39] Although Ricks claimed that she did not know the identity of her enemy, a later letter revealed that it was a woman. The Freedmen's Bureau rehired Ricks and her son to run an industrial school in November 1867, and Ricks claimed that her pupils were being poisoned by a "recapitulation of those charges preferred against me" by "the same individual or a member of her family."[40] Ricks's Southern heritage may have aroused the animosity of her accuser, but competition over meager resources and a limited number of positions also fueled discord among the women employed by the Freedmen's Bureau.

A fierce rivalry existed between Waity Harris, the teacher and agent affiliated with the Rhode Island Association for Freedmen, and Josephine Griffing. Griffing vied with Harris for the attention and funds of the Rhode Island Association, as Griffing frequently made fundraising and lecturing trips to that state. In November 1866, Mrs. R. M. Bigelow of Providence wrote to O. O. Howard to inquire whether or not Griffing was employed by the Freedmen's Bureau. She explained the reasons for her inquiry: "the ladies of the Relief Ass'n are so wedded to Mrs. Griffing that little or nothing can be done for our school unless it is positively known that Mrs. G is not employed by you at the Bureau. The funds which should have gone for the support of Miss H's school have gone in other directions and many are under the impression that Mrs. G has had more than her share."[41] After Harris became an employment agent, her resentment of Griffing drew the attention and involvement of the Freedmen's Bureau. Agent J. L. Roberts informed the Freedmen's Bureau that Harris and her brother were undermining the work of other agents and the bureau by influencing freedpeople to leave Washington "without respect to the orders & restrictions from Bureau Hd. Qtrs. provided they receive a fee for head." In addition, he reported that Harris abused her power as principal of an industrial school, which also served as a way station for freedpeople's journey to the North. He noted that Harris obstructed the migration process, refusing "to let parties sent here by Mrs. Griffing this evening occupy [the school]." Roberts commented that Harris could not make the excuse that she needed the rooms because "she [had] failed in executive ability to make her school either useful or profitable, but rather expensive." He recommended that Harris be turned out of her industrial school and her home.[42] Harris's conflict with Griffing clearly compromised her career as an employment agent. When combined with the exploitative elements of bureau-sponsored migration, competition between female agents hindered their ability to aid former slaves.

Freedpeople seconded criticisms of the bureau's migration policies. In the process of trying to help freedpeople, agents unwittingly separated families, mistreated freedpeople in transit, sent freedpeople to the wrong destination, or lost track of them altogether. Freedpeople reported to the Freedmen's Bureau when they were wronged and, since Josephine Griffing transported large numbers of freedpeople, the Freedmen's Bureau received many complaints about her. Freedpeople's grievances reveal the inadequacies in Griffing's efforts to secure justice for former slaves in the North.

Freedpeople primarily complained that Griffing separated black families before they could be reconstituted. In 1866, Griffing claimed that Octavio Randall received transportation to Richmond, Virginia, because his father had written for him. But bureau agent Rogers reported, "His mother came here a few days since inquiring for him and stated that herself and her husband are residing here and their consent was not given for him to be sent away."[43] In September 1867, General Howard asked Griffing to look into the case of Laura Jones, who was conveyed to Massachusetts against the will of her aunt.[44] In July 1868, Eliphalet Whittlesey asked Griffing to explain the case of Martha Williams, whom she had allegedly sent away without the consent of her parents.[45] As these examples demonstrate, Griffing often transported freedchildren to the North, a practice similar to apprenticeship. The Freedmen's Bureau encouraged this, if the parents permitted.[46] But Griffing and other agents made mistakes, believing these children were orphans or traveled with the blessing of their parents. In the aftermath of the Civil War, such accidents had tragic consequences, introducing disruptions to black family life that emancipation had promised to remedy.

The effects of migration policies on the African American family raised the ire of Quaker abolitionist Anna Earle, of Worcester, Massachusetts, who saw troubling resonance with the slave trade. In October 1867, Earle wrote to the Freedmen's Bureau to inquire into the whereabouts of

Kitty Brooks, a girl Griffing had transported to New York. Earle wrote on behalf of the girl's mother, Annie, who was with her in Worcester, stating her displeasure at the situation: "I pity the child's mother very much and I feel sorry that the Bureau should suffer as it does when its agents so wantonly violate the laws of humanity."[47] Earle requested that Mrs. Sarah Tilmon, the bureau's employment agent in New York City, search for Kitty. Earle wrote again in January 1868, and she noted that the date marked a year and a half since Annie had seen her child. Again, she urged the bureau to take action: "I feel sure that Mrs. Tillman [sic] can find her, if she can be made to do it. I refrain from expressing my feeling in regard to Mrs. Griffing, who it seems to me as clearly kidnaped little Kitty as if she had been a slave trader."[48] In one loaded phrase, Earle questioned Griffing's methods and her motives. She accused Griffing of undermining Annie's hard-won freedom and injuring the reputation of the Freedmen's Bureau. In March, the Freedmen's Bureau placed an advertisement for Kitty in the *People's Journal,* the organ of the African Civilization Society, but no evidence survives to show whether or not the mother and daughter were reunited.

The migration system also pushed freedpeople into specific employments that exacerbated the crisis of family disruption and recapitulated pre-emancipation domestic arrangements. Employment agents identified a shortage of domestic servants in the North, and seized the opportunity to relieve this shortage with freedwomen. Anna Lowell of the Howard Industrial School in Cambridge, Massachusetts, explained the purposes of her intelligence agency and training home to C. H. Howard: "There is a great demand here for female servants, and the object of the Association is to take girls and women and teach them and then get them good places."[49] But Lowell's aims included a number of presumptions about both freedwomen and domestic service. While opportunities for freedwomen were restricted by a race- and sex-segregated labor market, white employment agents never considered training freedwomen for any other type of job, viewing them instead as a natural servant class. Employment agents also overestimated the desirability of domestic service positions. Domestic servants often experienced intense isolation and exploitation. Because domestic servants usually boarded in the homes of their employers in the nineteenth century, freedwomen fought to reside with their families and establish their own households. By pushing domestic service as a route to economic independence, Lowell and other female agents instead recreated the race, class, and gender relationships of the plantation household in Northern homes. As servants, freedwomen's lives still would be controlled by the white families, particularly the white women, for whom they worked.[50]

Female agents juggled freedwomen's familial responsibilities with their efforts to train freedwomen for employment. Seeking to nurture "the moral good of the next generation," Lowell's association created a self-consciously female environment, with schoolrooms for teaching sewing and reading. Though Lowell requested that the Freedmen's Bureau send her young girls, preferably orphans, she also accepted women with small children, as "it is not difficult to get a place for a woman with a child over 18 months—when younger than that they will meet with much that is disappointing." Lowell told C. H. Howard that did not want men or boys, however, "as it interferes with all our arrangements."[51] Such strictures broke up married couples, including one preacher and his wife, and probably separated mothers and sons.[52]

In their enthusiasm to place freedwomen in domestic service positions, some agents even asked freedwomen to place their children in an asylum. Griffing explained this plan to C. H. Howard: "Homes and asylums for the younger children are being established in connexion with these branch offices, thus giving the multitudes of their class of sufferers an opportunity to better their condition—the mothers accepting good Homes and fair wages with facilities for improvement and when practicable contributing to the support of their children."[53] Griffing ideally wanted freedwomen to remain with their families, but she believed these orphanages fostered the worthy goal of economic independence, separating parents and children only temporarily. Employment agent A. F. Williams elaborated on Griffing's plan, writing that by "requiring the mother to devote a portion of her wages for the support of her children in the Institution, this plan would cause the mother to feel the responsibility resting upon her as the natural guardian of her children & keep alive the interest the mother should always feel in her offspring."[54] Though Griffing did not share Williams's condescending assumptions about freedwomen's maternal capacity, they both agreed that asylums were the only way to provide for women and their children.

Freedwomen unsurprisingly resisted agents' efforts to appropriate their children. At the African Civilization Society's Home for Freedchildren and Others in Brooklyn, the manager noticed that the mothers invariably tried to reclaim their daughters and sons. Henry M. Wilson of the Home for Freedchildren reported these problems to C. H. Howard: "We have considerable trouble with the parents of the children here. They often call for them in full determination to take them away from the home at fifteen minutes notice. . . . In most cases wherein the freedwomen are so urgent to take their children home they are entirely disqualified to take care of them."[55] Thus agents' desire to make freedpeople self-sufficient by finding them work often combined with their patronizing attitudes to override their concern about the fate of former slave families.

Though female agents contributed to the separation of African American families, white women's assistance sometimes intersected with the needs of freedwomen. For example, freedwoman Diana Williams enlisted the services of Josephine Griffing to her own end. In August 1868, Josephine Griffing reported to bureau agent Eliphalet Whittlesey on the current status of Williams, "a constant applicant for help and employment." After Griffing ascertained that Williams was truly destitute, she agreed to send Williams and her daughter to Hartford, Connecticut, where Williams had friends. Williams told Griffing that her husband approved of the move, but when the time of her departure arrived and she did not appear at the depot, Griffing discovered that Williams's husband had hidden the children, presumably to prevent her from leaving. A few days later, Williams again asked Griffing to find her a job near Washington because "she was suffering and could not live this way without work." After working in Philadelphia for a few days, Williams left her position and had not been heard from since. The Freedmen's Bureau fielded complaints from Williams's husband about the disappearance of his wife. Griffing responded that "Diana will return with money in her pocket & take care of her husband & children" and that Mr. Williams "was a worthless overbearing man to her" and she should have left long ago. Griffing counseled Mr. Williams to wait for his wife or find work in the meantime. Griffing suggested he "should be persuaded to take care of himself and one child."[56]

Griffing's assessment of Williams's case reflected her feminist views and her personal experience. Griffing had separated from her husband during the war and lived alone with her daughters in Washington, D.C., relying on her work with the Freedmen's Bureau and the National Freedmen's Relief Association to support her household. Griffing's financial situation was precarious, and grew even more insecure when she lost her salary with the Freedmen's Bureau in August 1868, the same month as Williams's disappearance.[57] Griffing's unhappy marriage and her fight for economic survival influenced her response to Diana Williams. In Griffing's opinion she was helping Williams escape from an unsatisfactory man, and, at the same time, offering her economic independence through domestic labor in the North. While most freedwomen fought to remain with their families, some sought to escape. Williams was intent on leaving her husband and Griffing's assistance helped her to accomplish this goal.

In addition to the involuntary separation of families, freedpeople complained of other forms of ill-treatment. The transportation system itself proved difficult, as the housing crisis in Washington created overwhelming demand. In April 1866, James Johnson, his family, and a number of other freedpeople were waiting at the Capitol Hill Barracks to travel to Rhode Island with Griffing. Johnson had sold all his belongings because he expected to leave in a couple of days. Instead, Johnson and his family had been in the barracks for two weeks and he had contracted an illness "lying on the damp floor without fire." After Johnson complained, Griffing informed the Freedmen's Bureau that she was giving him money until transportation was available to Providence.[58]

Freedwoman Harris objected to the treatment she received at the hands of another employment agent, H. G. Stewart, of the Rhode Island Association for Freedmen. Mrs. Harris charged that on their journey to Providence, Stewart herded freedpeople onto the steamboat like cattle and kept them on deck where they were exposed to a storm. Stewart blamed the influence of a free steward for Mrs. Harris's accusation: "In my opinion, the complaint made by Mrs. Harris was prompted if not wholly caused by the colored steward, who ordered the hack & took Mrs. Harris & family away & has since taken her daughter to N. York, after influencing Mrs. Harris to refuse an excellent home for her self and family."[59] Freedwomen did not take the infringement of their freedom and dignity lightly. They complained to the Freedmen's Bureau, demanded the return of their children, and, like Harris, took matters into their own hands. After experiencing Stewart's mistreatment, Harris decided her family's well-being was better entrusted to the black steward than to an unknown white family.

Such troubles in the Northern migration process contributed to Sojourner Truth's conclusion that "this was not the best mode of procedure, as it cost a great amount of labor, time, and money," and only helped the able-bodied population of freedpeople.[60] Truth turned her energy to petitioning the government to allot lands to freedpeople in the West. But despite freedpeople's complaints about family disruption, discrimination, and exploitation in the North, Griffing and other agents remained committed to aiding freedpeople to migrate to Northern jobs and homes. After the Freedmen's Bureau's employment office closed, its agents continued to direct inquiries from Northern employers to Griffing.

Griffing's faith in the liberating potential of Northern employment continued. In her reports to the National Freedmen's Relief Association, Griffing emphasized the positive outcomes and many benefits of freedpeople's migration to the North. She wrote that freedpeople who had gone to the North "with very few exceptions, express satisfaction with the country and the people, and encourage their friends in the city to follow their example." Griffing listed examples of economic mobility. Two brothers who migrated to Michigan had used their wages to purchase farms. Their wives earned $1.50 a day cleaning houses. Another freedman earned $30 a month in a rule factory, while yet another was commanding high wages as a house painter.[61] Another advantage of migrating to the North, Griffing pointed out, was the opportunity for an education. Frances Titus, a close friend of Sojourner Truth, ran an evening school for adults in Battle Creek, Michigan. She and five other teachers volunteered their time, finding "compensation for their labor in the good deportment and rapid improvement of these men and women who are to become citizens of their city and State." Griffing optimistically concluded, "Prejudice against color in the North is fast yielding before the presence of the black man."[62] Griffing related success stories, but the experiences of many freedpeople who migrated to the North belied her optimism.

Female employment agents did not succeed in achieving their twin goals of justice and economy. Women imagined that former slaves could achieve freedom and economic independence through Northern migration, a hope shared by many Southern blacks who undertook the journey during Reconstruction, the exodus to Kansas in 1879, and the Great Migration in the early twentieth century.[63] Yet the drive to find freedpeople jobs and homes in the North sometimes overwhelmed women's concern for the rights of former slaves. Female agents championed women's economic independence through paid labor, but by pushing freedwomen into domestic service positions, and separating families in the process, they limited a freedom already constrained by a sex- and race-segregated economy. Female agents' concern for freedwomen's economic independence reflected their own insecurities. Agents relied on their careers as intelligence agents for support. When they found their positions threatened by conflicts over funding, strategy, and politics, they fought to hold on to their jobs. In the end, economy proved the driving concern in the migration policies of the Freedmen's Bureau and its agents.

As the example of mothers at the Home for Freedchildren and Others demonstrates, freedpeople resisted reformers' attempts to limit or control their freedom. They accepted bureau-sponsored migration when it suited them, and protested when the Freedmen's Bureau and its agents infringed upon their rights. Freedpeople, especially freedwomen, emerged from slavery with a strong desire to put their families before work, especially work for a white person. In freedwomen's homes and in industrial schools, abolitionist women and freedwomen also struggled with the relationship between womanhood and free labor. Ultimately, female reformers' ideas about race, and their approach to racial equality, grew from their confrontations with freedwomen as well as with each other.

Chapter 8

The Limits of Women's Radical Reconstruction

Josephine Griffing asserted that Northern and Western women "understood" freedwomen's "wants and necessities," presuming sisterhood with former slaves.[1] But as the decade of the 1860s drew to a close, women confronted the limits of this vision. As freedmen's agents and industrial school teachers, white women sought to shape freedwomen's work and family lives in ways that reflected their own goals for political influence and economic independence. But while the women's rights movement allowed white middle-class women to look beyond the home for fulfillment, emancipation gave freedwomen their first opportunity to place their personal and family lives above the demands of a slaveholder or an employer.[2] Accepting assistance when it met their needs, freedwomen resisted white reformers' efforts to dictate either their domestic or labor arrangements. These interactions challenged white women's assumptions about their connection to freedwomen, exposing the racial and class dimensions of their relationship.

The alliance between black and white abolitionist-feminists was also tested over the course of the freedmen's aid movement. Though women worked closely as teachers, distributors of relief, and employment agents, the experiences of black and white reformers began to diverge. Marked by society's racism, free black women joined elite African American men in their struggle for equality, just as white women restricted their fight for suffrage along racial lines. Rather than achieving an interracial movement for women's rights and freedmen's aid, as many abolitionist-feminists had hoped, the freedmen's aid movement set the stage for the separate trajectory of black and white women's reform after the 1870s.[3]

White abolitionist women entered the freedmen's aid movement with a specific interest in freedwomen and children, an interest that was sanctioned by policy and the gender conventions of the North. Freedmen's aid societies and the Freedmen's Bureau encouraged female teachers and agents to investigate the home life of freedpeople. The New York National Freedmen's Relief Association directed its teachers to "interest themselves in the moral, religious and social improvement of the families of their pupils, to visit them in their homes, to instruct the women and girls in sewing and domestic economy."[4] While Northern white women empathized with freedwomen as mothers, daughters, and sisters, they often criticized freedwomen's homes and families, especially if they interfered with the Protestant work ethic. As a result, white women and freedwomen clashed over the proper balance between home and work, charity and independence.

From the beginning, freedmen's aid reformers viewed domestic habits as crucial to the success of emancipation. At Port Royal, South Carolina, Massachusetts abolitionist Susan Walker described her daily home visits to preach industry and cleanliness. On March 25, 1862, she wrote,

Again at the Jenkins' plantation to look into cabins, talk with women and see what can be done to improve them. Katy has 7 ragged, dirty children, what shall be done? No husband and nothing. Some clothes are given for her children— one naked, and must have it at once. Is Katy lazy? Very likely. Does she tell the truth, perhaps not. I must have faith and she must, at least, cover her children. She promises to make her cabin and herself clean and to wash her children before putting on the new clothes.[5]

In the aftermath of slavery, abolitionists found illegitimacy, single motherhood, nakedness, and dirt. Though they blamed the slaveholders for this situation, they also chided the victims, accusing them of laziness and deceit, and making charity dependent on black families adopting the minimum standards of Northern domesticity.[6]

The earliest efforts at education reflected these attitudes toward domesticity. Walker noted the importance of teaching freedwomen how to sew. "Comparatively few of the freed-women here can sew," Walker remarked. "We hope to teach many to do it, but they need the clothing now." She believed that freedwomen needed to sew to provide clothing for their families, but she also viewed domesticity as a training ground for economic independence. White women hoped to prepare freedwomen to earn wages to support their families.[7] Lucy Chase, who had access to sewing machines in Norfolk, Virginia, wrote of the employment opportunities available to skilled freedwomen: "Now, if the Government will let the machines sew for it, the machine-worker can be furnished with present means of support and those who become experts, may secure here, or elsewhere, permanent situations in manufacturing establishments."[8]

Efforts at domestic and vocational education ran headlong into an unexpected reality: most freedwomen were already skilled at sewing. While reformers imagined that enslaved women had worked largely in the fields, many slaves had worked in houses, and all had been responsible for sewing clothes for their families. Walker later amended her statement, noting that "nearly all can" sew, but assumptions about black women's domestic habits influenced nearly every such interaction.[9]

Female reformers continued to emphasize freedwomen's need for white guidance in their homes. In January 1865, teacher Laetitia Campbell explained to her sponsor, Mrs. Mary K. Wead, that her work with freedpeople extended outside the schoolroom: "there is a work of almost as much importance to be done in the homes of our children, as in the schools." Campbell wrote that she visited every family once a week: "We must see that those who cannot work receive rations, wood and clothing, words of instruction and sometimes even of admonition are needed." Teachers' visits to the families of their pupils served two purposes. While teachers would "admonish" freedwomen to meet certain standards in the home, they also provided material aid to the destitute. Campbell ended her letter by emphasizing the neediness of families: "It is not infrequent in our visits to find a mother with her whole family in heel to keep from perishing with cold, and sometimes we may find them shivering over a kettle of coals a fire place or stove being an unattainable luxury."[10] Stressing domestic order, both Campbell and Walker also relieved the immediate wants of former slaves.

Despite the empathy white women felt for freedwomen and their families, they struggled to understand the actions and motivations of freedwomen. Freedwomen's commitment to their families astonished Northern white women, especially when they felt freedwomen's attachment to their families undermined the values of industry and economy that Northerners tried to instill. Carrie Lacy wanted to provide for "the comfort of the old people and helpless children."[11] But she was also disheartened by one elderly freedwomen, "Aunt Lucy," to whom she gave a pair of shoes in 1870. She complained to Emily Howland that giving relief to Aunt Lucy would only encourage the lazy, dependent behavior of Lucy's young relatives. She listed her reservations: "There is no use in giving much at once to Aunt L. as she has Millie & all her family in her house. I am afraid as it is that Henry will wear her shoes." Lacy had given Aunt Lucy rations enough to last one person two weeks, but, "Afterward I heard that she 'cooked' it all upon return and next day was begging in another quarter." Lacy tried to convince Aunt Lucy to move into the Home for Aged Colored Women and Children in Washington, D.C., but she refused. Finally Lacy voiced her frustrations at Aunt Lucy's determination to support Millie and her family: "I cannot understand her. Millie has a lot of babies who have no two of the same father, and Aunt L. feels 'bound' to take care of them. Joanna is still in jail."[12] This case demonstrates Aunt Lucy's commitment to keeping her family together at all costs, even if it meant a greater struggle for survival. Lacy, on the other hand, expressed disgust with Aunt Lucy's willingness to support younger relatives who did not work and, by Lacy's standards, had questionable morals. Schooled in the virtues of free labor and self-reliance, Lacy's priorities clearly differed from Aunt Lucy's. Slavery had divided Aunt Lucy's family, and having seen her family reunited, Aunt Lucy was unwilling to leave them. Her "bonds" were of a different nature.[13]

Untroubled by this gap in understanding, white women formulated policies that profoundly affected the family lives of freedwomen. They encouraged freedwomen and girls to migrate to the North, seeing it as a place of "real Freedom" and "civilization."[14] They also pushed freedwomen to obtain economic independence through wage labor. But the Northern migration of freedwomen and girls often came at the expense of their family relationships, and this created friction between African American women and white reformers.

White women purposefully separated children from their parents in their drive to establish freedwomen's self-reliance. In 1865, Anna Searing, a white teacher in Washington, D.C., wrote of the difficulties she faced with the mother of Louisa Allen. Louisa had migrated to the North to live with a white woman, Georgia Willets. Her mother had been so "importunate" that they brought Louisa to Washington for a visit. Naturally, the mother wanted to take Louisa home. As Searing reported, "Louisa screamed declaring she would not go; that she would through [sic] herself out the window and making various other threats, and appealing so strongly to our sympathies that we thought we would see if any effort could be made in her behalf." Searing asked the Freedmen's Bureau to mediate the dispute. Since the mother refused to meet with a bureau officer, Searing expected the worst: "I did not think from the first that anything could be done because the law of course gives the mother authority over the child." Searing explained her opposition to Louisa's mother: "Her mother admits that she wishes her [Louisa] to support her: says she has been taking in sewing but does not intend to do that any longer. I am perfectly disgusted with the woman, she is downright lazy." Louisa refused to go with her mother, however, even struggling out of her mother's grasp as her mother tried to drag her from the schoolhouse. For Searing, the case ended happily, with Louisa returning to the North: "Mrs. Thomas has now gone to put the child on the cars for New Jersey as light hearted as if restored from some great calamity."[15]

Searing's account of the dispute emphasized the alliance between Louisa and Northern white women against the demands of Mrs. Allen. Searing viewed Louisa's fight for autonomy as comparable to her own struggle for independence through freedmen's aid. She and her friends consequently dismissed Mrs. Allen's "authority" over her daughter in favor of the educational, moral, and economic benefits of life in the North. But Mrs. Allen, with the Freedmen's Bureau, viewed the conflict as a product of emancipation, which replaced masters control over their slaves with parents "authority" over their children. To further subvert

Mrs. Allen's parental rights, Searing criticized her character. Yet Mrs. Allen's fight for Louisa echoed freedwomen's struggle against the involuntary apprenticeship of their children. Searing did not remark on these disturbing similarities.[16]

When they could not send freedwomen and girls to jobs in the North, white women established industrial sewing schools to train freedwomen to be self-supporting. Established in conjunction with the Freedmen's Bureau, industrial schools provided freedwomen with instruction in sewing, ironing, and other domestic arts, preparing them for positions as domestic servants. Officially called a school, industrial schools also operated as factories and a form of charity. Freedwomen earned a small amount for their work, and were paid in cash, food, or clothing. The Freedmen's Bureau bought clothing sewn in industrial schools and distributed it to the destitute or sold it cheaply to freedpeople. The bureau also paid the rent on these schools, offering the teachers housing in the same rooms.

Industrial schools combined the two main obsessions of Northern reformers: education for economic independence and work for relief. Reformers had founded similar institutions for men and women prior to emancipation. These schools not only presumed that manual labor instilled a work ethic and contributed to intellectual achievement, but also that outright charity fostered pauperism. As African Americans of both sexes enrolled in such schools after the Civil War, these institutions became a battleground for debates over poverty, dependency, race, and gender.[17] White women claimed industrial sewing schools promoted the self-reliance of freedwomen, but the schools created one form of economic independence for the white teachers and principals and another for freedwomen. As industrial school teachers, white women achieved status as school principals and businesswomen. They also gained access to government power and policy. By comparison, white women conceptualized self-support for freedwomen as merely the right to subsistence. They viewed potential "careers" for freedwomen as limited to domestic service and plantation labor, a view that was reinforced by a segregated labor market. Rather than furthering economic independence for freedwomen, industrial schools endorsed freedwomen's dependence on white women.

After leaving Port Royal, Susan Walker opened her industrial sewing school in Washington, D.C., in December 1865. Walker's goals for her school were "to encourage in them [freedwomen] habits of industry, economy, cleanliness. To elevate them in character & condition generally. To inspire an ambition for self-improvement and an earnest desire to be faithful to their responsibilities as freedwomen."[18] On average her school had seventy women students. From October 1866 to October

1867, Walker instructed 315 women and 12 men and boys and produced 819 items of clothing. Walker also claimed success in placing freedwomen in jobs. She reported that "Service places in and around Washington were found for 100 women, and 30 others were provided with employment outside of the District . . . *to help the freedwomen help themselves.*"[19] Walker thus noted her school's value in aiding African American women to become free laborers. She provided job training and placement for freedwomen, and sometimes freedmen.

Despite Walker's good intentions, freedwomen complained to the Freedmen's Bureau about the treatment they received at her school. In June 1867, Lavinia Coleman reported that she had worked for Walker for twenty days and only obtained three pounds of meat and some flour as pay. Coleman demanded payment in cash, rejecting Walker's system of work for food, which too closely resembled slave allowances. The bureau investigator concluded that Coleman's grievance was one of many: "there are a great number of women in these Barracks who have worked for Miss Walker and who invariably complain of receiving no pay except a little meat & flour."[20] Walker later explained that she gave out food as

Figure 8. Industrial sewing school—the Freedmen's Union Industrial School, Richmond, Virginia, 1866 (drawn by Jas. E. Taylor). Courtesy Library of Congress, Prints and Photographs Division, LC-USZ62-33264.

part payment instead of clothing to those who wished it. More importantly, she did not view herself as freedwomen's employer, but rather
their guardian. As Walker commented, "It is not so much to furnish
employment & do a large quantity of work, as to teach them how to do
well whatever they undertake."[21] Oblivious to the contradiction inherent
in her position, Walker saw herself as a teacher of the values of independence and self-reliance, even though she undermined these lessons
by not providing fair remuneration. Walker also infantilized adult freedwomen as dependent on her guidance. Freedwomen clearly saw Walker
as their employer, however, and called upon the Freedmen's Bureau to
intercede when they felt Walker treated them unjustly.

In May 1868, Virginia Johnson complained to the bureau that she had
worked at Walker's industrial school for one month and was paid $10,
but that Walker subsequently took back $5 of that money. The Freed-
men's Bureau investigator concluded that Walker should be ordered to
give back the $5 or be prosecuted for the amount. The investigator
noted, "This is but one of many similar cases that have been referred to
me by the colored women employed by Miss Walker, and I am satisfied
that justice to the poor colored women demands that Miss Walker be
called to account for her knavery (I cannot use a milder term in this connection) as the treatment of her women employees has become outra-
geously notorious."[22] Bureau officials believed that Walker was taking
advantage of her employees. Another agent wrote, "For months complaints have been made to me in regard to the way Miss Walker has paid
her employees, i.e. in old clothes, and new clothes, drawn through this
office, and charged against the people, and the money paid to them by
Maj. Brown, subsequently taken from them by Miss Walker."[23] The school
inculcated free labor ideology all too well, for freedwomen expected
wages and fair treatment in exchange for their labor, not a return to the
paternalism of slavery.

Walker justified her policies by drawing on the fears of white America
that black women were withdrawing from the labor force in large numbers. She claimed that Virginia Johnson had not done a month's work
but had quit because Johnson's "husband was displeased" with the idea
of her working.[24] In part, Walker's expectation that Johnson should work
for wages reflected her own beliefs regarding women's wage labor and professional employment. As Walker was unmarried, she undoubtedly relied
on her employment as an industrial school teacher and financial contributions from benevolent friends to support herself. Self-supporting single women were not uncommon in the Civil War era. But Walker clearly
held different standards and expectations for African American women.
Johnson was a married woman. While freedwomen were more likely to
find employment in cities than freedmen, emancipation allowed black

families to determine who should work and when, a prerogative African Americans guarded vigilantly.[25] Placed in "service" in and around the District, freedwomen also remained subordinate to members of white families, and the employees of white women. Walker's perspective thus combined economic reality, her own feminism, and her patronizing assumptions about the capabilities of former slaves. In the end, Walker confidently defended her mission: "I am not wholly disheartened by the many disagreeables of the last two weeks, because I have infinite faith in the end for which I labor and in the sincerity of my purpose." The bureau continued to support Walker's school.[26]

Freedwomen likewise asked the Freedmen's Bureau to investigate Waity Harris's industrial school, also located in Washington, D.C. Far more than Griffing and other reformers, Harris's sense of economic and social insecurity governed her relationship with her parent society and her employees; her status depended on freedwomen's poverty and need for employment. Harris complained that her school was underfunded, even though she received a large salary of $60 per month from the Rhode Island Association for Freedmen. Harris tried to prove her worth to the Rhode Island Association by forwarding recommendations from O. O. Howard, commissioner of the Freedmen's Bureau, and others.[27] But these references did not end Harris's fight for support from her parent society, and she continued to claim her school was wanting in "proper material."[28]

Harris's concerns for her industrial school infected her relationship with freedwomen, who reported that Harris failed to compensate them for their work. One woman, Sophia Johnson, engaged to iron for Harris at a dollar a day and worked for two days, but did not receive any payment. Harris responded that Johnson's work was not well done, arguing that Johnson had ironed only the fronts of shirts, not the backs or the sleeves. Mr. Roberts, a bureau agent, reported to C. H. Howard, assistant commissioner of the Freedmen's Bureau, that he thought the case was an important one: "I regard the principle acted upon as involving a question of considerable magnitude & the parties upon both sides seem anxious to be heard."[29] Howard assigned a committee to investigate the case.

In making her statement to the Freedmen's Bureau's special committee, Sophia Johnson described the erratic and aggressive behavior Harris showed in dealing with her:

I called to see Miss Harris last Monday, She sent for me, she commenced to quarrel so I started to leave, she was in a rage and halloed to me as if I were a dog, I left and went to Mrs. Baker's where I live, Miss Baker sent me back, told me not to have a fuss; I went back and asked Miss Harris, will you please pay me? she told me she would not; told me to take myself out of the house, I thought she would throw me out; I was scared; she slammed the door in my face, caught the kitten thereon.[30]

Johnson had done everything in her power to seek a fair redress of her grievances, but Harris's violence drove her to seek the aid of the Freedmen's Bureau. Johnson's complaint asserted her basic rights against the arbitrary, paternalistic, and violent authority of Waity Harris. Having been a slave, Sophia Johnson sought nothing more than the fair and impersonal exchange of cash for labor promised by Northern reformers. Though abolitionist-feminists viewed the Freedmen's Bureau as *their* agency, the bureau regulated white reformers' relationship with freedwomen, just as it did the relationship between planters and freedpeople in the South. Such regulation often proved ineffective and equally arbitrary, as the committee decided in Johnson's favor but did not discipline Harris for her behavior.

To retain her employment as an industrial school teacher working for the Freedmen's Bureau and the Rhode Island Association, Harris depended on freedwomen's poverty, "ignorance," and especially need.[31] Her ill-treatment of Johnson reconfirmed her position in the hierarchy of their working relationship. Although the dispute between Harris and Johnson was an extreme instance, all women in the freedmen's aid movement viewed freedwomen as the beneficiaries of their benevolence, or dependents on their aid.[32] When freedwomen challenged this benevolence and rejected this dependent position, they upset white women's understanding of the nature of womanhood and their role in Reconstruction.

White women's abolitionist and feminist ideals foundered when confronted with the complexity of African American lives, their skills, their histories, and their family connections and struggles. Both reformers and freedwomen internalized aspects of free labor ideology, but they pursued economic independence in ways that reflected their experience of race, class, gender, and region. Insecure about their status, female agents and teachers affirmed their own authority through their relationship with freedwomen. Freedwomen rejected any situation that resembled slavery, demanding fair, consistent policies that offered material assistance, wages, and acknowledged the integrity of black families. Though white women presumed a gendered bond with freedwomen, these conflicts over standards of domesticity, and the relationship between benefactor and client, employer and employee, divided women. When white women discovered they did not always "understand" freedwomen, they abandoned their search for commonalities and established a patronizing guardianship over freedwomen.

As an experiment in interracial activism, the freedmen's aid movement also allowed black and white reformers to explore the possibility of gender solidarity. Most free African American women probably viewed sisterhood with skepticism, but, prompted by emancipation, they reevaluated their relationship to both white women and former slaves. While Frances Harper, Charlotte Forten, Rebecca Primus, and other African American women identified former slaves as "mine own people," they felt some ambivalence about this connection.[33] As free black women struggled for economic independence and equality, their differences from white women also became more pronounced. The evolving relationship between black and white reformers, like the interactions between reformers and freedwomen, influenced the course of women's reform after Reconstruction.

Letters from Emma V. Brown (c.1843–1902) to Emily Howland communicated one free African American woman's frustrating search for equal sisterhood on a personal level. This unusual correspondence grew from the close friendship between Brown, a freedmen's teacher, and Howland, a white woman who was Brown's mentor as well as her friend.[34] The letters illuminate Brown's relationship to both Howland and former slaves, and thus reveal the changing status of middle-class black women during Reconstruction. Brown struggled with her ties to former slaves, but she also noted the growing distance between herself and Howland. By 1870, Brown gradually turned away from Howland, and thus away from sisterhood, and toward a new African American elite for support in her fight for full citizenship.

The friendship of Emma Brown and Emily Howland developed out of their mutual interest in black education. They met at Myrtilla Miner's school for free black girls in Washington, D.C., in 1857, where Brown was a student and Howland a teacher. Both women disapproved of Miner's paternalistic approach to black education, and their conflicts with Miner cemented their friendship. Howland hired Brown as her assistant over the protests of Miss Miner, who preferred she hire a white woman for the job.[35] Howland and Miner clashed further over the management of the school. According to Howland, Miner began charging a $1.50 per month fee for every student who wanted to attend her school. Miner did not institute this fee in order to keep the school in operation, which would have been acceptable to Howland, but rather so she could afford to build herself a new house. Howland reported to a school trustee that the fee had reduced the number of students from fifty to fourteen in one week, and some of the most promising students could no longer attend.[36] Angry over Miner's policies, Howland moved back to New York in 1859, yet she remained on good terms with the trustees, who urged her to return to the District to teach.[37]

Following these conflicts with Miner, Brown left to teach in another school. As a former student, however, Brown found it more difficult to extricate herself from Miner's sphere of influence. In July 1859, she wrote to Howland that Miner's school was still in operation and "some days they have 9 scholars, sometimes less and never more than 14."

Brown reflected, "I cannot help thinking how strange it is that my school is larger than Miss Miner's."[38] Brown felt she owed Miner a "universal debt of gratitude" for providing her with an education, but she informed Howland that did not "like or respect" Miner and she would "never teach [at Miner's school] while she has anything to do with it."[39] Though she initially supported Brown's goal of attending Oberlin College, Miner resented Brown's success and retaliated by trying to deter her acquaintances from contributing to Brown's tuition.[40]

Inspired by Howland's example, Brown became an avid proponent of black education, viewing education as a way for free African Americans to aid those still enslaved. In 1859, she described her commitment to education in response to proposals to colonize free blacks in Africa: "It is our duty to be elevated by education and remain just where we are. Surely every intelligent one is needed here to do what he can toward helping his deeper crushed brother in bonds." She aimed "to teach the colored people that it is their duty to remain in America." In this letter, Brown also suggested that African Americans were of great "account" to the country: "As they thus shake the country to the very centre, colored people must be of some importance. I close by saying Africa, *never*! America, our native land *forever*!"[41] Brown saw herself as an educated woman with a duty to enslaved African Americans, an identity that allied her with Howland.

Brown's political beliefs shaped her desire to attend Oberlin, and her enrollment at the famous Ohio seminary, in 1860, brought her closer to Howland, as they reveled in the union between the antislavery and feminist causes that her attendance represented. At Oberlin, Brown was stimulated by visiting lecturers, including Antoinette Brown Blackwell and Carl Schurz, and by her political disagreements with President Charles Grandison Finney and other students.[42] Despite ill health, lack of funds, and the "considerable prejudice" she faced, she reiterated her dedication to an Oberlin education: "I guess no one could persuade me to leave here. I am perfectly charmed, each day I like the place better—This is the grand fountain of knowledge. There is no danger of my giving up."[43] Brown was thrilled with the opportunity for higher education, but also by the chance to leave Washington, D.C., which she "loathed."[44] Though Brown's mother told her she could remain in Oberlin until the fall of 1861, Brown left at the end of June 1861, when health and financial problems forced her to return to a city and life she hated. At home, she resumed teaching in order to support her family. One friend told Howland that "E said she wished she had died before she left Oberlin."[45]

Back in Washington, Brown grew frustrated with her duty to her race. She expressed weariness with teaching and described her students as "savage" and "stupid," comments that reveal Brown's class identification and sense of superiority.[46] She begged Howland to find her a school in Canada, or "*anywhere, anywhere out of*—the District of Columbia," but she added "anywhere but to Africa."[47] Brown remained in Washington, becoming one of the first teachers in Washington's "colored" public school system in 1864. Still, she asked Howland, "Would you believe I hate school now?" "How can I overcome this loathing, this hatred of teaching?"[48] Unhappiness cost Brown her health. A physician told her what she already knew: "that I am worn out—& that my liver is disordered."[49]

Brown's poor health, while undoubtedly real and debilitating, was also driven by class and racial anxieties provoked by the war and emancipation. Brown felt new financial pressures after her return to Washington. Her family had been fairly comfortable at one point, but by the beginning of the Civil War, they depended on her income. She told Howland that "I scarcely care for anything—yet it is necessary that I should work— that I should keep up. I am impatient, crass, and hateful. My brother can get no work of any kind. He is moody and disagreeable because of this. My mother cannot collect any money—The whole burden falls on me. Of course I am glad to help them but it seems as if everything goes wrong. I cannot make them economical."[50] While Brown resented the necessity of teaching, she declined the economic security that marriage would have provided. Like her friend Howland, she explicitly rejected "the smooth path" of domesticity in favor of "the rugged one" of education and a career.[51] Brown's financial problems were no different from many single women, but they were compounded by racial discrimination. Unemployment was high in wartime Washington, especially for African American men like her brother. In addition, middle-class black women, frequently compelled to work out of financial necessity, faced limited career choices. Much to her dismay, Brown's struggle for economic survival placed her only marginally above former slaves.

Before and during the Civil War, Brown maintained her class and color differences from enslaved African Americans. In an 1862 letter to Howland, Brown indicated her racial self-conception when describing a male acquaintance: "He is allied to the colored race, and like myself the blood of the Caucasian and Indian flows in his veins."[52] Brown used the word "Negro" only in relation to the racial epithets others directed at her, she considered herself and other middle-class blacks "colored."[53] Brown commented on her white blood and her long hair, yet she also found it "strange" that she and Anna Searing, a white woman who also taught at Myrtilla Miner's school, were "fellow students" at Oberlin.[54] When comparing herself to both Anna Searing and Myrtilla Miner, Brown used the word "strange," pinpointing the distance between their respective positions in American society. Brown saw herself occupying a social space between these white women and most African Americans, due to her class, race, and education. As a result, Brown fought constant battles on behalf of "colored" people. At Oberlin, she witnessed a "colored man [who] spoke as well as any other much better than many. I felt proud that he did so nobly."[55] When the women in her hall at Oberlin formed a soldier's aid society, she told them "not one whit of aid would she give them if they would not permit colored persons to join their ranks."[56] Brown's efforts on behalf of "colored" people generally were also a personal struggle for equality with Howland and her white friends.

After emancipation, Brown found that her identity as an educated free "colored" woman did not prevent whites from degrading and insulting her. She faced regular reminders of her race and her unequal position in American society. Brown informed Howland that young men, "laying aside their manhood," harassed and threw stones at her as she walked to school.[57] Brown's womanhood did not protect her from the insults of these men. She also experienced the racial prejudice of white allies in the freedmen's aid movement. She attended a meeting at which General O. O. Howard, commissioner of the Freedmen's Bureau, and the Rev. John Kimball, superintendent of education for the District, addressed the "N.T.s", or "Nigger Teachers."[58] In her letter to Howland, Brown mocked Howard's speech as unoriginal and sentimental, and then described Kimball as a "consummate fool." Apparently, Kimball asked the teachers if black children were as honest as white children. The teachers responded with silence: "The colored teachers as if they had known of this ridiculous performance beforehand had together resolved on their course, declined taking any part in the debate—None of us voted—all looked just what they thought." Brown wryly commented, "At the close I wished I had remained in school teaching my children to be as honest as white folks."[59] In addition to Kimball's racial preconceptions, Brown noted his tendency toward outright discrimination: "I know he [Kimball] would gladly have all white teachers if he had the power to turn out colored ones."[60] Despite Brown's efforts to construct her own identity, such interactions reinforced Brown's race and her association with former slaves.

Brown's first response to her changing circumstances was to escape her life in Washington. She had opposed colonization before the Civil War, but the intractability of racial divisions made the prospect of leaving the United States more appealing: "Some of my friends are going to Africa and recently I have been tempted to go where there is perfect freedom. Again, I thought it wiser to remain. I am restless, weary and dissatisfied. It is impossible for me to think clearly to do anything."[61] Brown's search for perfect freedom led to her brief employment at the Pension Office, to a school in Charleston, South Carolina, and finally to Jackson, Mississippi, which in 1870 became the first state to send an

African American man to the U.S. Senate.[62] Brown supported herself
by copying the acts of the state legislature and she boarded with a friend,
Secretary of State James Lynch. Brown's letters to Howland in this
period portray the vibrancy of black political life, and testify to the
radical potential of Reconstruction. Though she enjoyed the compan-
ionship of Secretary of State Lynch and other members of Mississippi's
political elite, Brown still did not feel at home. She informed Howland
that she was tired of being the object of male pursuit ("the negro men
have annoyed me almost beyond endurance") and that she planned to
return to Charleston.[63]

As her comment about "negro men" implies, gender also influenced
Brown's search for perfect freedom. During her time in the South,
between 1869–70, Brown probably reconsidered her decision to remain
unmarried. She wrote Howland that she had numerous admirers and a
marriage proposal from a prominent member of the lower house of the
Mississippi legislature. Though Brown rejected these advances and fled
from Mississippi in order to protect her single status, her letters indicate
growing recognition of her sexual vulnerability. In her letters to Howland, she downplayed this vulnerability by mocking her suitors. But as
with the white men who harassed her on her way to school, her womanhood did not protect her in the way it protected Howland. She told Howland of one invitation from a former suitor, a fellow teacher, who asked
her to join him in New Orleans. Brown believed a move to New Orleans
would be like "jumping into the lion's mouth."[64] Some of Brown's suitors
may have been white, as she mentioned a "German flame" in two letters,
but she was clearly aware of the dangers white men posed to black
women.[65] For example, Brown told Howland of the situation of Kate
Baker: "I have tried to save her from ruin but in vain. This girl got herself into trouble with some white man as I verily believe—she could not
force him to marry her—then she tempted my brother."[66] Brown's willingness to share such information with Howland affirmed the strength of
their relationship. In the racially and sexually charged atmosphere of
Reconstruction, black women vigilantly protected their reputations from
whites. Brown's honesty with Howland showed that she did not fear negative judgment from her friend.[67] Her frank discussions of romance also
demonstrate that she was opening to the possibility of marriage, and the
safety and security it could provide.

Brown's letters from the South hint that a new chapter in her life was
about to begin. In Mississippi, she participated fully in African American
political and cultural life, and, upon her return to Washington, she continued her association with black political leaders. After 1870, the fre-
quency of Brown's letters to Howland decline dramatically. In 1875,
Brown wrote that she was principal of the Charles Sumner School in

Washington. In this position, Brown finally expressed satisfaction with
her place in postwar America: "this school is a success. I glory in it. It is
just the field I like—wide enough for my ambition."[68] As a principal,
Brown commanded a good salary and received new status. Brown's pride
in her achievement encouraged her to write to Howland, but while they
kept in touch and saw each other occasionally, their friendship never
reached the same intensity. Instead, Emma Brown directed her focus
elsewhere, to her new school, to the African American political and
intellectual elite, and then to a husband. In 1879, the thirty-six-year-old
spinster married Henry P. Montgomery, principal of the John F. Cook
school in Washington. Montgomery was a former slave from Mississippi,
who joined the Union army during the war.[69] Brown's marriage signaled
an important change from her earlier stance on marriage and "Negro"
men, another indication that she began to identify more closely with
African Americans. Her friendship with Howland grew more distant as
she allied with other educated blacks in pursuit of freedom and uplift.

Her decision to marry also ended a major part of her relationship with
Howland. At the beginning of their friendship, they shared their status
as single women, seeking fulfillment through political activism and teaching. Despite their relative independence, both women discovered family
demands and social limitations on their freedom. The expectations of
her parents forced Howland to hire another teacher for the school she
founded in Heathsville, Virginia, and return to the North. Brown was
bound to teach in order to support herself and her family. In Brown's
complaints of weariness and dissatisfaction, Howland probably recognized the condition of women generally. Brown's struggle for autonomy
linked her to Howland, but, following emancipation, the social and economic gulf between the two women grew.

While Brown turned to the new black political and intellectual elite,
Howland's response to racial inequality was to continue her philanthropic activities, a response rooted in her position as a wealthy white
woman. Until her death in 1929, Howland remained a benefactor of
black schools in the South and sponsored women's attendance at Oberlin and other colleges. While Howland maintained her interest in former
slaves, their lives were not connected to hers. Howland could, and did,
leave teaching and the South. In New York State, Howland threw her
energies into the woman suffrage movement, and her interests in racial
and sexual equality, once joined, divided.

Emma Brown's friendship with Emily Howland roughly parallels
the history of the freedmen's aid movement, and their relationship has
significance for the movement as a whole. In 1870, after Emily Howland's return to the North and Emma Brown's journey to the deep South,
the Freedmen's Bureau and the branches of the American Freedmen's

Union Commission had already begun their withdrawal from the South. Of the secular organizations, only the New England Freedmen's Aid Society functioned until 1876. While a number of white women remained in the South, including Howland's friends Sallie Holley and Caroline Putnam, most women reformers turned their political ambitions to the racially segregated movements for suffrage, temperance, organized charity, and the club movement. White women continued to aid black schools, but largely through financial contributions. In contrast, African American women sustained their commitment to aiding and elevating former slaves through education and the black women's club movement. Like Emma Brown, their commitment was based on their race, class, and gender identity, and on their own struggle for full inclusion in American society. The freedmen's aid movement set black and white women on separate paths toward achieving independence, economic opportunity, and political rights.

At the beginning of the freedmen's aid movement, white abolitionist women assumed that their interests coincided with freedwomen's. Reformers brought their abolitionist and women's rights principles to freedmen's aid, but their lives as Northern, middle-class, white women influenced their views of Reconstruction, benevolence, free labor, paid employment, and domestic economy. Although white women believed they understood freedwomen, they discovered that their interests were divided by racial experience. Freedwomen's goals grew from the history of slavery. Family reconstitution, self-ownership, independence from whites, and the right to compensation for their labor, among other things, shaped freedwomen's conception of freedom. Though abolitionist women made a conscious effort to build a movement around sisterhood, the experiences of reformers and freedwomen during Reconstruction revealed the racial and class divisions among women, and the challenges that any such movement must face.

Conclusion

During Reconstruction, women asserted a national political vision for the first time. Women in the freedmen's aid movement conceived a federal government that assumed responsibility for all its citizens. The state, through the Freedmen's Bureau, would protect those who had recently been exploited and inaugurate a new era in which political equality and economic opportunity were possibilities for all Americans, rather than a few. Female reformers advocated aid to the neediest former slaves, those least able to accommodate free labor ideology: single mothers, widows, the elderly, the poor, and the sick. Their radical vision for Reconstruction confronted familiar political obstacles: fears of big government and questions about its legitimacy, criticism of women's political ambitions and disregard for their ideas, and an unwillingness to address the glaring inequalities in America's political economy.

In the freedmen's aid movement, we see the origins of contemporary political debates. African American poverty is only one legacy of timid federal Reconstruction policies, the preoccupations of the post-emancipation era still guide lawmakers seeking to alleviate poverty without compromising American values such as thrift, sobriety, and hard work. The experience of women reformers shows the prehistory of the so-called "gender gap" in public attitudes toward social policy.[1] Yet it also shows the very real limits on a unified women's movement that presumes a universal female subject. The complexities of women's vision for Reconstruction is essential to understanding American political history as well as current events.

The history of the freedmen's aid movement is an early example of women's efforts to reconstruct the relationship between the federal government and its citizens.[2] Abolitionist women adapted the precepts of Radical Republicanism, political and civil rights, free labor, and a powerful federal government, asserting women's equality as they pursued justice for former slaves. In addition to arguing for universal suffrage, they viewed the Freedmen's Bureau as the vehicle through which they could ease the transition from slavery, shape the condition of freedom, and remind the nation of its obligation to former slaves. Women in the freedmen's aid movement also lobbied Congress, founded aid societies, distributed relief, bought land to sell to freedpeople, and taught in normal and industrial schools.

These white and black women created a national women's political culture that challenged the male political culture of the Republican Party, the Freedmen's Bureau, and male reformers. Though men and women in the freedmen's aid movement shared a commitment to education and self-reliance, they disagreed over the appropriate place of women and the consequences of charity. In freedmen's aid societies, men and women also grappled with the rise of more centralized, scientific, and professional forms of charity. Women embraced the new partnership between private benevolence and the government, but they resisted national "commissions" like the American Freedmen's Union Commission, which wanted to place women's benevolence under the authority of male reformers.[3] Freedmen's Bureau agents and male politicians reiterated male reformers' disapproval of women's approach to poverty and material relief, linking their opposition to welfare to their antagonism to women's political power. Skeptical of prolonged government intervention, Republican politicians and male reformers put their faith in public education, economic development, and universal male suffrage to solve the problems posed by emancipation.

Women based their proposals for Reconstruction on the assumption that women shared interests across race, class, region, and religion, but they found their vision of sisterhood taxed by their interaction with freedwomen and with each other. Josephine Griffing argued that the salvation of the country "lay in its speedy recognition and admission of the counterpoising moral element of the woman nature."[4] Feminists promoted economic independence, equal suffrage, and women's full participation in government and policymaking, yet race and class limited their definition of women's rights. Abolitionist women built their postwar careers on their advocacy for former slaves, basing their moral authority in part upon their supervisory relationship to freedpeople. Middle-class women, white and black, believed former slaves needed their guidance and direction, but freedwomen resisted this guidance as often as they accepted it.[5] As they established professional careers, and searched for economic security, women also competed for positions and influence in the freedmen's aid movement, exposing important strategic differences. Though the conflicts between reformers and freedwomen revealed the limits of sisterhood as a premise for freedmen's aid, these struggles also gave birth to a dynamic, if still divided, postwar women's political culture.

After Reconstruction, women in the freedmen's aid movement extended their influence in American reform, participating in the charity organization movement, the women's club, temperance, and suffrage movements, and educational reform. All of these efforts placed women at the forefront of national efforts to grapple with industrialization, urbanization, immigration, and the changing status of women and African Americans.[6] Though Josephine Griffing died during Reconstruction, Ednah Dow Cheney established the New England Women's Club, Cornelia Hancock founded the Philadelphia Society for Organizing Charity and the Children's Aid Society, and Frances Ellen Watkins Harper and Charlotte Forten Grimké helped launch the National Association of Colored Women. Before her marriage, Charlotte Forten had also worked briefly as a clerk in the U.S. Treasury Department. Julia Wilbur served in the U.S. Patent Office from 1869 until her death in 1895, continuing women's identification with the federal government. In addition, Emily Howland became a leader in women's education and suffrage.

While black and white women participated in similar postwar activities, their efforts often took place in separate contexts and contained different meanings. Most white reformers retreated to the North after the disappointments of Reconstruction, joining organizations and clubs that frequently emphasized white women's racial and class superiority. In addition, white feminists began to base their arguments for suffrage and political influence on racial difference, though many also maintained their interest in the education and welfare of former slaves, donating money to African American schools and protesting lynching.[7] Only Sallie Holley, Caroline Putnam, and a few other white women chose to stay in the South and teach the children of former slaves. Emma Brown and other black women did not have the same choices as white women. In their own minds, and in the eyes of American society, the future of middle-class blacks and former slaves were intricately connected. As they worked to improve the welfare and status of all African Americans, black women created a place for themselves in American politics and reform. As Glenda Gilmore argues, these women became the diplomats of the African American community.[8]

The fight for universal suffrage also weakened the historic link between antislavery and women's rights, contributing to the declining cooperation between white and black women after Reconstruction. When abolitionists supported the Fourteenth and Fifteenth Amendments, Elizabeth Cady Stanton and Susan B. Anthony formed the National Woman Suffrage Association, offending former allies by using racist arguments in support of woman suffrage. Their opponents established the American Woman Suffrage Association, and the two organizations did not unite until 1890. Although black women joined both organizations, they often had to work for suffrage in the face of objections from white suffragists.[9] Many historians of women's reform have investigated the racism that precipitated this split, noting its significance for the history of the women's rights movement. Louise Michele Newman concludes that the women's rights movement was inherently racist, arguing that feminists based arguments for women's equality on the role of white middle-class women as "experts on racial questions and 'protectors' of vulnerable peoples."[10]

As Newman suggests, women in the freedmen's aid movement also asserted their political power as advisors and teachers of former slaves, thus reinforcing freedpeople's dependency. But the history of women's activism in freedmen's aid is more than the story of white women's racism.[11] The freedmen's aid movement occurred in a larger political and social context, in which whites and blacks, men and women, Northerners and Southerners, struggled with the meaning of freedom, equality, and independence, but also with the meaning of race, manhood, and womanhood.[12] As abolitionist-feminists lobbied for education, employment, land reform, political rights, and material aid, they challenged the political rhetoric of dependency more often than they succumbed to it. Though they sometimes resorted to paternalistic and racist views of former slaves, their vision for Reconstruction, which included universal suffrage and a strong Freedmen's Bureau, made them true political radicals during Reconstruction.

Historians have long explored the connections between women's rights and African American freedom, from antislavery through the Civil Rights movement, but with recent studies of the racism of the feminist movement and "whiteness," the relationship between racial identity, gender, and feminism demands further exploration.[13] Yet studies of the relationship between feminism and racism must also consider the historical context, and not discount the real experiences of women. As Barbara Jeanne Fields argues, ideology is created in the daily lives of individuals.[14] Indeed, the realities of Reconstruction—political disagreement, fighting over resources, poverty, and disillusionment—shaped race and gender ideology, as much as that ideology influenced the strategies of women reformers.

Reconstruction politics, rather than racism or internal factionalism, ultimately limited abolitionist-feminists' ability to assert their vision of government protection and a moral national political culture. They confronted politicians and reformers hostile to women's inroads into Reconstruction policy and fearful of dependency and pauperization among the newly emancipated. To a certain extent, both women and former slaves accepted the ideal of economic independence as a route to equality, further constraining their ability to challenge the power of free labor ideology. Popular opposition to the growth of the federal government, and in particular, to a national agency dedicated to freedpeople, strengthened the reaction against Radical Reconstruction and its female advocates. In addition, the push for reconciliation, a reconciliation based on the mutual interests of Northern and Southern whites, overwhelmed the case for civil rights.[15]

Though the freedmen's aid movement occurred in a specific time, its history has significance for the present. Americans still debate the appropriate relationship between welfare and the federal government, using political language that associates race and sex with dependency. As is true of the "gender gap" in today's political culture, women in the freedmen's aid movement accepted the idea of state protection, believing that it offered a path to political inclusion for groups that had previously been excluded. Abolitionist-feminists were among the first to argue for a national debt for slavery, similar to today's arguments for reparations and affirmative action. During Reconstruction, women in the freedmen's aid movement sought to radically transform American politics. Their vision for Reconstruction included political equality for women and African Americans, protection for former slaves, and national responsibility for slavery and its consequences.

Notes

Introduction

1. Benjamin Butler applied the term "contraband" to slave refugees at Fortress Monroe, Virginia, in 1861. One of the first moves toward the Emancipation Proclamation in 1863, his classification of slaves as enemy property allowed the federal government to resist Southern efforts to retrieve runaways, while employing African Americans as laborers for the Union Army.

2. Henrietta S. Jacquette, ed., *South After Gettysburg: Letters of Cornelia Hancock from the Army of the Potomac, 1863–65* (Philadelphia: University of Pennsylvania Press, 1937), 42–43.

3. Josephine Griffing Petition, presented May 9, 1864, HR38A-G10.5, Records of the House of Representatives, Record Group 233, National Archives and Records Administration.

4. Jacqueline Jones, *Soldiers of Light and Love: Northern Teachers and Georgia Blacks, 1865–1873* (Athens: University of Georgia Press, 1980, 1992); Henry Lee Swint, *The Northern Teacher in the South, 1862–1870* (1941; New York: Octagon Books, 1967); Ronald E. Butchart, *Northern Schools, Southern Blacks, and Reconstruction: Freedmen's Education, 1862–1875* (Westport, Conn.: Greenwood Press, 1980); Robert C. Morris, *Reading, 'Riting, and Reconstruction: The Education of Freedmen in the South, 1861–1870* (Chicago: University of Chicago Press, 1981). On African American teachers see Farah Jasmine Griffin, *Beloved Sisters and Loving Friends: Letters from Rebecca Primus of Royal Oak, Maryland, and Addie Brown, of Hartford, Connecticut, 1854–1868* (New York: Knopf, 1999); Clara Merritt DeBoer, *His Truth Is Marching On: African Americans Who Taught the Freedmen for the American Missionary Association, 1861–1877* (New York: Garland, 1995); Adam Fairclough, "'Being in the Field of Education and Also Being a Negro . . . Seems . . . Tragic': Black Teachers in the Jim Crow South," *Journal of American History* 87 (June 2000): 65-91.

5. For example, Joe M. Richardson, *Christian Reconstruction: The American Missionary Association and Southern Blacks, 1861–1890* (Athens: University of Georgia Press, 1986); Butchart, *Northern Schools, Southern Blacks, and Reconstruction*; Paul A. Cimbala and Randall M. Miller, eds., *The Freedmen's Bureau and Reconstruction: Reconsiderations* (New York: Fordham University Press, 1999). James M. McPherson includes some discussion of women in *The Struggle for Equality: Abolitionists and the Negro in the Civil War and Reconstruction* (Princeton, N.J.: Princeton University Press, 1964). Freedmen's aid societies used both "freedmen" and "freedman" in

their titles, sometimes varying between the two. Like other historians, I have standardized the names of freedmen's aid societies with "freedmen." See McPherson, *Struggle for Equality*; Butchart, *Northern Schools, Southern Blacks*, 5. Because the American Missionary Association was part of the evangelical wing of the antislavery movement, the Association's leadership was even more conservative about gender roles than the AFUC. As a result, I have found no women in active leadership positions within the AMA, and I have not considered their organization in this study.

6. Julie Roy Jeffrey, *The Great Silent Army of Abolitionism: Ordinary Women in the Antislavery Movement* (Chapel Hill: University of North Carolina Press, 1998), 1, passim. In chapter 6, Jeffrey offers a preliminary discussion of abolitionist women's activism in freedmen's aid. See also Blanche Glassman Hersh, *The Slavery of Sex: Feminist-Abolitionists in America* (Urbana: University of Illinois Press, 1978); Jean Fagan Yellin, *Women and Sisters: The Antislavery Feminists in American Culture* (New Haven, Conn.: Yale University Press, 1989); Jean Fagan Yellin and John C. Van Horne, *The Abolitionist Sisterhood: Women's Political Culture in Antebellum America* (Ithaca, N.Y.: Cornell University Press, 1994).

7. David Montgomery, *Beyond Equality: Labor and the Radical Republicans, 1862–1872* (New York: Knopf, 1967); Eric Foner, *Reconstruction: America's Unfinished Revolution, 1863–1877* (New York: Harper and Row, 1988), 228–39.

8. For the abolitionist view of slavery as a sin, see Robert Abzug, *Cosmos Crumbling: American Reform and the Religious Imagination* (New York: Oxford University Press, 1994), chap. 6.

9. Eric Foner, *Free Soil, Free Labor, Free Men: The Ideology of the Republican Party Before the Civil War* (New York: Oxford University Press, 1970). For the contradictions between free labor ideology and African American rights, see Willie Lee Rose, *Rehearsal for Reconstruction: The Port Royal Experiment* (New York: Oxford University Press, 1964); Foner, *Reconstruction*, chaps. 2, 4; Julie Saville, *The Work of Reconstruction: From Slave to Wage Laborer in South Carolina, 1860–1870* (New York: Cambridge University Press, 1996), chaps. 1, 2; Thomas C. Holt, "'An Empire over the Mind': Emancipation, Race, and Ideology in the British West Indies and the American South," in J. Morgan Kousser and James M. McPherson, eds., *Region, Race, and Reconstruction: Essays in Honor of C. Vann Woodward* (New York: Oxford University Press, 1982), 283–313. Heather Cox Richardson explores the strength of free labor ideology and its relationship to racism through the end of the nineteenth century. See Richardson, *The Death of Reconstruction: Race, Labor and Politics in the Post-Civil War South, 1865–1901* (Cambridge, Mass.: Harvard University Press, 2001).

10. Nancy Fraser and Linda Gordon, "A Genealogy of *Dependency*: Tracing a Keyword of the U.S. Welfare State," *Signs* 19, no. 2 (1992): 309–36; Amy Dru Stanley, *From Bondage to Contract: Wage Labor, Marriage, and the Market in the Age of Slave Emancipation* (New York: Cambridge University Press, 1998); Joanne Pope Melish, *Disowning Slavery: Gradual Emancipation and "Race" in New England, 1780–1860* (Ithaca, N.Y.: Cornell University Press, 1998).

11. Southerners and Northerners had different perspectives on freedpeople's "dependency"; this manuscript focuses on Northern reformers and policymakers. The best analysis of the problems "dependency" posed for Southern blacks is Laura Edwards, *Gendered Strife and Confusion: The Political Culture of Reconstruction* (Urbana: University of Illinois Press, 1997), 7, 66–80. See also Leslie A. Schwalm, *A Hard Fight for We: Women's Transition from Slavery to Freedom in South Carolina* (Urbana: University of Illinois Press, 1997), chap. 7; Stanley, *From Bondage to Contract*, chap. 3; Foner, *Reconstruction*, 152–53. Saidiya V. Hartman

refers to Northern anxieties over freedpeople's capacity for free labor as the "discourse of idleness"; see Hartman, *Scenes of Subjection: Terror, Slavery, and Self-Making in Nineteenth-Century America* (New York: Oxford University Press, 1997), 126–30. For manumission laws, dependency, and race see, for example, George Fredrickson, *White Supremacy: A Comparative Study in American & South African History* (New York: Oxford University Press, 1981), 85–86; David Brion Davis, *Slavery and Human Progress* (New York: Oxford University Press, 1984), 207–23; Melish, *Disowning Slavery*, chaps. 2, 3.

12. Schwalm, *A Hard Fight for We*, chaps. 6, 7; Edwards, *Gendered Strife and Confusion*, chaps. 1, 4; Stanley, *From Bondage to Contract*, chap. 4; Hartman, *Scenes of Subjection*, 156–61; Jacqueline Jones, *Labor of Love, Labor of Sorrow: Black Women, Work, and the Family from Slavery to the Present* (New York: Vintage Books, 1986), chap. 2; Noralee Frankel, *Freedom's Women: Black Women and Families in Civil War Era Mississippi* (Bloomington: Indiana University Press, 1999), 29, 52, 179, passim; Tera Hunter, *To 'Joy My Freedom: Southern Black Women's Lives and Labors After the Civil War* (Cambridge, Mass.: Harvard University Press, 1997).

13. Foner, *Reconstruction*, chaps. 2–4; Saville, *The Work of Reconstruction*; Schwalm, *Hard Fight for We*, chaps. 6, 7; Edwards, *Gendered Strife and Confusion*, chaps. 1, 2; Frankel, *Freedom's Women*, chap. 3; Ira Berlin, Barbara J. Fields, Steven F. Miller, Joseph P. Reidy, and Leslie S. Rowland, *Slaves No More: Three Essays on Emancipation and the Civil War* (New York: Cambridge University Press, 1993), 79–186; Catherine Clinton, "Reconstructing Freedwomen," in Catherine Clinton and Nina Silber, eds., *Divided Houses: Gender and the Civil War* (New York: Oxford University Press, 192), 306–19.

14. Carol Faulkner, "'A Proper Recognition of Our Manhood': The African Civilization Society and the Freedmen's Aid Movement," *Afro-Americans in New York Life and History* (January 2000): 41–62; Wilson Jeremiah Moses, *The Golden Age of Black Nationalism, 1850–1925* (New York: Oxford University Press, 1978), chap. 4; William S. McFeely, *Frederick Douglass* (New York: W.W. Norton, 1991), chaps. 18, 19. See also James O. Horton, *Free People of Color: Inside the African American Community* (Washington, D.C.: Smithsonian Institution Press, 1993).

15. John Murray Forbes to Edward Atkinson, February 9 and February 15, 1865, Edward Atkinson Papers, Massachusetts Historical Society.

16. For this definition of women's political culture see Ruth Bogin and Jean Fagan Yellin, "Introduction," and Kathryn Kish Sklar, "'Women Who Speak for an Entire Nation': American and British Women at the World Anti-Slavery Convention, London, 1840," in Yellin and Van Horne, *Abolitionist Sisterhood*, 2, 301–33. Paula Baker, "The Domestication of Politics: Women and American Political Society, 1780–1920," in Ellen Carol DuBois and Vicki L. Ruiz, eds., *Unequal Sisters: A Multicultural Reader in U.S. Women's History* (New York: Routledge, 1990), 66–91; Kathryn Kish Sklar, "Historical Foundations of Women's Power in the Creation of the American Welfare State, 1830–1930," in Seth Koven and Sonya Michel, eds., *Mothers of a New World: Maternalist Politics and the Origins of Welfare States* (New York: Routledge, 1990), 43–93. On women and antebellum benevolence see Mary P. Ryan, *Cradle of the Middle Class: The Family in Oneida County, New York, 1790–1865* (New York: Cambridge University Press, 1981); Nancy Hewitt, *Women's Activism and Social Change: Rochester, New York, 1822–1872* (Ithaca, N.Y.: Cornell University Press, 1984); Lori D. Ginzberg, *Women and the Work of Benevolence: Morality, Politics, and Class in the Nineteenth-Century United States* (New Haven, Conn.: Yale University Press, 1990), chaps. 1–3. For the racial and class implications of women's political culture, see Peggy Pascoe, *Relations of Rescue: The Search for Female Moral Authority in the American West, 1874–1939* (New

York: Oxford University Press, 1990); Louise Michele Newman, *White Women's Rights: The Racial Origins of Feminism in the United States* (New York: Oxford University Press, 1999). For the class dimensions of black women's reform, see especially Deborah Gray White, *Too Heavy a Load: Black Women in Defense of Themselves, 1894–1994* (New York: W.W. Norton, 1999), chaps. 1, 2.

17. See George Fredrickson, *The Inner Civil War: Northern Intellectuals and the Crisis of the Union* (New York: Harper Torchbooks, 1965), 188, 199–201, 211–16; Ginzberg, *Women and the Work of Benevolence*, chaps. 5, 6; Stanley, *From Bondage to Contract*, chap. 3. Historians who write about women and party politics deplore the idea of a women's political culture in the Gilded Age. See Rebecca Edwards, *Angels in the Machinery: Gender in American Party Politics from the Civil War to the Progressive Era* (New York: Oxford University Press, 1997), 8. The historiography of black women's reform after emancipation does not address the issue of scientific or organized charity. Because of the close association of scientific charity with the social elite and government and politics, African Americans may not have had access to the means or power to engage in this type of charitable activity. However, Glenda Gilmore notes that African American women participated in Associated Charities branches in North Carolina. Glenda Elizabeth Gilmore, *Gender and Jim Crow: Women and the Politics of White Supremacy in North Carolina* (Chapel Hill: University of North Carolina Press, 1996), 171–72.

18. Judith Ann Giesberg, *Civil War Sisterhood: The U.S. Sanitary Commission and Women's Politics in Transition* (Boston: Northeastern University Press, 2000). As historians have noted, however, the rise of a national women's political culture created gender tensions. See Jeanie Attie, *Patriotic Toil: Northern Women and the American Civil War* (Ithaca, N.Y.: Cornell University Press, 1998); Elizabeth Leonard, *Yankee Women: Gender Battles in the Civil War* (New York: W.W. Norton, 1994), xix–xxv, chap. 2.

19. Joan Waugh, *Unsentimental Reformer: The Life of Josephine Shaw Lowell* (Cambridge, Mass.: Harvard University Press, 1997), 2–12; Ginzberg, *Women and the Work of Benevolence* 202–6; Ruth Bordin, *Woman and Temperance: The Quest for Power and Liberty, 1873–1900* (New Brunswick, N.J.: Rutgers University Press, 1981, 1990); Karen J. Blair, *The Clubwoman as Feminist: True Womanhood Redefined, 1868–1914* (New York: Holmes and Meier, 1980); Paula Giddings, *When and Where I Enter: The Impact of Black Women on Race and Sex in America* (New York: Bantam Books, 1984), chaps. 4, 5, 6; Gilmore, *Gender and Jim Crow*, chaps. 2, 6. Lyde Cullen Sizer argues that nineteenth-century women writers entered the political debate over the meaning of the Civil War and Reconstruction, attempting to redefine the place of women in the nation. See *The Political Work of Northern Women Writers and the Civil War, 1850–1872* (Chapel Hill: University of North Carolina Press, 2000).

20. For the history of the women's rights movement during Reconstruction see Ellen Carol DuBois, *Feminism and Suffrage: The Emergence of an Independent Women's Movement in America, 1848–1869* (Ithaca, N.Y.: Cornell University Press, 1978). See also Newman, *White Women's Rights*, chap. 2.

21. Roslyn Terborg-Penn, *African American Women in the Struggle for the Vote, 1850–1920* (Bloomington: Indiana University Press, 1998), 42; Nell Irvin Painter, *Sojourner Truth: A Life, a Symbol* (New York: W.W. Norton, 1996), 226, 229, 232.

22. Lee Virginia Chambers-Schiller, *Liberty, a Better Husband: Single Women in America: The Generations of 1780–1840* (New Haven, Conn.: Yale University Press, 1984).

23. Louise Michele Newman argues that the women's rights movement developed concurrently with the rise of social Darwinism, and that women's efforts to

civilize former slaves, Native Americans, and others grew from their beliefs in white supremacy. Racist beliefs thus enabled women's entrance into the public sphere. Newman gives the freedmen's aid movement as one example of women's civilizing mission. Newman, *White Women's Rights*, 23, 26–27. The views of feminists in the freedmen's aid movement thus demand closer examination, as scholars suggest that racial attitudes should be studied in relationship to social and economic context. See Holt, "'An Empire over the Mind,'" 306–7; Barbara Jeanne Fields, "Slavery, Race, and Ideology in the United States of America," *New Left Review* 181 (May/June 1990): 95–118.

24. Newman, *White Women's Rights*, chap. 2; Yellin, *Women and Sisters*, 24–25. See also Pascoe, *Relations of Rescue*, xxi–xxii, passim; Christine Stansell, *City of Women: Sex and Class in New York, 1789–1860* (Urbana: University of Illinois Press, 1987), 70–75. Class position informed reformers' relationship with freedwomen, but, as Amy Dru Stanley has argued, it was racial ideology which shaped Yankees' understanding of the different domestic rights of working-class whites and African Americans. Stanley, *From Bondage to Contract*, 190.

25. In order to include some African American reformers I have loosely defined "Northern" to comprise the border states and those free blacks who maintained class differences from former slaves. Giddings, *When and Where I Enter*; Evelyn Brooks Higginbotham, *Righteous Discontent: The Women's Movement in the Black Baptist Church, 1880–1920* (Cambridge, Mass.: Harvard University Press, 1993); Gilmore, *Gender and Jim Crow*; Stephanie J. Shaw, *What a Woman Ought To Be and Do: Black Professional Women Workers During the Jim Crow Era* (Chicago: University of Chicago Press, 1996); White, *Too Heavy a Load*.

Chapter 1. Dependency, Gender, and Freedmen's Aid During the Civil War

1. Willie Lee Rose, *Rehearsal for Reconstruction: The Port Royal Experiment* (New York: Oxford University Press, 1964). See also Julie Saville, *The Work of Reconstruction: From Slave to Wage Laborer in South Carolina, 1860–1870* (New York: Cambridge University Press, 1996); Leslie A. Schwalm, *A Hard Fight for We: Women's Transition from Slavery to Freedom in South Carolina* (Urbana: University of Illinois Press, 1997).

2. James M. McPherson, *The Struggle for Equality: Abolitionists and the Negro in the Civil War and Reconstruction* (Princeton, N.J.: Princeton University Press, 1964); Jacqueline Jones, *Soldiers of Light and Love: Northern Teachers and Georgia Blacks, 1865–1873* (Athens: University of Georgia Press, 1980, 1992).

3. George Fredrickson, *The Inner Civil War: Northern Intellectuals and the Crisis of the Union* (New York: Harper and Row, 1965); Morton Keller, *Affairs of State: Public Life in Late Nineteenth-Century America* (Cambridge, Mass.: Belknap Press, 1977); Robert H. Bremner, *The Public Good: Philanthropy and Welfare in the Civil War Era* (New York: Knopf, 1980); Lori D. Ginzberg, *Women and the Work of Benevolence: Morality, Politics and Class in the Nineteenth- Century United States* (New Haven, Conn.: Yale University Press, 1990); Elizabeth D. Leonard, *Yankee Women: Gender Battles in the Civil War* (New York: W.W. Norton, 1994); Joan Waugh, *Unsentimental Reformer: The Life of Josephine Shaw Lowell* (Cambridge, Mass.: Harvard University Press, 1997).

4. McPherson, *Struggle for Equality*, 164–65, 172–73, 396.

5. Bremner, *The Public Good*, 98–109. On dependency, see Laura Edwards, *Gendered Strife and Confusion: The Political Culture of Reconstruction* (Urbana: University of Illinois Press, 1997), chap. 2; Schwalm, *Hard Fight for We*, chap. 7; Amy

Dru Stanley, *From Bondage to Contract: Wage Labor, Marriage, and the Market in the Age of Slave Emancipation* (New York: Cambridge University Press, 1998), chap. 3; Saidiya Hartman, *Scenes of Subjection: Terror, Slavery, and Self-Making in Nineteenth-Century America* (New York: Oxford University Press, 1997), chap. 4.

6. Edward Hooper to Ellen Hooper, April 17, 1862, Hooper Papers, Houghton Library, Harvard University. Charlotte Forten, a teacher on St. Helena Island, described Hooper as "the most anti-slavery of the Superintendents." Charlotte L. Forten, *The Journals of Charlotte Forten Grimké*, ed. Brenda Stevenson (New York: Oxford University Press, 1988), 428. James Freeman Clarke, a prominent Unitarian minister and member of the Commission, recommended Hooper to Edward L. Pierce by stating that he was "a young man every way suited to this work, one of some conscience, love of usefulness & religious purpose. He is a teacher & superintendent of my Sunday School, & a faithful worker among the poor, & in every sort of benevolent action." James Freeman Clarke to Edward L. Pierce, February 14, 1862, Edward Pierce Papers, Houghton Library.

7. American Freedmen's Inquiry Commission, *Final Report May 15, 1864*. American Freedmen's Inquiry Commission, Letters Received by the Adjutant General (RG 94, M619), Roll 199, National Archives and Records Administration (hereafter AFIC).

8. Edward Hooper to Robert Hooper, June 6, 1862, Hooper Papers.

9. *First Annual Report of the Educational Commission* (Boston: Prentiss and Deland, 1863).

10. Edward Hooper to Robert Hooper, January 10, 1863, Hooper Papers.

11. *Facts Concerning the Freedmen, Their Capacity, and Their Destiny, Collected and Published by the Emancipation League* (Boston: Commercial Printing House, 1863).

12. Saville, *The Work of Reconstruction*; Edwards, *Gendered Strife and Confusion*, 66–80; David Roediger, *The Wages of Whiteness: Race and the Making of the American Working Class* (New York: Verso, 1991), chap. 4; Jonathan A. Glickstein, "Pressures from Below: Pauperism, Chattel Slavery, and the Ideological Construction of Free Market Labor Incentives in Antebellum America," *Radical History Review* 69 (1997): 114–59.

13. McPherson, *Struggle for Equality*, chap. 6; George Fredrickson, *The Black Image in the White Mind: The Debate on Afro-American Character and Destiny, 1817–1914* (New York: Harper & Row, 1971), 174; Glickstein, "Pressures from Below," 144–45; Thomas Holt, "'An Empire over the Mind': Emancipation, Race, and Ideology in the British West Indies and the American South," in J. Morgan Kousser and James M. McPherson, eds., *Region, Race, and Reconstruction: Essays in Honor of C. Vann Woodward* (New York: Oxford University Press, 1982), 283–313. Joanne Pope Melish, *Disowning Slavery: Gradual Emancipation and "Race" in New England, 1780–1860* (Ithaca, N.Y.: Cornell University Press, 1998), 86–87, 109–118.

14. Entry for April 13, 1862, "Journal of Miss Susan Walker," *Quarterly Publication of the Historical and Philosophical Society of Ohio* 7 (1912): 30.

15. Quoted in Mrs. A. M. French, *Slavery in South Carolina and the Ex-Slaves; or, The Port Royal Mission* (New York: Winchell M. French, 1862), 26. See also E. L. Pierce to Salmon Chase, March 1, 1862, Edward Pierce Papers.

16. Maria Mann to Aunt Mary, August 14, 1863, Mary Tyler Peabody Mann Papers, Library of Congress.

17. Ann B. Earle to Dear Friend, March 25, 1864, in Henry Swint, ed., *Dear Ones at Home: Letters from Contraband Camps* (Nashville: Vanderbilt University Press, 1966), 105.

18. American Freedmen's Inquiry Commission, *Preliminary Report Touching the*

Condition and Management of Emancipated Refugees; Made to the Secretary of War by the American Freedmen's Inquiry Commission, June 30, 1863 (New York: John F. Trow, 1863).

19. Lucy Chase to Dear Ones at Home, April 1, 1863, *Dear Ones at Home*, 67.

20. Chase to Dear Ones, April 1, 1863, 68. The "discourse of idleness" refers to the language surrounding the debate over freedpeople's conduct and fitness for freedom in the context of a free labor system. See Hartman, *Scenes of Subjection*, 127.

21. Sarah Chase to Mr. May, March 9, 1866, *Dear Ones at Home*, 201.

22. Letter from Sarah Chase, April 18, 1865, *Dear Ones at Home*, 156. Saidiya Hartman notes the prevalence of this strain of thought in advice manuals to freedpeople. She argues that "only industry, diligence, and a willingness to work, proved one's worthiness of freedom," and concludes that reformers' emphasis on freedpeople's worthiness replaced "the nation's duty to guarantee, at minimum, their exercise of liberty and equality, if not opportunities for livelihood other than debt-peonage." Hartman, *Scenes of Subjection*, 135, 118.

23. *First Annual Report of the Barnard Freedmen's Aid Society of Dorchester*, 1865, Kroch Library, Cornell University.

24. M. E. Shearman to John Alvord, History of the Friends' Freedmen's Relief Association, November 27, 1867, Letters Received, Records of the Education Division (M803), Bureau of Refugees, Freedmen, and Abandoned Lands (RG105), National Archives and Records Administration (hereafter BRFAL).

25. *Freedmen's Bulletin* 1, no. 1 (February 1865), 9.

26. *Annual Report of the National Freedmen's Relief Association of New York* (New York: Holman, 1866).

27. *Annual Report of the National Freedmen's Relief Association*, 1866; Bremner, *Public Good*, 98–109.

28. Fragment of Maria Mann letter, possibly February 10, 1863, Mary Tyler Peabody Mann Papers.

29. Maria Mann to Aunt Mary, May 18 1863, Mary Tyler Peabody Mann Papers.

30. Julia A. Wilbur to Anna M. C. Barnes, October 24, 1862, Rochester Ladies' Anti-Slavery Society Papers, William L. Clements Library, University of Michigan (hereafter RLASS).

31. Wilbur to Barnes, October 24, 1862.

32. Maria Webb to Anna Barnes, October 10, 1859, Account Book, Box 2, RLASS.

33. Julie Roy Jeffrey, *The Great Silent Army of Abolitionism: Ordinary Women in the Antislavery Movement* (Chapel Hill: University of North Carolina Press, 1998); Jean Fagan Yellin and John C. Van Horne, eds., *The Abolitionist Sisterhood: Women's Political Culture in Antebellum America* (Ithaca, N.Y.: Cornell University Press, 1994).

34. *Twelfth Annual Report of the Rochester Ladies' Anti-Slavery Society* (Rochester, N.Y.: A. Strong, 1863), 3–4.

35. Julia Wilbur to Anna Barnes, February 27, 1863, RLASS; Lee Virginia Chambers-Schiller, *Liberty, a Better Husband: Single Women in America: The Generations of 1780–1840* (New Haven, Conn.: Yale University Press, 1984), chap. 6.

36. *Liberator*, August 21, 1857. The New York State Teachers' Association also introduced Wilbur to Susan B. Anthony. See Journal Brief, August 2, 1853; Journal Brief, August 5, 1857, Box 1, Julia A. Wilbur Papers, Haverford College (hereafter Wilbur Papers). At the same convention, Susan B. Anthony resolved "that it is the duty of all our schools, colleges, and universities, to open their

doors to woman, and to give her equal and identical educational advantages, side by side, with her brother, man." For more information on Anthony and the New York State Teachers' Association see Ann D. Gordon, ed. *The Selected Papers of Elizabeth Cady Stanton and Susan B. Anthony*, vol. 1, *In the School of Anti-Slavery 1840–1866* (New Brunswick, N.J.: Rutgers University Press, 1997), 228–29, 278–79, 323–24, 351, 374–77.

37. Journal Brief, May 3, 1858, Box 1, Wilbur Papers. Wilbur's family problems included the death of her brother, the death of her sister in childbirth, the death of her sister's baby, a custody struggle over her sister's remaining daughter, the death of her stepmother, and the remarriage of her father. See Journal Briefs, November 20, 1857, August 21 and September 11, 1858, July 16 and December 31, 1859, Box 1, Wilbur Papers.

38. *Twelfth Annual Report*, 7. Ira Berlin, Steven F. Miller, Joseph P. Reidy, and Leslie S. Rowland, *Freedom: A Documentary History of Emancipation, 1861–1867*, series 1, vol. 2, *The Wartime Genesis of Free Labor: The Upper South* (New York: Cambridge University Press, 1993), 78, 275.

39. Wilbur to Barnes, October 24 1862, and November 26, 1862, RLASS.

40. *Twelfth Annual Report*, 8–9. For more information on Julia Wilbur's work in Alexandria see Berlin et al., *Freedom*, 250–51, 275–76, 280–82, 284–87.

41. *Thirteenth Annual Report of the Rochester Ladies' Anti-Slavery Society* (Rochester, N.Y.: Democrat Steam Printing, 1864), 24.

42. *Twelfth Annual Report*, 12–13. Berlin et al., *Freedom*, 275–6, 280–84.

43. Wilbur to Barnes, October 24, 1862, February 27, 1863.

44. *Thirteenth Annual Report*, 3.

45. *Thirteenth Annual Report*, 22.

46. Wilbur to Barnes, November 13, 1862.

47. Wilbur to Barnes, November 12, 1862, November 13, 1862. See also November 26, 1862.

48. Wilbur to Barnes, February 27, 1863.

49. Wilbur to Barnes, November 13, 1862, February 27, 1863, December 22-24, 1862.

50. Wilbur to Barnes, November 25, 1862.

51. Wilbur to Barnes, February 27, 1863. See also *Twelfth Annual Report*, 12–14.

52. Wilbur to Barnes, November 13, 1862, February 27, 1863. *Twelfth Annual Report*, 8.

53. Wilbur, quoting a letter from Harriet Jacobs, to Barnes, August 8, 1863.

54. Wilbur to Barnes, March 10, 1863.

55. Wilbur to Barnes, February 27, 1863.

56. Wilbur to Barnes, November 5, 1863.

57. Wilbur to Hon. E. M. Stanton, March 24, 1863, quoted in Berlin et al., *Freedom*, 280–82. Wilbur was not always happy with her RLASS salary; see Wilbur to Barnes, December 15, 1862, March 5, 1864.

58. Jeanie Attie, *Patriotic Toil: Northern Women and the American Civil War* (Ithaca, N.Y.: Cornell University Press, 1998), prologue.

59. Lt. Col. H. H. Wells to Brig. Gen. J. P. Slough, April 23, 1863, quoted in Berlin et al., *Freedom*, 284–86.

60. Lt. Col. H. H. Wells to Gen. John P. Slough, April 11, 1863, quoted in Berlin et al., *Freedom*, 286.

61. Slough's endorsement of the letter of Wells to Slough, April 11, 1863, quoted in Berlin et al., *Freedom*, 286.

62. *Thirteenth Annual Report*, 23.

63. *Thirteenth Annual Report,* 22.

64. *Thirteenth Annual Report,* 23–24. See also *Twelfth Annual Report,* 12. Former slaves also asserted their independence from government support. See Peter Rachleff, *Black Labor in Richmond, 1865–1890* (1984; Urbana: University of Illinois Press, 1989), 24–25.

65. *Thirteenth Annual Report,* 23.

66. *Thirteenth Annual Report,* 23–24.

67. Wilbur to Barnes, January 15–17, 1863.

68. Wilbur to Barnes, January 15–17, 1863.

69. Wilbur to Barnes, December 15, 1862, RLASS.

70. Journal Brief, January 15, 1857, Box 1. See also Journal Briefs September 30–31, 1853; February 8, 1856, Box 1; Diary, October 2, 1853, April 1, 1854, Box 3, Wilbur Papers.

71. Julia Griffiths Crofts to Barnes, February 20, 1863; Wilbur to Barnes, January 23, 1863.

72. Julia Wilbur to Emily Howland, February 5, 1863, Emily Howland Papers, Kroch Library, Cornell University.

73. *Twelfth Annual Report,* 17. Wilbur and Jacobs also worked together in Alexandria hospitals. See *Thirteenth Annual Report,* 12–13.

74. Wilbur to Barnes March 10, 1863.

75. Wilbur to Barnes, March 10, 1863.

76. Wilbur to Barnes, August 8, 1863.

77. Wilbur to Barnes, November 20 1863, March 5 1864. Although Wilbur notes in her 1865 report that "Mr. G." had been dismissed, in her letter to Maria G. Porter, dated February 8, 1865, she said "we think Gen. Slough will do all he can to get him another place, in Savannah perhaps." RLASS, *Fourteenth Annual Report of the Rochester Ladies' Anti-Slavery Society* (Rochester, N.Y.: William S. Falls, 1865), 7.

78. Wilbur to Barnes, December 27, 1863, March 5, 1864; *Fourteenth Annual Report,* 9.

Chapter 2. The Freedmen's Aid Movement Reorganized

1. Julia A. Wilbur to Maria G. Porter, February 8, 1865, Rochester Ladies' Anti-Slavery Society Papers, William L. Clements Library, University of Michigan (RLASS).

2. Victoria Olds, "The Freedmen's Bureau as a Social Agency," Ph.D. dissertation, Columbia University School of Social Work, 1966. See also George Fredrickson, *The Inner Civil War: Northern Intellectuals and the Crisis of the Union* (New York: Harper and Row, 1965), 191; Walter I. Trattner, *From Poor Law to Welfare State: A History of Social Welfare in America* (New York: Free Press, 1979), chap. 5; Charles Gray, "The Freedmen's Bureau: A Missing Chapter in Social Welfare History," Ph.D. dissertation, Yeshiva University, 1994, 1–10.

3. Eric Foner, *Reconstruction: America's Unfinished Revolution, 1863-1877* (New York: Harper and Row, 1988), 68–69.

4. American Freedmen's Inquiry Commission Papers, Houghton Library, Harvard University.

5. American Freedmen's Inquiry Commission Papers. For a similar questionnaire see Ira Berlin, Barbara Jeanne Fields, Steven F. Miller, Joseph P. Reidy, and Leslie S. Rowland, eds., *Free at Last: A Documentary History of Slavery, Freedom, and the Civil War* (New York: New Press, 1992), 186–200.

6. Vincent Colyer to Robert Dale Owen, May 25, 1863, in Ira Berlin, Steven F. Miller, Joseph P. Reidy, and Leslie S. Rowland, *Freedom: A Documentary History of Emancipation, 1861–1867*, series 1, vol. 2, *The Wartime Genesis of Free Labor: The Upper South* (New York: Cambridge University Press, 1993), 123–126. See also American Freedmen's Inquiry Commission Papers (RG 94, M619), File 4, Roll 200, National Archives and Records Administration (hereafter AFIC).

7. Samuel G. Howe, *The Refugees from Slavery in Canada West: Report to the American Freedmen's Inquiry Commission* (Boston: Wright and Potter, 1864).

8. *Facts Concerning the Freedmen, Their Capacity, and Their Destiny, Collected and Published by the Emancipation League* (Boston: Commercial Printing House, 1863).

9. Testimony of Miss Lucy Chase, File 2, AFIC, Roll 200.

10. Testimony of Miss Laura Towne, File 3, AFIC, Roll 200.

11. Willie Lee Rose, *Rehearsal for Reconstruction: The Port Royal Experiment* (New York: Oxford University Press, 1964), chaps. 7, 10, 13; see my discussion of land reform in chap. 6.

12. Testimony of Mrs. Daniel Breed, File 1, AFIC, Roll 200.

13. Testimony of the Ladies' Contraband Relief Society, File 7, AFIC, Roll 201; Leslie A. Schwalm, "Encountering Emancipation: Slave Migration to the Midwest During the Civil War," presented at the Southern Historical Association 65th Annual Meeting, Fort Worth, Texas, November 3–6, 1999.

14. Testimony of the Ladies' Contraband Relief Society, File 7, AFIC, Roll 201.

15. Historians have noted that government agents and reformers considered freedwomen to be dependents on their male relatives and shaped their policies accordingly. But historians have not investigated Northern white women's interest and concern for freedwomen and their children. See Jacqueline Jones, *Labor of Love, Labor of Sorrow: Black Women, Work, and the Family, from Slavery to the Present* (New York: Vintage Books, 1985), 62; Saidiya V. Hartman, *Scenes of Subjection: Terror, Slavery, and Self-Making in Nineteenth-Century America* (New York: Oxford University Press, 1997), 156; Leslie A. Schwalm, *A Hard Fight for We: Women's Transition from Slavery to Freedom in South Carolina* (Urbana: University of Illinois Press, 1997), 249–50.

16. *Preliminary Report Touching the Condition and Management of Emancipated Refugees; Made to the Secretary of War by the American Freedmen's Inquiry Commission, June 20, 1863* (New York: John F. Trow, 1863).

17. American Freedmen's Inquiry Commission, *Final Report*, American Freedmen's Inquiry Commission Papers (RG 94, M619), reel 201, National Archives and Records Administration.

18. Elizabeth Cady Stanton, Susan B. Anthony, and Matilda Joslyn Gage, eds., *History of Woman Suffrage* (1881; New York: Source Book Press, 1970), 2: 37, 29. See Keith E. Melder, "Josephine Sophia White Griffing," in Edward T. James, Janet Wilson James, and Paul S. Boyer, eds., *Notable American Women* (Cambridge, Mass.: Harvard University Press, 1971); Melder, "Angel of Mercy in Washington: Josephine Griffing and the Freedmen, 1864–1872," *Records of the Columbia Historical Society of Washington, D.C.*, 1863–65: 243–72; James M. McPherson, *The Struggle for Equality: Abolitionists and the Negro in the Civil War and Reconstruction* (Princeton, N.J.: Princeton University Press, 1964), 171, 188, 389, 391–92.

19. Stanton, Anthony, Gage, *History of Woman Suffrage*, 2: 27.

20. Josephine Griffing to William Lloyd Garrison, March 24, 1864, Ms. A.1.2.v.33 p. 32b, Boston Public Library (BPL). During the Civil War, government agencies offered new employment opportunities for middle-class women. See Cindy Sondik Aron, *Ladies and Gentlemen of the Civil Service: Middle-Class Workers in Victorian America* (New York: Oxford University Press, 1987).

21. Wilbur to Anna M. C. Barnes, October 2, 1863, RLASS.

22. Emma V. Brown to Emily Howland, January 20, no year, Box 10, Emily Howland Papers, Cornell University.

23. Laura Towne to Susan Walker, March 25, 1862, Susan Walker Papers, Sterling Library, Yale University.

24. *First Annual Report of the Educational Commission* (Boston: Prentiss and Deland, 1863).

25. Thomas C. Holt, "'An Empire over the Mind': Emancipation, Race, and Ideology in the British West Indies and the American South," in J. Morgan Kousser and James M. McPherson, eds., *Region, Race, and Reconstruction: Essays in Honor of C. Vann Woodward* (New York: Oxford University Press, 1982), 283–313.

26. McPherson, *Struggle for Equality*, chap. 13; Lawrence J. Friedman, *Gregarious Saints: Self and Community in American Abolitionism, 1830–1870* (New York: Cambridge University Press, 1982), chap. 9; William Cohen, "James Miller McKim: Pennsylvania Abolitionist," Ph.D. dissertation, New York University, 1968.

27. McKim Collection 2, Box 7, Freedmen's Aid Organizations, No. 1, Samuel May Anti-Slavery Collection, Cornell University.

28. Garrison to McKim, September 11, 1865, Ms. A.1.1. v. 6 p. 118, BPL.

29. McKim Collection 2, Box 7, Freedmen's Aid Organizations, No. 9. On the American Union Commission see Robert H. Bremner, *The Public Good: Philanthropy and Welfare in the Civil War Era* (New York: Knopf, 1980), 94.

30. In addition to believing in the value of "self-reliance," Lyman Abbott and other leaders of the AFUC believed that more harm was done to freedpeople by making them the sole focus of their work. See Lyman Abbott, *Reminiscences* (New York: Houghton Mifflin, 1915), 251, 274.

31. William Lloyd Garrison wrote Theodore Parker that he held Hannah Stevenson in "highest respect in regard to her rare womanly culture, her intellectual vigor, her moral excellence, and her sympathetic nature, drawing her closely to the side of the distressed and suffering, the poor and perishing. Tell her she is in my eyes very beautiful, in the highest and noblest sense of the term." See Louis Ruchames, ed., *The Letters of William Lloyd Garrison* (Cambridge, Mass.: Belknap Press, 1975), 4: 607–8.

32. Hannah Stevenson to Ednah Dow Cheney, February 7 1866?, Ms. A.10.1. No. 127, BPL; Willie Lee Rose, *Rehearsal for Reconstruction: The Port Royal Experiment* (Athens: Brown and Thrasher Books of the University of Georgia Press, 1964, 1999), 375.

33. For a discussion of Josephine Shaw Lowell's freedmen's aid work and its impact on the rest of her career as a reformer see Joan Waugh, *Unsentimental Reformer: The Life of Josephine Shaw Lowell* (Cambridge, Mass.: Harvard University Press, 1997), 87–91.

34. Amy Swerdlow, "Abolition's Conservative Sisters: The Ladies' New York Anti-Slavery Societies, 1834–40," in Jean Fagan Yellin and John C. Van Horne, eds., *The Abolitionist Sisterhood: Women's Political Culture in Antebellum America* (Ithaca, N.Y.: Cornell University Press, 1994), 31–44; Lori D. Ginzberg, *Women and the Work of Benevolence: Morality, Politics, and Class in the Nineteenth-Century United States* (New Haven, Conn.: Yale University Press, 1990), 28–32.

35. Fredrickson, *Inner Civil War*, 188, 189–94; Ginzberg, *Women and the Work of Benevolence*, 139, chap. 5 passim. J. Matthew Gallman observes that most benevolent organizations in the Civil War era, especially the Sanitary Commission, were managed by a male hierarchy but run by women reformers. See Gallman, *Mastering Wartime: A Social History of Philadelphia During the Civil War* (New York: Cambridge University Press, 1990), chap. 5.

36. Lucretia Mott to Martha Coffin Wright, April 9, 1865, Mott Collection, Friends Historical Library, Swarthmore College, in Beverly Wilson Palmer, ed., *Selected Letters of Lucretia Coffin Mott* (Urbana: University of Illinois Press, 2002), 357–58; Ginzberg, *Women and the Work of Benevolence*, chap. 4.

37. John White Chadwick, ed., *A Life for Liberty: Anti-Slavery and Other Letters of Sallie Holley* (New York: Negro Universities Press, 1899, 1969), 32; Katherine Lydigsen Herbig, "Friends for Freedom: The Lives and Careers of Sallie Holley and Caroline Putnam," Ph.D. dissertation, Claremont Graduate School, 1977, 119–122; Anna M. Speicher, *The Religious World of Antislavery Women: Spirituality in the Lives of Five Abolitionist Lecturers* (Syracuse, N.Y.: Syracuse University Press, 2000), 38–45, 73, 107, 141–150.

38. Herbig, "Friends for Freedom," 66–68.

39. Chadwick, *A Life for Liberty*, 53; Herbig, "Friends for Freedom," 47.

40. Chadwick, *A Life for Liberty*, 59–60.

41. Herbig, "Friends for Freedom," 104–8.

42. Chadwick, *A Life for Liberty*, 68–69, 76, 87; Sallie Holley to Maria G. Porter, June 3, 1852, RLASS.

43. Chadwick, *A Life for Liberty*, 189.

44. *National Anti-Slavery Standard*, March 7, 1868. See also Herbig, "Friends for Freedom," 229; Julie Roy Jeffrey, *The Great Silent Army of Abolitionism: Ordinary Women in the Antislavery Movement* (Chapel Hill: University of North Carolina Press, 1998), 230.

45. Sallie Holley to Emily Howland, April 3, 1865, Emily Howland Papers.

46. Chadwick, *A Life for Liberty*, 209–10.

47. *National Anti-Slavery Standard*, March 12, 1870.

48. Chadwick, *A Life for Liberty*, 203.

49. Chadwick, *A Life for Liberty*, 211.

50. *National Anti-Slavery Standard*, March 12, 1870; Herbig, "Friends for Freedom," 240–41, 267.

51. *National Anti-Slavery Standard*, December 12, 1868, February 20, 1869.

52. Jacqueline Jones, *Soldiers of Light and Love: Northern Teachers and Georgia Blacks, 1865–1873* (Athens: University of Georgia Press, 1980, 1992), 144–149.

53. *National Anti-Slavery Standard*, December 12, 1868.

54. *National Anti-Slavery Standard*, October 30, 1869, December 4, 1869.

55. *National Anti-Slavery Standard*, November 27, 1869, February 26, 1870.

56. *National Anti-Slavery Standard*, February 20, 1869.

57. *National Anti-Slavery Standard*, July 10, 1869, October 9, 1869.

58. Chadwick, *A Life for Liberty*, 220.

59. Chadwick, *A Life for Liberty*, 115.

60. Chadwick, *A Life for Liberty*, 257.

61. Chadwick, *A Life for Liberty*, 217–18.

62. Holly later joined the National Woman Suffrage Association, but during Reconstruction neither she nor Caroline Putnam spoke actively on behalf of votes for white or black women. See "Appeal to Women Citizens of the United States, Tract No. 1," September 1879, in Patricia G. Holland and Ann D. Gordon, eds., *The Papers of Elizabeth Cady Stanton and Susan B. Anthony* (Wilmington, Del.: Scholarly Resources, 1992), reel 20; Herbig, "Friends for Freedom," 236–63.

63. Chadwick, *Life for Liberty*, 257, 217–18. Herbig, "Friends for Freedom," 378–82.

Chapter 3. Women and the American Freedmen's Union Commission

1. Jeanie Attie, *Patriotic Toil: Northern Women and the American Civil War* (Ithaca, N.Y.: Cornell University Press, 1998), 12–18; George Fredrickson, *The Inner Civil War: Northern Intellectuals and the Crisis of the Union* (New York: Harper and Row, 1965), 188; Lori D. Ginzberg, *Women and the Work of Benevolence: Morality, Politics, and Class in the Nineteenth- Century United States* (New Haven, Conn.: Yale University Press, 1990), 5, chaps. 5, 6; Joan Waugh, *Unsentimental Reformer: The Life of Josephine Shaw Lowell* (Cambridge, Mass.: Harvard University Press, 1997); Elizabeth D. Leonard, *Yankee Women: Gender Battles in the Civil War* (New York: W.W. Norton, 1994); Judith Ann Giesberg, *Civil War Sisterhood: The U.S. Sanitary Commission and Women's Politics in Transition* (Boston: Northeastern University Press, 2000). The professionalization and feminization of teaching had begun before the war. This factor certainly stimulated women's interest in freedmen's schools—as teachers and as the administrators of aid societies. Kathryn Kish Sklar, *Catharine Beecher: A Study in American Domesticity* (New York: W.W. Norton, 1976), 180–82; Carl F. Kaestle, *Pillars of the Republic: Common Schools and American Society, 1780–1860* (New York: Hill and Wang, 1983), 123–27; Jacqueline Jones, *Soldiers of Light and Love: Northern Teachers and Georgia Blacks, 1865–1873* (Athens: University of Georgia Press, 1980, 1992), 36.

2. *Fifth Annual Report* of the New York Branch of the AFUC, 1867, reprinted in *American Freedman* 2, no. 1 (April 1867); see also Hannah Stevenson to Dear Friends, August 30, 1866, in Henry Swint, ed., *Dear Ones at Home: Letters from Contraband Camps* (Nashville: Vanderbilt University Press, 1966), 206.

3. J. Miller McKim, *American Freedman* 1, no. 12 (March 1867): 181; see also *American Freedman* 1, no. 1 (April 1866): 10.

4. See James M. McPherson, *The Struggle for Equality: Abolitionists and the Negro in the Civil War and Reconstruction* (Princeton, N.J.: Princeton University Press, 1964), chap. 17; Ronald E. Butchart, *Northern Schools, Southern Blacks, and Reconstruction: Freedmen's Education, 1862–1875* (Westport, Conn.: Greenwood Press, 1980), chap. 5. For the AMA's influential role in black education see James M. McPherson, *The Abolitionist Legacy: From Reconstruction to the NAACP* (Princeton, N.J.: Princeton University Press, 1975), 143–160; Joe M. Richardson, *Christian Reconstruction: The American Missionary Association and Southern Blacks, 1861–1890* (Athens: University of Georgia Press, 1986).

5. *American Freedman* 1, no. 6 (September 1866): 95–96. For more information of the competition between evangelical and secular freedmen's aid societies see Butchart, *Northern Schools, Southern Blacks,* esp. chaps. 1–5.

6. *American Freedman* 2, no. 2 (May 1867): 215.

7. See Butchart, *Northern Schools, Southern Blacks,* 204; McPherson, *Struggle for Equality,* 403.

8. Stevenson, Cheney, et al. to Edward Atkinson, October 24, 1866, Edward Atkinson Papers, Massachusetts Historical Society (MHS).

9. Joanne Pope Melish, *Disowning Slavery: Gradual Emancipation and "Race" in New England, 1780–1860* (Ithaca, N.Y.: Cornell University Press, 1998), 3.

10. Ednah Dow Cheney to Mr. Manly, April 8, 1868, New England Freedmen's Aid Society Daily Journal, January 1868–September 1869, NEFAS papers, MHS.

11. Ellen Collins to General O. O. Howard, October 19, 1868. Letters to the Commissioner (M752), Bureau of Refugees, Freedmen, and Abandoned Lands (RG105), National Archives and Records Administration.

12. *American Freedman* 2, no. 7 (October 1867): 292; 2, no. 5 (August 1867): 258–59.

13. *Seventh Annual Report of the Friends' Association for the Aid and Elevation of the Freedmen* (Philadelphia: Brinckloe and Marot, 1871).

14. Ellen Collins to J. Miller McKim, September 10, 1866, Alphabetical Correspondence, Box 12, Samuel J. May Anti-Slavery Collection, Cornell University; Robert H. Bremner, *The Public Good: Philanthropy and Welfare in the Civil War Era* (New York: Knopf, 1980), 131–132. James D. Anderson argues that freedpeople wanted independence from Northern aid societies. See Anderson, *The Education of Blacks in the South, 1860–1935* (Chapel Hill: University of North Carolina Press, 1988), 12.

15. John Alvord, *Fifth Semi-Annual Report on Schools for Freedmen,* January 1, 1868 (Washington, D.C.: Government Printing Office, 1868), 16; Educational Commission (NEFAS) Records, esp. September 13, 1866 and September 10, 1867, MHS.

16. History of the Friends' Freedmen's Relief Association of Philadelphia, November 27, 1867, Letters Received, Records of the Education Division (M803), Bureau of Refugees, Freedmen, and Abandoned Lands (BRFAL), (RG105), National Archives and Records Administration.

17. John Alvord, *Fifth Semi-Annual Report,* January 1, 1868, 48.

18. *American Freedman,* final number of 1868, 2. As the end was drawing near the AFUC cut back on the publication of the *Freedman.* The July and August numbers were combined and there was only one more number in 1868. *The American Freedman* was issued twice in 1869, in April and July.

19. John Alvord, *Sixth Semi-Annual Report* (Washington, D.C.: Government Printing Office, 1868), 6–7. Eliphalet Whittlesey to Francis George Shaw, December 13, 1867. Alphabetical Correspondence, Box 26, May Anti-Slavery Collection. The following all give examples of black communities with self-sustaining schools: Jones, *Soldiers of Light and Love,* 71–76; Anderson, *The Education of Blacks in the South,* 7–12; Butchart, *Northern Schools, Southern Blacks,* chap. 9; Robert C. Morris, *Reading, 'Riting, and Reconstruction: The Education of Freedmen in the South, 1861-1870* (Chicago: University of Chicago Press, 1981), 119–126.

20. Anderson notes Alvord's support for freedpeople's independent educational efforts. See *The Education of Blacks in the South,* 6–7, 13–15.

21. John Alvord, *Ninth Semi-Annual Report* (Washington, D.C.: Government Printing Office, 1870), 21, 26, 42. Robert Morris writes that when Samuel Armstrong, founder of Hampton Institute, began to require a weekly tuition fee from his students in 1869, one-third of the students were forced to leave the school. *Reading, 'Riting, and Reconstruction,* 155–156.

22. *American Freedman,* final number of 1868, 2.

23. *American Freedman* (April 1869): 3.

24. *Sixth Annual Report of the Friends' Association of Philadelphia for the Aid and Elevation of the Freedmen* (Philadelphia: Thomas William Stuckey, 1870).

25. Ellen Collins to Mary K. Wead, September 18, 1865. Wead Papers, Sophia Smith Collection, Smith College (SS). For Ellen Collins's work on the Sanitary Commission see Jeanie Attie, *Patriotic Toil: Northern Women and the American Civil War* (Ithaca, N.Y.: Cornell University Press, 1998), 42–43, 109–10, 254–55, 270. See also Ginzberg, *Women and the Work of Benevolence,* chap. 5; Elizabeth Leonard, *Yankee Women: Gender Battles in the Civil War* (New York: Norton, 1994), chap. 2.

26. Circular of the Women's Branch, reprinted in *Pennsylvania Freedmen's Bulletin* 1, no. 4 (December 15, 1865): 91.

27. E. C. Putnam to Ednah Dow Cheney, *Freedmen's Record* (December 1867): 182–184.

28. Lucretia Mott to Martha Coffin Wright, December 27, 1862, Mott Collection, Friends Historical Library, Swarthmore College. Quakers raised awareness for their freedmen's aid activities by placing notices in Quaker papers and including descriptive accounts of reformers' travels among freedpeople. See, for example, *Friends' Intelligencer* (January 2, 1864): 680; (January 9, 1864): 692–95.

29. Lucretia Mott to Martha Wright, Martha Lord, and Anna Brown, January 21, 1864, Mott Collection.

30. *Twelfth Annual Report of the Rochester Ladies' Anti-Slavery Society* (Rochester, N.Y.: A. Strong, 1863), 3–5.

31. Hannah Stevenson to Mr. May, March 5, 1866, May Anti-Slavery Collection.

32. Stevenson to May, March 5, 1866.

33. Lyman Abbott, *Reminiscences* (New York: Houghton Mifflin, 1915), ix.

34. Stevenson to Octavius B. Frothingham, February 26, 1866; J. Miller McKim to Stevenson, July 6, 1866, McKim Letterbooks; both in May Anti-Slavery Collection.

35. Stevenson to McKim, July 16, 1866, and July 20, 1866, May Anti-Slavery Collection. George Fredrickson, *The Black Image in the White Mind: The Debate on Afro-American Character and Destiny, 1817–1914* (Hanover, N.H.: Wesleyan University Press by the University Press of New England, 1971, 1987), 171–74.

36. Stevenson to McKim, July 20, 1866, Samuel J. May Anti-Slavery Collection.

37. Mary Mann to Edward L. Pierce, undated, Pierce papers, Houghton Library, Harvard University (HU).

38. *Pennsylvania Freedmen's Bulletin* 1, no. 1 (February 1865): 2. This division between abolitionists who appealed on behalf of destitute freedpeople and abolitionists who touted the self-reliance of former slaves had existed before emancipation. The changes in benevolent reform and the antislavery movement during and after the Civil War heightened the gendered aspects of this division. See, for example, Michael F. Hembree, "The Question of 'Begging': Fugitive Slave Relief in Canada, 1830–1865," *Civil War History* 37, no. 4 (1991): 314–27.

39. Mrs. Martha Canfield to the Rev. J. M. Walden, February 17, 1866, McKim Collection 2, Folder 43, May Anti-Slavery Collection. Agent John Eaton of the Freedmen's Bureau recommended Mrs. Canfield to Edward Everett Hale, of the Soldier's Memorial Society, as worthy of his society's support. He described her as "prudent, trustworthy, self-sacrificing, and efficient," and told her story as follows: "Her husband had a prominent connection with the excellent reformatory institutions of Ohio, and lost his life as Col. at Shiloh. After his death, Mrs. C. devoted herself as a relief for herself and a fulfillment of her husband's cherished purposes to the good of the army, and so, the preservation of the country. These efforts brought, in connection, the suffering of the poor whites and negroes. After a seasons labor for the whites she undertook this institution for colored orphans. She has worked successfully amid great difficulties." See Eaton to E. E. Hale, November 6, 1865. Letters Sent, Records of the Assistant Commission for the District of Columbia M1055 (ACDC), BRFAL.

40. *Pennsylvania Freedmen's Bulletin* (June 1866).

41. *Pennsylvania Freedmen's Bulletin* (January 1867). As Jeannie Attie has shown, the Sanitary Commission also had trouble enlisting and retaining the voluntary labor of Northern women. See Attie, *Patriotic Toil: Northern Women and the American Civil War* (Ithaca, N.Y.: Cornell University Press, 1998), 98–114, 128–40.

42. McPherson, *Struggle for Equality*, 172–73, 396.

43. Elizabeth P. Breck, letter published in the *Daily Hampshire Gazette*, November 8, 1866, New England Freedmen's Aid Society (NEFAS) Papers, Sophia Smith Collection, Smith College (SS).

44. Other examples of appeals which balanced freedpeople's self-reliance with freedpeople's poverty include, *First Annual Report of the Executive Committee of the Barnard Freedmen's Aid Society of Dorchester*, 1865; *Extracts from Letters of Teachers and Superintendents of the New England Education Commission for Freedmen* (Boston: David Clap, 1864); pamphlet of the Cleveland Freedmen's Union Commission, September, 1866, Correspondence, Box 12, May Anti-Slavery Collection.

45. Stevenson to Breck, October 8, 1864, NEFAS Papers, SS.

46. Stevenson to Breck, October 12, 1864, NEFAS Papers, SS.

47. Stevenson to M. A. Cochran, December 9, 1864, NEFAS Papers, SS. For the negative connotations of the word beggar during Reconstruction, see Amy Dru Stanley, *From Bondage to Contract: Wage Labor, Marriage, and the Market in the Age of Emancipation* (New York: Cambridge University Press, 1998), 103.

48. See Jones, *Soldiers of Light and Love*, 146–47 on teachers' letters encouraging aid.

49. Breck to Cochran, December 23, 1864, NEFAS Papers, SS.

50. Letter from Breck printed in the *Hampshire Gazette*, October 31 1865, NEFAS Papers, SS.

51. Letter from Miss Breck printed in the *Hampshire Gazette*, July 23, 1866, NEFAS Papers, SS.

52. Letter from Miss Breck printed in the *Hampshire Gazette*, November 20, 1866, NEFAS Papers, SS.

53. Breck to Cochran, published in the *Hampshire Gazette*, February 23, 1867, NEFAS Papers, SS. Jean Fagan Yellin, *Women and Sisters: The Anti-Slavery Feminists in American Culture* (New Haven, Conn.: Yale University Press, 1989); Kristin Hoganson, "Garrisonian Abolitionists and the Rhetoric of Gender, 1850-1860," *American Quarterly* 45 (December 1993): 558–95.

54. *Fourth Annual Report of the National Freedmen's Relief Association for the District of Columbia* (Washington, D.C.: McGill and Witherow, 1866), 12. For a discussion of compulsion to work in order to receive aid in the postwar years see Stanley, *From Bondage to Contract*, chap. 3.

55. Leslie A. Schwalm, *A Hard Fight for We: Women's Transition from Slave to Wage Laborer in South Carolina* (Urbana: University of Illinois Press, 1997), 249–54. Southern states also enforced this definition of marriage, see Laura F. Edwards, *Gendered Strife and Confusion: The Political Culture of Reconstruction* (Urbana: University of Illinois Press, 1997), 31-45. For the equation of manhood and freedom and its consequences, see Martha Hodes, *White Women, Black Men: Illicit Sex in the Nineteenth Century South* (New Haven, Conn.: Yale University Press, 1997), 143–44, 166; Saidiya Hartman, *Scenes of Subjection: Terror, Slavery, and Self-Making in Nineteenth Century America* (New York: Oxford University Press, 1997), 152–57.

56. Jacob R. Shipherd to Gen. C. H. Howard, July 13, 1865. Letters Received, ACDC, BRFAL.

57. J. Miller McKim to William Lloyd Garrison, February 7, 1866, May Anti-Slavery Collection.

58. *Pennsylvania Freedmen's Bulletin* (April 1866).

59. Nettie Sanford to Annie Wittenmeyer, November 12, 1863, War Correspondence of Annie Wittenmeyer, Iowa State Historical Library, as quoted in Leonard, *Yankee Women*, 81. See also Attie, *Patriotic Toil*, chap. 5.

60. John Murray Forbes to Edward Atkinson, February 9 and February 15, 1865, Edward Atkinson Papers, MHS.

61. McKim to Shipherd, January 10, 1866, McKim letterbooks, May Anti-Slavery Collection; Shipherd to O. O. Howard, October 30, 1865, Letters Received, Office of the Commissioner, BRFAL; "This Week," *The Nation*, December 7, 1865, 708.

62. Jones describes the freedmen's aid movement as "women's work." She also argues that the women teachers resisted the more impersonal policies of the organizations which employed them. See Jones, *Soldiers of Light and Love*, 36, chap. 4.

63. *Freedmen's Record* 1, no. 2 (February 1865): 18.

64. Laetitia Campbell to Mary K. Wead, December 19, 1865, Wead Papers, SS.

65. Hannah Stevenson to Elizabeth Breck, October 8, 1864, NEFAS Papers, SS.

66. Sarah Allaback, "'Better than Silver and Gold': Design Schools for Women in America, 1848–1860," *Journal of Women's History* 10, no. 1 (Spring 1988): 88–107; Nina de Angeli Walls, "Art and Industry in Philadelphia: Origins of the Philadelphia School of Design for Women 1848-1876," *Pennsylvania Magazine of History and Biography* 67 (July 1993): 177–99.

67. Ednah Dow Cheney, *Reminiscences of Ednah Dow Cheney (born Littlehale)* (Boston: Lee and Shepard, 1902), 155. See also Karen J. Blair, *The Clubwoman as Feminist: True Womanhood Redefined, 1868–1914* (New York: Holmes and Meier, 1980), 32–37. On women's political culture see Paula Baker, "The Domestication of Politics: Women and American Political Society, 1780–1820," *American Historical Review* 89 (June 1984): 620–47; Kathryn Kish Sklar, " 'Women Who Speak for an Entire Nation': American and British Women at the World Anti-Slavery Convention, London, 1840," in Jean Fagan Yellin and John C. Van Horne, eds., *The Abolitionist Sisterhood: Women's Political Culture in Antebellum America* (Ithaca, N.Y.: Cornell University Press, 1994), 301–333.

68. *Index*, April 26, 1873.

69. Meetings of March 10 and October 25, 1865, Records of the Educational Commission 1862–76. NEFAS Papers, MHS.

70. Meetings of September 18, 1865, September 13, 1866, and September 10, 1867, Records of the Educational Commission 1862–76.

71. *Freedmen's Record* 2, no. 9 (September 1866): 157.

72. *Freedmen's Record* 3, no. 9 (September 1867): 141.

73. *Freedmen's Record* 4, no. 8 (August 1868): 121.

74. *Freedmen's Record* 4, no. 11 (November 1868): 169, and 4, no. 12 (December 1868): 185.

75. *Freedmen's Record* 5, no. 4 (November 1869): 41.

76. *Freedmen's Record* 5, no. 10 (April 1873): 133, and 5, no. 11 (April 1874): 148; Cheney, *Reminiscences*, 97.

77. Cheney to Mr. Jillison, September 29, 1869. Daily Record of the NEFAS January 1868–September 1869, NEFAS Papers, MHS.

78. Annual Meeting, March 10, 1870, Educational Commission Records, 1862–76. NEFAS Papers, MHS.

79. Letter to Josephine Shaw Lowell, January 19, 1870. Copied into the Daily Record of the NEFAS, HU.

80. Letter to Josephine Shaw Lowell, January 19, 1870.

81. Daily Record of the NEFAS, November 14, 1870, HU.

82. Daily Record of the NEFAS, December 7, 1870.

83. Daily Record of the NEFAS December 9, 1870.

84. Daily Record of the NEFAS September 29, 1870; November 25, 1870; April 21, 1871.

85. Constitution of the Cheney Educational Association, undated, Ednah Dow Cheney Papers 13, Boston Public Library.

86. Anderson, *The Education of Blacks in the South*, chap. 5.

87. Ednah Dow Cheney, *Memoirs of Lucretia Crocker and Abby W. May* (Boston, 1893), 36. A few male reformers hung on to the end as well. These included Rev.

John Parkman and Edward Hooper. But although they attended meetings, they never appear to have an active role in the Society's affairs, through correspondence, tours of the schools, or meeting teachers.

Chapter 4. Mothers of the Race: Black Women in the Freedmen's Aid Movement

1. Elizabeth Keckley, *Behind the Scenes; or, Thirty Years a Slave, and Four Years in the White House* (New York: Oxford University Press, 1988), 112–13.

2. Deborah Gray White points out the class implications of African American women's reform in *Too Heavy a Load: Black Women in Defense of Themselves, 1894–1994* (New York: W.W. Norton, 1999), 69–82.

3. As Glenda Gilmore argues for the Progressive era, "black women became the black community's diplomats to the white community." See Glenda Elizabeth Gilmore, *Gender and Jim Crow: Women and the Politics of White Supremacy in North Carolina, 1896–1920* (Chapel Hill: University of North Carolina Press, 1996), 148; see also Stephanie J. Shaw, *What a Woman Ought to Be and Do: Black Professional Women Workers During the Jim Crow Era* (Chicago: University of Chicago Press, 1996), 2.

4. For the important theme of self-help see White, *Too Heavy a Load*, 27; Lyde Cullen Sizer, *The Political Work of Northern Women Writers and the Civil War, 1850–1872* (Chapel Hill: University of North Carolina Press, 2000), 276, 270–78.

5. *Christian Recorder*, January 7, 1865. Peggy Lamson, "Richard Harvey Cain," in Rayford Logan and Michael Winston, eds., *Dictionary of American Negro Biography* (New York: W.W. Norton, 1982), 84–85. Harry C. Silcox points out that black communities' support for black teachers presented a threat to whites during Reconstruction. See Silcox, "Nineteenth-Century Philadelphia Black Militant: Octavius V. Catto (1839–1871)," in Joe William Trotter, Jr., and Eric Ledell Smith, eds., *African Americans in Pennsylvania: Shifting Historical Perspectives* (University Park: Pennsylvania State University Press, 1997), 205–7.

6. See James Oliver Horton, *Free People of Color: Inside the African American Community* (Washington, D.C.: Smithsonian Institution Press, 1993), 102; and, for example, *Christian Recorder*, April 12 and 26, 1862, September 7, 1862, October 4, 1862.

7. *Constitution of the African Civilization Society and the Anniversary Address by Rev. J. P. Thompson* (New Haven, Conn.: Thomas J. Stafford, 1861), 1, 35; Carol Faulkner, "'A Proper Recognition of Our Manhood': The African Civilization Society and the Freedmen's Aid Movement," *Afro-Americans in New York Life and History* 24, no. 1 (January 2000): 41–62; Benjamin Quarles, *Black Abolitionists* (New York: Oxford University Press, 1969), 217, 221. For brief discussions of the ACS freedmen's aid work see Robert C. Morris, *Reading, 'Riting, and Reconstruction: The Education of Freedmen in the South, 1861–1870* (Chicago: University of Chicago Press, 1976, 1981), 116; Ronald Butchart, *Northern Schools, Southern Blacks, and Reconstruction: Freedmen's Education, 1862–1875* (Westport, Conn.: Greenwood Press, 1980), 70, 154–55.

8. *Christian Recorder*, December 12, 1863. "Junius" was probably Junius C. Morrell or Morel, principal of public school no. 2 in the Weeksville section of Brooklyn, an all-black neighborhood where the offices of the ACS were located. See *Christian Recorder*, January 26, 1866; and Carleton Mabee, *Black Education in New York State* (Syracuse, N.Y.: Syracuse University Press, 1979), 86.

9. For the relationship of feminism to black nationalism see E. Frances White, "Africa on My Mind: Gender, Counter Discourse, and African American

Nationalism," *Journal of Women's History* 2, no. 1 (Spring 1990): 73–97; Wilson Jeremiah Moses, *The Golden Age of Black Nationalism, 1850–1925* (New York: Oxford University Press, 1978), chap. 5.

10. As Wilson Jeremiah Moses has pointed out, Douglass also disapproved of the ACS's belief in racial purity and black identity, which he felt was as bad as white chauvinism. Moses, *Golden Age*, 86. See also William S. McFeely, *Frederick Douglass* (New York: W.W. Norton, 1991), 241–52. August Meier argues that integration and separation are two separate and conflicting impulses in African American thought. He believes that during Reconstruction, integration was the dominant strain. However, the ACS and other African American freedmen's aid efforts shows that the philosophy of self-help and racial unity was also strong. See August Meier, *Negro Thought in America, 1880–1915: Racial Ideologies in the Age of Booker T. Washington* (1963; Ann Arbor: University of Michigan Press, 1988), chap. 1.

11. *Christian Recorder*, February 13, 1864.

12. Frederick Douglass to J. Miller McKim, May 1865, Box 13, Samuel J. May Anti-Slavery Collection, Cornell University. See also James M. McPherson, *The Struggle for Equality: Abolitionists and the Negro in the Civil War and Reconstruction* (Princeton, N.J.: Princeton University Press, 1964), 397; McFeely, *Frederick Douglass*, 241–42.

13. Roslyn Terborg-Penn, *African American Women in the Struggle for the Vote, 1850–1920* (Bloomington: Indiana University Press, 1998), 27, 24–34. Ellen Carol DuBois, *Feminism and Suffrage: The Emergence of an Independent Women's Movement in America, 1848–1869* (Ithaca, N.Y.: Cornell University Press, 1978), 59, 187–88, chap. 6.

14. Frances Ellen Watkins Harper, *Iola Leroy; or, Shadows Uplifted* (New York: Oxford University Press, 1988), 262. Harper was born in Baltimore, but she lectured throughout the North in the years preceding the Civil War. During her marriage she resided briefly in Ohio, and later in life she lived in Philadelphia. See also Carla L. Peterson, *"Doers of the Word": African- American Women Speakers and Writers in the North (1830–1880)* (New York: Oxford University Press, 1995), chaps. 5, 6, 8; Hazel V. Carby, *Reconstructing Womanhood: The Emergence of the Afro-American Woman Novelist* (New York: Oxford University Press, 1988), chap. 4; Farah Jasmine Griffin, "Frances Ellen Watkins Harper in the Reconstruction South," *Sage: A Scholarly Journal on Black Women* (Supplement, 1988): 45-47; Sizer, *Political Work of Northern Women Writers*, 270–78; William Still, *The Underground Railroad* (New York: Arno Press, 1968), 755–80.

15. Frances Ellen Watkins Harper, letters, December 29, 1870, and February 20, 1870, in Frances Smith Foster, *A Brighter Coming Day: A Frances Ellen Watkins Harper Reader* (New York: Feminist Press, 1990), 130, 127.

16. William Still, introduction to Harper, *Iola Leroy*, 2.

17. Frances Ellen Watkins Harper, letter, March 29, 1870, in Foster, *Brighter Coming Day*, 127.

18. Harper, writing from Alabama in 1871, Foster, *Brighter Coming Day*, 134.

19. African American women responded to Harper's cry, and generations dedicated themselves to uplifting their race. White, *Too Heavy a Load*, 24; Paula Giddings, *When and Where I Enter: The Impact of Black Women on Race and Sex in America* (New York: Bantam Books, 1984); Shaw, *What a Woman Ought to Be*; Evelyn Brooks Higginbotham, *Righteous Discontent: The Women's Movement in the Black Baptist Church, 1880–1920* (Cambridge, Mass.: Harvard University Press, 1993); Glenda Elizabeth Gilmore, *Gender and Jim Crow*.

20. Foster, *Brighter Coming Day*, 217.

21. Foster, *Brighter Coming Day*, 217–18; Griffin, "Frances Ellen Watkins Harper," 46.

22. DuBois, *Feminism and Suffrage*, Nell Irvin Painter, *Sojourner Truth: A Life, a Symbol* (New York: W.W. Norton, 1996), 224–25; Terborg-Penn, *African American Women*, 32–33. As Carla L. Peterson writes, by reminding white suffragists of the continuing problems of racial oppression and discrimination, Harper rejected feminists' "unitary category of 'woman.'" Peterson, *"Doers of the Word"*, 229.

23. Harper, *Iola Leroy*, 114.

24. Harper, *Iola Leroy*, 276, 234. As Deborah Gray White argues, black women identified white women as "part of the problem." White, *Too Heavy a Load*, 40–42.

25. *Christian Recorder*, August 20, 1864.

26. William J. Wilson, Report to American Freedmen's Inquiry Commission, 1863. American Freedmen's Inquiry Commission Papers, Ms. Am 629, Houghton Library, Harvard University.

27. *Christian Recorder*, April 7, 1866.

28. Charlotte L. Forten, *The Journals of Charlotte Forten Grimké*, ed. Brenda Stevenson (New York: Oxford University Press, 1988), 376.

29. See Stevenson, "Introduction," *Journals of Charlotte Forten Grimké*, Lisa A. Long, "Charlotte Forten's Civil War Journals and the Quest for 'Genius, Beauty, and Deathless Fame'" *Legacy* 16, no. 1 (1999): 37–48; Peterson, *Doers of the Word*, 177–79; Sizer, *Political Work*, 159–63.

30. *Journals of Charlotte Forten Grimké*, 44, and see, for example, 460, 464, 467; Peterson, *Doers of the Word*, chap. 7.

31. *Journals of Charlotte Forten Grimké*, 419, 428; Forten, "Life on the Sea Islands," *Atlantic Monthly* (May 1864): 67.

32. Forten, "Life on the Sea Islands," *Atlantic Monthly* (May 1864): 72, 82–83. The second part of Forten's article appeared in the *Atlantic Monthly* (June 1864): 666–76.

33. Forten, "Life on the Sea Islands," (May 1864): 71.

34. Forten, "Life on the Sea Islands," (May 1864): 86.

35. Forten, "Life on the Sea Islands," (May 1864): 86.

36. Farah Jasmine Griffin, *Beloved Sisters and Loving Friends: Letters from Rebecca Primus of Royal Oak, Maryland, and Addie Brown of Hartford, Connecticut, 1854–1868* (New York: Knopf, 1999), 12, 215–17.

37. Griffin, *Beloved Sisters*, 77–79, 99–100, chaps. 5–10, passim.

38. Griffin, *Beloved Sisters*, 118.

39. Griffin, *Beloved Sisters*, 128.

40. Griffin, *Beloved Sisters*, 216.

41. Griffin, *Beloved Sisters*, 148.

42. Griffin, *Beloved Sisters*, 147.

43. Griffin, *Beloved Sisters*, 181, 185.

44. Griffin, *Beloved Sisters*, 204.

45. Noralee Frankel, *Freedom's Women: Black Women and Families in Civil War Era Mississippi* (Bloomington: Indiana University Press, 1999), 95–96.

46. Griffin, *Beloved Sisters*, 172–73.

47. Griffin, *Beloved Sisters*, 134; *Journals of Charlotte Forten Grimké*, 464. For more on African American teachers see Clara Merritt DeBoer, *His Truth Is Marching On: African Americans Who Taught the Freedmen for the American Missionary Association, 1861–1877* (New York: Garland Publishing, 1995).

48. Painter, *Sojourner Truth*, 261.

49. Sojourner Truth, *Narrative of Sojourner Truth: A Bondswoman of Olden Time, with a History of Her Labors and Correspondence Drawn from Her "Book of Life"* (New York: Oxford University Press, 1991), 182–83.

50. Truth, *Narrative*, 181–2.

51. Truth, *Narrative*, 191. Her work as an employment agent will be discussed more fully in chap. 7.

52. For more on the Freedmen's Bureau's migration policies see William Cohen, *At Freedom's Edge: Black Mobility and the Southern White Quest for Racial Control* (Baton Rouge: Louisiana State University Press, 1991), chap. 4.

53. Truth, *Narrative*, 193.

54. Truth, *Narrative*, 194–95.

55. Truth, *Narrative*, 198.

56. Griffing to Truth, January 7, 1869, Post Family Papers, Department of Rare Books and Special Collections, University of Rochester Library.

57. Painter, *Sojourner Truth*, 218–19; Carleton Mabee, "Sojourner Truth Fights Dependence on Government: Moves Freed Slaves Off Welfare in Washington to Jobs in Upstate New York," *Afro-Americans in New York Life and History* 14 (January 1990): 7–26.

58. Griffing to Truth, January 7, 1869, Post Papers.

59. *Fourth Annual Report of the National Freedmen's Relief Association of the District of Columbia* (Washington, D.C.: McGill and Witherow, 1866), 15. For example, Griffing to Sojourner Truth, January 7, 1869, Post Papers.

60. *Fourth Annual Report*, 15.

61. *Fourth Annual Report*, 15–16.

62. *Fifth Annual Report of the National Freedmen's Relief Association of New York* (Washington, D.C.: McGill and Witherow, 1867), 13; For Truth's struggle to support herself see Painter, *Sojourner Truth*, 197.

63. *Christian Recorder*, November 1, 1862; Keckley, *Behind the Scenes*, 113.

64. Keckley, *Behind the Scenes*, 39.

65. Keckley, *Behind the Scenes*, 49; Elizabeth Young points out that Keckley not only resided in a border state, but she was in a metaphorical border state in terms of region, race, and class. See Young, *Disarming the Nation: Women's Writing and the American Civil War* (Chicago: University of Chicago Press, 1999), 123–25.

66. Keckley, *Behind the Scenes*, 19–20.

67. Keckley, *Behind the Scenes*, 140.

68. Keckley, *Behind the Scenes*, 254, 257. In another comment on white racism, Keckley points out that Lincoln's son Tad was a slow learner. Keckley concluded that "had Tad been a negro boy, not the son of a President, and so difficult to instruct, he would have been called thick-skulled, and would have been held up as an example of the inferiority of race" (219).

69. Keckley, *Behind the Scenes*, 115.

70. Keckley, *Behind the Scenes*, 112.

71. Keckley, *Behind the Scenes*, 143.

72. Keckley, *Behind the Scenes*, 45.

73. Keckley, *Behind the Scenes*, 313. Young, *Disarming the Nation*, 143.

74. Keckley, *Behind the Scenes*, 257.

75. As Elizabeth Young points out, Keckley destroys any claim for sisterhood between white and black women as well. Young, *Disarming the Nation*, 147.

76. Gilmore, *Gender and Jim Crow*.

Chapter 5. The Freedmen's Bureau and Material Aid

1. Michael B. Katz, *The Undeserving Poor: From the War on Poverty to the War on Welfare* (New York: Pantheon Books, 1989), 5, 7–8, 9–15; Megan J. McClintock,

"Civil War Pensions and the Reconstruction of Union Families," *Journal of American History* 83 (September 1996): 456–80; Theda Skocpol, *Protecting Soldiers and Mothers: The Political Origins of Social Policy in the United States* (Cambridge, Mass.: Harvard University Press, 1992).

2. Oliver Otis Howard, *Autobiography of Oliver Otis Howard* (New York: Baker and Taylor, 1908), 2: 226. William S. McFeely, *Yankee Stepfather: General O. O. Howard and the Freedmen* (1968; New York: W.W. Norton, 1994), 208–9, 265; Robert H. Bremner, *The Public Good: Philanthropy and Welfare in the Civil War Era* (New York: Knopf, 1980), chap. 6; George R. Bentley; *History of the Freedmen's Bureau* (1944; New York: Octagon Books, 1974), 76–79, 139–44; Eric Foner, *Reconstruction: America's Unfinished Revolution, 1863–1877* (New York: Harper and Row, 1988), 152–53. For the expansion of the State during the Civil War era and the tensions expansion provoked, see Morton Keller, *Affairs of State: Public Life in Late Nineteenth-Century America* (Cambridge, Mass.: Belknap Press, 1977), chaps. 1–3; Richard Frankel Bensel, *Yankee Leviathan: The Origins of Central State Authority in America 1859–1877* (New York: Cambridge University Press, 1990). David Montgomery notes the important role of the state for Radical Republicans. See *Beyond Equality: Labor and the Radical Republicans, 1862–1872* (New York: Knopf, 1967), 78–80.

3. Kathryn Kish Sklar, "The Historical Foundations of Women's Power in the Creation of the American Welfare State, 1830–1930," in Seth Koven and Sonya Michel, eds., *Mothers of a New World: Maternalist Politics and the Origins of Welfare States* (New York: Routledge, 1993), 45. See also Koven and Michel, "Introduction: Mother Worlds," in *Mothers of a New World*, 2–4. Women's work with the Freedmen's Bureau coincided with women's entrance into government employment in general. See Cindy Sondik Aron, *Ladies and Gentlemen of the Civil Service: Middle-Class Workers in Victorian America* (New York: Oxford University Press, 1987). Sklar points out that the tradition of limited government in the United States promoted women's autonomous political institutions (p. 54). Certainly in the case of the Freedmen's Bureau, women acted on their own because they perceived the Freedmen's Bureau to be powerless and inadequate to much of the task of aiding former slaves. The Freedmen's Bureau encouraged private benevolence to aid former slaves in ways they could not.

4. For additional treatments of Josephine Griffing's freedmen's aid work see Keith Melder, "Angel of Mercy in Washington: Josephine Griffing and the Freedmen, 1864–1872," *Records of the Historical Society of the District of Columbia*, 1863–65; James M. McPherson, *The Struggle for Equality: Abolitionists and the Negro in the Civil War and Reconstruction* (Princeton, N.J.: Princeton University Press, 1964), 389–92; Phebe A. Hanaford, *Daughters of America; or, Women of the Century* (Augusta, Me.: True and Co., 1882), 353–55.

5. Dorothy Sterling, *Ahead of Her Time: Abby Kelley and the Politics of Antislavery* (New York: W.W. Norton, 1991), 261. For the Women's National Loyal League see Wendy Hamand Venet, *Neither Ballots Nor Bullets: Women Abolitionists and the Civil War* (Charlottesville: University Press of Virginia, 1991). Griffing and her husband likely got a divorce. After Griffing's death Belva Lockwood, the first woman admitted to argue cases before the Supreme Court, helped Griffing's three daughters petition the court that Josephine Emma Griffing, her eldest daughter, be made administratrix of Griffing's estate. In the records of this petition, Emma describes Griffing as a femme sole at the time of her death in 1872. Charles Griffing did not die until 1880. See Records of the U.S. District Court in the District of Columbia, RG 21, Entry 115, Box 118, No. 7679, National Archives and Records Administration.

6. HR38A-G10.5, Records of the House of Representatives, Record Group 233, National Archives and Records Administration. These sentiments are also echoed in Griffing to William Lloyd Garrison, March 24, 1864, Ms. A.1.2.v.33 p. 32b, Boston Public Library.

7. Josephine Griffing to O. O. Howard, May 8, 1865, Office of the Commissioner, Letters Received M752, Bureau of Refugees, Freedmen, and Abandoned Lands (BRFAL), RG105, National Archives and Records Administration.

8. Julia Wilbur to Anna M. Barnes, March 5, 1864, Rochester Ladies' Anti-Slavery Society papers, William L. Clements Library, University of Michigan (RLASS).

9. *Fourteenth Annual Report of the Rochester Ladies' Anti-Slavery Society* (Rochester, N.Y.: William S. Falls, 1865), 10; *Seventeenth Annual Report of the Rochester Ladies' Anti-Slavery and Freedmen's Aid Society* (Rochester, N.Y.: William S. Falls, 1868), 12.

10. *Fourteenth Annual Report*, 4.

11. *Fourteenth Annual Report*, 13; *Fifteenth Annual Report of the Rochester Ladies' Anti- Slavery Society* (Rochester, N.Y.: William S. Falls, 1866), 17.

12. *Fourteenth Annual Report*, 16–17.

13. *Fourteenth Annual Report*, 25–26. For freedwomen's struggle against the apprenticeship of their children see Karin L. Zipf, " Reconstructing 'Free Woman': African-American Women, Apprenticeship, and Custody Rights During Reconstruction," *Journal of Women's History* 12 (Spring 2000): 8–31.

14. Allan Johnston, *Surviving Freedom: The Black Community of Washington, D.C., 1860–1880* (New York: Garland Publishing, 1993), 107–8.

15. *Fourteenth Annual Report*, 10.

16. Julia Wilbur to Maria G. Porter, February 8, 1865, RLASS.

17. *Fifteenth Annual Report*, 8.

18. *Fifteenth Annual Report*, 14.

19. *Fifteenth Annual Report*, 23.

20. *Fourteenth Annual Report*, 4.

21. *Fifteenth Annual Report*, 3.

22. *Fifteenth Annual Report*, 7.

23. "Appeal in behalf of the Freedmen of Washington, D.C.," *Liberator*, November 3, 1865.

24. *Third Annual Report of the National Freedmen's Relief Association of the District of Columbia* (Washington, D.C.: McGill and Witherow, 1865), 4–5.

25. McClintock, "Civil War Pensions," 456–80; Skocpol, *Protecting Soldiers and Mothers*, chap. 2.

26. *Sixteenth Annual Report of the Rochester Ladies' Anti-Slavery Society* (Rochester, N.Y.: William S. Falls, 1867), 27; *Seventeenth Annual Report*, 27–28.

27. "A Plea for Humanity," in the *Third Annual Report of the National Freedmen's Relief Association of the District of Columbia*, 4–5.

28. *Fourth Annual Report of the National Freedmen's Relief Association of the District of Columbia* (Washington, D.C.: McGill and Witherow, 1866), 11. For a similar description of Washington's destitute freedpeople see Laura S. Haviland, *A Woman's Life Work: Labors and Experiences of Laura S. Haviland* (Chicago: C.V. Waite, 1887), 457–62, in which she describes a number of families living in "squalid wretchedness."

29. *Fourteenth Annual Report*, 24. Interestingly, opponents of "dependency" did not discuss the dependence of white refugees on the bureau. During the hard winter of 1867, Wilbur noted that whites received far more assistance from a congressional appropriation to alleviate destitution than did African Americans.

"Some persons seem to think it is harder to whites to suffer and be poor than it is for the colored people. In many cases white persons asked for help when, if colored people were as well off, they would not think of applying for help." *Sixteenth Annual Report*, 11. For Northern white belief that dependency was an innate characteristic in African Americans see Joanne Pope Melish, *Disowning Slavery: Gradual Emancipation and "Race" in New England, 1780–1860* (Ithaca, N.Y.: Cornell University Press, 1998), 77, 86, 97.

30. *Sixteenth Annual Report*, 10.

31. *Sixteenth Annual Report*, 9–10.

32. *Seventeenth Annual Report*, 16–17.

33. *Fourteenth Annual Report*, 11.

34. *Fourteenth Annual Report*, 12; *Fifteenth Annual Report*, 9; Howard, *Autobiography*, 2: 264. For more information on the Contraband Fund see Ira Berlin et al., *Freedom: A Documentary History of Emancipation, 1861–1867*, series I, vol. 3, *The Wartime Genesis of Free Labor: The Upper South* (New York: Cambridge University Press, 193), 251–55.

35. *Seventeenth Annual Report*, 11–12.

36. Aron, *Ladies and Gentlemen*, 5, 70–71; See also Elizabeth Cady Stanton, Susan B. Anthony, and Matilda Joslyn Gage, *History of Woman Suffrage* (New York: Source Books Press, 1970), 3: 814.

37. *Revolution*, March 24, 1870.

38. Josephine Griffing to Elizabeth Cady Stanton, December 27, 1870, in Ann D. Gordon, ed., *The Selected Papers of Elizabeth Cady Stanton and Susan B. Anthony*, vol. 2, *Against an Aristocracy of Sex, 1866–1873* (New Brunswick, N.J.: Rutgers University Press, 2000), 390–91.

39. *Revolution*, May 25, 1871. See also issue of May 26, 1870.

40. Lucretia Mott to Josephine Griffing, December 25, 1869, and May 17, 1870, Griffing Collection, Columbia University. See also Beverly Wilson Palmer, ed., *Selected Letters of Lucretia Coffin Mott* (Urbana: University of Illinois Press, 2002), 429–30.

41. *Sixteenth Annual Report*, 22; *Fifteenth Annual Report*, 16.

42. *National Anti-Slavery Standard*, May 1, 1869. Gordon, *Selected Papers of Stanton and Anthony*, 2: 647, app. C. Wilbur attended every National Woman Suffrage Association Meeting in Washington, D.C., from 1869 to 1895. Susan B. Anthony and Ida Husted Harper, *History of Woman Suffrage* (New York: Source Books Press, 1970), 4: 260. On Wilbur and the right to vote see also Nancy Hewitt, *Women's Activism and Social Change: Rochester, New York, 1822–1872* (Ithaca, N.Y.: Cornell University Press, 1984), 207; Lori D. Ginzberg, *Women and the Work of Benevolence: Morality, Politics, and Class in the Nineteenth-Century United States* (New Haven, Conn.: Yale University Press, 1990), 180.

43. *Sixteenth Annual Report*, 12.

44. *Seventeenth Annual Report*, 27.

45. Jacob. R. Shipherd to C. H. Howard, July 13, 1865, Letters Received, M1055, Assistant Commissioner for the District of Columbia (ACDC), BRFAL.

46. Shipherd to O. O. Howard, October 30, 1865. Letters Received, Office of the Commissioner, BRFAL. J. Miller McKim also objected to Griffing's appeal. See McKim to Shipherd, January 10, 1866, McKim Letterbooks, Samuel J. May Anti-Slavery Collection, Cornell University; "This Week," *The Nation*, December 7, 1865, 708. After Reconstruction, Shipherd had an interesting and scandalous career as a businessman, lawyer, "adventurer," and ladies' man. For example, see the *New York Times*, February 16, 1882, 5, and June 25, 1905, 7.

47. S. N. Clark to the Associated Press, December 19, 1865, Letters Sent, ACDC, BRFAL.

48. Clark to Mr. E. Carpenter, December 5, 1865, Letters Sent, ACDC, BRFAL.

49. Josephine Emma Griffing was probably twenty-five at the time. After her work with the Freedmen's Bureau ended, Josephine Emma worked in the federal pension office. Like her mother, she was active in the woman suffrage movement. Gordon, *Selected Papers of Stanton and Anthony*, 2: 403, 482.

50. Howard, *Autobiography*, 2: 221.On the transformation of charity in the Civil War era, see Amy Dru Stanley, *From Bondage to Contract: Wage Labor, Marriage, and the Market in the Age of Slave Emancipation* (New York: Cambridge University Press, 1998), 98, 104; Joan Waugh, *Unsentimental Reformer: The Life of Josephine Shaw Lowell* (Cambridge, Mass.: Harvard University Press, 1997), chaps. 5 and 6; Ginzberg, *Women and the Work of Benevolence*, chap. 6; George Fredrickson, *The Inner Civil War: Northern Intellectuals and the Crisis of the Union* (New York: Harper and Row, 1965), 211–16. On women's resistance to this transformation see Elizabeth D. Leonard, *Yankee Women: Gender Battles in the Civil War* (New York: W. W. Norton, 1994), 81, 85; Jeanie Attie, *Patriotic Toil: Northern Women and the American Civil War* (Ithaca, N.Y.: Cornell University Press, 1998). Attie points out that the male directors of the Sanitary Commission were violating an antebellum "compromise" on gender relations which gave women authority over benevolent work.

51. W. F. Spurgin to S. N. Clark, November 1, 1865, Letters Received, ACDC, BRFAL.

52. Saville, *Work of Reconstruction*, 4, 47.

53. Spurgin to Clark, November 1, 1865, Letters Received, ACDC, BRFAL. Wilbur had a more favorable impression of Spurgin: "It is a pleasure to bear testimony to the kindness, capability and efficiency of this officer. His duties are perplexing and require great patience, and perhaps no one could perform them better than does Capt. S." See *Fifteenth Annual Report*, 10.

54. Spurgin to Clark, January 1, 1866, Letters Received, ACDC, BRFAL.

55. See reports from Josephine Griffing, October and November 1867, Letters Received, ACDC, BRFAL.

56. Will Coulter to C. H. Howard, November 5, 6, 7, 1867; Major Vandenburgh to Will Coulter, November 7, 1867, Letters Received, ACDC, BRFAL.

57. Howard, *Autobiography*, 2: 226. Howard instructed his agents to cut back on relief as early as 1865, see Bentley, *History of the Freedman's Bureau*, 76. For a bureau officer's reluctance to issue rations, see John William De Forest, *A Union Officer in the Reconstruction* (New Haven, Conn.: Yale University Press, 1948), 58–60. For more on the bureau's reluctance to be a pauper agency see Foner, *Reconstruction*, 152–53.

58. Howard, *Autobiography*, 2: 346.

59. *Sixteenth Annual Report*, 7; Howard, *Autobiography*, 2: 268.

60. *Sixteenth Annual Report*, 3–4.

61. *Fifteenth Annual Report*, 16; *Seventeenth Annual Report*, 4.

62. *Seventeenth Annual Report*, 27. Wilbur's efforts to secure employment in government service were tied to her support for woman suffrage. See Diary entries March 12, April 8, April 26, May 1, May 13, and May 17, 1869, Box 1, Julia A. Wilbur Papers, Collection 1158, Haverford College Library, Quaker Collection. Aron, *Ladies and Gentlemen*, 152.

63. Griffing to O. O. Howard, April 20, 1869, Letters Received by the Commissioner, BRFAL.

64. Josephine Griffing to O. O. Howard, November 23, 1870, Letters Received by the Commissioner, BRFAL; Josephine S. Griffing, "Work of the National Freedmen's Relief Association for the Year," 1868, Senate 41A-H5.2, National Archives and Records Administration.

65. Griffing to O. O. Howard, September 15, 1868. Letters Received by the Commissioner, BRFAL. In 1868, only one of Griffing's daughters brought in an income. Josephine Emma was twenty-seven years of age, Helen was twenty, and Cora was twelve. Records of the U.S. District Court in the District of Columbia, RG 21, Entry 115, Box 118, No. 7679, National Archives and Records Administration; Entry for Josephine Griffing; p. 35, line 40, p. 36, lines 1-3, Enumeration District 87, Washington, D.C., Census of Population; (National Archives Microfilm Publication M593, roll 306); Ninth Census of the United States, 1870; Records of the Bureau of the Census, Record Group 29; National Archives and Records Administration—Great Lakes Region, Chicago.

66. Griffing to O. O. Howard, November 22, 1869. Letters Received by the Commissioner, BRFAL.

67. Griffing to Horace Greeley, September 12, 1870, reprinted in Elizabeth Cady Stanton, Susan B. Anthony, and Matilda Joslyn Gage, eds., *History of Woman Suffrage* (1881; New York: Source Books Press, 1970), 2: 36.

68. Griffing to the Mayor of Washington, April 8, 1871, *History of Woman Suffrage*, 2: 35.

69. *Friends Intelligencer*, December 15, 1877; *Revolution*, April 7, 1870; Lucretia Mott to Josephine Griffing, December 25, 1869, Griffing Collection, Columbia University; Josephine S. Griffing, "Work of the National Freedmen's Relief Association for the Year," 1868, Senate 41A-H5.2, National Archives and Records Administration. Stacey M. Robertson, *Parker Pillsbury: Radical Abolitionist, Male Feminist* (Ithaca, N.Y.: Cornell University Press, 2000).

70. Horace Greeley to Griffing, September 7, 1870, Griffing Collection. See also *History of Woman Suffrage*, 2: 36–37.

71. For example, Louise Michele Newman, *White Women's Rights: The Racial Origins of Feminism in the United States* (New York: Oxford University Press, 1999), 8; Jacqueline Jones, *Soldiers of Light and Love: Northern Teachers and Georgia Blacks, 1865–1873* (1980; Athens: Brown and Thrasher Books of the University of Georgia Press, 1992), 117–18, 141, 166; Peggy Pascoe, *Relations of Rescue: The Search for Female Moral Authority in the American West* (New York: Oxford University Press, 1990), xxi–xxii.

Chapter 6. Land Schemes

1. *National Anti-Slavery Standard*, October 9, 1869.

2. Eric Foner, *Reconstruction: American's Unfinished Revolution, 1863–1877* (New York: Harper and Row, 1988), 159–60, 245–46; Foner, *Free Soil, Free Labor, Free Men: The Ideology of the Republican Party Before the Civil War* (New York: Oxford University Press, 1970), 27–29. For Southern blacks who succeeded in buying land after the Civil War, see Loren Schweninger, *Black Property Owners in the South, 1790–1915* (1990; Urbana: University of Illinois Press, 1997), chap. 5.

3. *National Anti-Slavery Standard*, February 20, 1869.

4. On Fanny Wright's reputation and radicalism see Lori D. Ginzberg, "'The Hearts of Your Readers Will Shudder': Fanny Wright, Infidelity, and American Freethought," *American Quarterly* 46, no. 2 (June 1994):195–226; Celia Morris, *Fanny Wright: Rebel in America* (1984; Chicago: University of Illinois Press, 1992), 105, 100–40.

5. John Stauffer notes the significance of this precedent in his book, which examines the radical friendship of Gerrit Smith, John Brown, Frederick Douglass, and James McCune Smith. See *The Black Hearts of Men: Radical Abolitionists*

and the Transformation of Race (Cambridge, Mass.; Harvard University Press, 2002), 144, 134–58.

6. Edward Hooper to Dr. Robert William Hooper, March 7, 1863, Edward William Hooper Papers, Houghton Library, Harvard University. See also Willie Lee Rose, *Rehearsal for Reconstruction: The Port Royal Experiment* (New York: Oxford University Press, 1964), chap. 10, 297–313, 346–58; Foner, *Reconstruction,* 50–60, 69, 109–10, 158–64, 190; Julie Saville, *From Slave to Wage Laborer in South Carolina, 1860–1870* (New York: Cambridge University Press, 1996), chap. 3.

7. Foner, *Reconstruction,* 246.

8. Judith Colucci Breault, *The World of Emily Howland: Odyssey of a Humanitarian* (Millbrae, Calif.: Les Femmes, 1976), 2, 10–11; see also Florence Woolsey Hazzard, "Emily Howland," in Edward T. James, Janet Wilson James, and Paul S. Boyer, eds., *Notable American Women* (Cambridge, Mass.: Belknap Press, 1971).

9. *National Anti-Slavery Standard,* April 4, 1868. Howland gained more support from Washington's free black and white reform communities than Miner, causing Miner to become jealous. See Breault, *World of Emily Howland,* 36–39.

10. Emily Howland, *Early History of Friends in Cayuga County, New York, Read Before the Cayuga County Historical Society, April 8, 1880,* Collections of the Cayuga County, New York Historical Society, No. 2, 1888, 10, 17.

11. Howland, *Early History,* 16, 29.

12. Howland, *Early History,* 29. Howland pointed out that the Scipio meetinghouse reflected this equality of men and women: "The form of the edifice, though not pleasing to the eye, gives in material shape, one of the distinctive principles of the Society, the quality of men and women in affairs of the church; the square building being convertible at will, into two equal rooms, where these co-ordinate bodies deliberate separately." See Howland, *Early History,* 17.

13. Quoted in Breault, *World of Emily Howland,* 44; see also 128–29.

14. Breault describes Howland as a bridge between the NWSA and the AWSA, but suggests that she remained in the background of the national suffrage movement due to nervousness and anxiety. See *World of Emily Howland,* 137, 139. I believe Howland's reluctance to play a role in the national suffrage scene may reflect her political independence rather than personal fears.

15. Breault, *World of Emily Howland,* 70, 93.

16. Francis George Shaw to Emily Howland, February 25, 1863. Emily Howland Papers, Friends Historical Library, Swarthmore College. Read on microfilm at Kroch Library, Cornell University, Collection 2760, Reel 1 (hereafter referred to as Swarthmore).

17. Emily Howland to Slocum Howland, April 29, 1866, Emily Howland Papers, Swarthmore. Howland clearly disapproved of contributions being used to pay the salaries of the secretaries of the aid societies, as did Hannah Stevenson.

18. Breault, *World of Emily Howland,* 74–75.

19. Emily Howland to Slocum Howland, May 28, 1863, Emily Howland Papers, Swarthmore. In an article written for the *National Anti-Slavery Standard,* Howland described the residents of the Arlington camp as "self-sustaining." This could be an effort to portray freedpeople in a positive light, or because the end of the war had brought some stability to the Arlington camp. See issue of August 19, 1865.

20. "Appeal of the National Association for the Relief of Colored Women and Children," Emily Howland's correspondence, 1863, Emily Howland Papers, Kroch Library, Cornell University.

21. Emily Howland to Hannah Howland (sister-in-law), May 15, 1866, Emily Howland Papers, Swarthmore.

22. Emily Howland to Hannah Howland, April 16, 1866. Emily Howland Papers, Swarthmore.

23. Sallie to Emily Howland, November 18, 1865, Emily Howland Papers, Cornell.

24. Emily Howland to her mother, Hannah Howland, June 29 and August 23, 1866, Emily Howland Papers, Swarthmore.

25. Anna Searing to Emily Howland, December 31, 1865, Emily Howland Papers, Cornell.

26. Lizzie Bailey to Emily Howland, written from Arlington, Va., February 6, 1866, Emily Howland Papers, Cornell.

27. Breault, *World of Emily Howland*, 62.

28. J. P. Read to Emily Howland, August 3, 1864, and Betsey Read to Emily Howland, October 23, 1864, Emily Howland Papers, Cornell.

29. *National Anti-Slavery Standard*, March 2, 1867; Breault, *World of Emily Howland*, 80–82.

30. L. Edwin Dudley to Gen. O. Brown, July 13, 1867, Emily Howland Papers, Swarthmore.

31. *National Anti-Slavery Standard*, December 12, 1868.

32. Emily Howland to Aunt, January 16, 1871, Emily Howland Papers, Swarthmore.

33. Henrietta S. Jaquette, ed., *South After Gettysburg: Letters of Cornelia Hancock from the Army of the Potomac, 1863–65* (Philadelphia: University of Pennsylvania Press, 1937), x. See also Jaquette, "Cornelia Hancock," in Edward T. James, Janet W. James, and Paul S. Boyer, eds., *Notable American Women* (Cambridge, Mass.: Belknap Press, 1971). Lori D. Ginzberg points out that Hancock and other Quakers, who viewed the Civil War as a "moral struggle," continued women's antebellum benevolence in "settings that were defined by government action." See *Women and the Work of Benevolence: Morality, Politics, and Class in the Nineteenth-Century United States* (New Haven, Conn.: Yale University Press, 1990), 177–79. Other women also made the transition between freedmen's aid and charity organization; see Joan Waugh, *Unsentimental Reformer: The Life of Josephine Shaw Lowell* (Cambridge, Mass.: Harvard University Press, 1997).

34. Jaquette, *South After Gettysburg*, 35, 40. Howland was already friends with Hancock's sister, Ellen Child. See Breault, *World of Emily Howland*, 24–25.

35. Jaquette, *South After Gettysburg*, 31.

36. Jaquette, *South After Gettysburg*, 33.

37. Jaquette, *South After Gettysburg*, 34.

38. Jaquette, *South After Gettysburg*, 35; Joanne Pope Melish, *Disowning Slavery: Gradual Emancipation and "Race" in New England, 1780–1860* (Ithaca, N.Y.: Cornell University Press, 1998), chap. 3.

39. Jaquette, *South After Gettysburg*, 40, 42.

40. Jaquette, *South After Gettysburg*, 35, 40.

41. Jaquette, *South After Gettysburg*, 42.

42. Jaquette, *South After Gettysburg*, 43.

43. *Friends Intelligencer*, February 1, 1868.

44. *Friends Intelligencer*, December 28, 1867; February 1, 1868.

45. *Friends Intelligencer*, February 1, 1868.

46. *Friends Intelligencer*, April 23, 1870.

47. *Friends Intelligencer*, April 23, 1870.

48. Cornelia Hancock to Emily Howland, January 14, 1869; Hancock to Slocum Howland, December 5, 1870, Emily Howland Papers, Swarthmore.

49. Hancock to Emily Howland, April 13, 1870, Emily Howland Papers,

Swarthmore; Hancock to Howland, April 11, 1869, Emily Howland Papers, Cornell.

50. Hancock to Howland, May 6, 1869, Emily Howland Papers, Swarthmore. On the capitalist/free labor intentions of many of the Gideonites see Rose, *Rehearsal for Reconstruction,* 212–18.

51. Hancock to Howland, August 18 and September 14, 1875, Emily Howland Papers, Swarthmore.

52. Hancock to Howland, May 30, 1878, Emily Howland Papers, Swarthmore.

53. Hancock to Howland, August 18, 1875, Emily Howland Papers, Swarthmore.

54. Amy Dru Stanley, *From Bondage to Contract: Wage Labor, Marriage, and the Market in the Age of Slave Emancipation* (New York: Cambridge University Press, 1998), chap. 3.

55. Sojourner Truth, *Narrative of Sojourner Truth; A Bondwoman of Olden Time, with a History of Her Labors and Correspondence Drawn from Her "Book of Life"* (New York: Oxford University Press, 1991), 199; Nell Irvin Painter, *Sojourner Truth: A Life, a Symbol* (New York: W.W. Norton, 1996), 234–42.

56. Truth, *Narrative of Sojourner Truth,* 197; Painter, *Sojourner Truth,* 218; Carleton Mabee, "Sojourner Truth Fights Dependence on Government: Moves Freed Slaves off Welfare in Washington to Jobs in Upstate New York," *Afro-Americans in New York Life and History* 14, no. 1 (January 1990): 7–26.

57. Truth, *Narrative,* 195.

58. Truth, *Narrative,* 197.

59. Truth, *Narrative,* 197.

60. Truth, *Narrative,* 200–201.

61. Truth, *Narrative,* 209.

62. Elizabeth Cady Stanton, Susan B. Anthony, and Matilda Joslyn Gage, *History of Woman Suffrage* (1881; New York: Source Books, 1970), 2: 193–94; Painter, *Sojourner Truth,* 148, 197, 242.

63. Painter, *Sojourner Truth,* 241–42, 243–46. Nell Irvin Painter, *Exodusters: Black Migration to Kansas After Reconstruction* (New York: W.W. Norton, 1976, 1986).

64. Foner, *Reconstruction,* 235–37, 245–46.

Chapter 7. Female Employment Agents and African American Migration to the North

1. Waity Harris to Samuel Austin, September 11, 1866, Records of the Rhode Island Association for Freedmen, Rhode Island Historical Society (RIHS).

2. Elizabeth Pleck argues that freedpeople did not benefit in the long run from migration to the North during Reconstruction. She found that African Americans who migrated to Boston under the auspices of the Freedmen's Bureau were impoverished and endured intense racial discrimination. Elizabeth Pleck, *Black Migration and Poverty, Boston, 1865–1900* (New York: Academic Press, 1979). William Cohen describes the Freedmen's Bureau as a giant employment agency, which encouraged the relocation of black labor in the interests of free labor and fewer dependent freedpeople. William Cohen, *At Freedom's Edge: Black Mobility and the Southern White Quest for Racial Control, 1861–1915* (Baton Rouge: Louisiana State University Press, 1991), 84–85, chap. 4. For an examination of black migration to the Midwest see Leslie A. Schwalm, "Encountering Emancipation: Slave Migration to the Midwest during the Civil War," paper delivered at the Southern Historical Association 65th Annual Meeting, Fort Worth, Texas, November 3–6, 1999.

3. *Fourth Annual Report of the National Freedmen's Relief Association of the District of Columbia* (Washington, D.C.: McGill and Witherow, 1866), 7.

4. Cohen, *At Freedom's Edge*, 84–85.

5. Keith Melder, "Angel of Mercy in Washington: Josephine Griffing and the Freedmen, 1864-1872," *Records of the Columbia Historical Society of the District of Columbia*, 1863–65, 259; James M. McPherson, *Struggle for Equality: Abolitionists and the Negro in the Civil War and Reconstruction* (Princeton, N.J.: Princeton University Press, 1964), 389–92; Nell Irvin Painter, *Sojourner Truth: A Life, a Symbol* (New York: W.W. Norton, 1996), 217.

6. Anna Lowell to General C. H. Howard September 1, 1867, Letters Received, Records of the Assistant Commissioner for the District of Columbia (ACDC), M1055, Bureau of Refugees, Freedmen, and Abandoned Lands (BRFAL), RG105, National Archives and Records Administration.

7. Allan Johnston, *Surviving Freedom: The Black Community of Washington, D.C., 1860–1880* (New York: Garland Publishing, 1993), 107–8.

8. *Third Annual Report of the National Freedmen's Relief Association for the District of Columbia* (Washington: McGill and Witherow, 1865), 4; James Borchert, *Alley Life in Washington: Family, Community, Religion, and the Folklife in the City, 1850–1970* (Urbana: University of Illinois Press, 1980).

9. O. O. Howard, Circular Letter, February 24, 1867, in *Circulars, Etc. Issued by the Commissioner of the Bureau of Refugees Freedmen and Abandoned Lands from Its organization to Dec. 31 1867* (Washington, D.C.: 1867).

10. C. H. Howard to Max Woodhull, July 16, 1866; C. H. Howard to Anna Lowell, October 29, 1866, Letters Sent, ACDC, BRFAL.

11. Circular Letter issued February 24, 1867 in *Circulars, Etc. Issued by the Commissioner.* General O. O. Howard reported that he spent $1,320,000.00 on transportation in the fiscal year ending June 1867. In the year ending October 1869, Howard reported that he provided transportation to 6,481 people. See O. O. Howard, *Autobiography of Oliver Otis Howard* (New York: Baker and Taylor, 1907), 2: 331, 362. Interestingly, the bureau also subsidized the efforts of the American Colonization Society to encourage freedpeople to migrate to Liberia.

12. Howard, *Autobiography*, 2: 213–14. See also George R. Bentley, *A History of the Freedmen's Bureau* (1944; New York: Octagon Books, 1974), 76–79; William S. McFeely, *Yankee Stepfather: General O. O. Howard and the Freedmen* (1968; New York: W. W. Norton, 1994); Eric Foner, *Reconstruction: America's Unfinished Revolution, 1863–1877* (New York: Harper & Row, 1988), 152–53.

13. C. H. Howard to Griffing, October 15, 1866, Letters Sent, ACDC, BRFAL. Cohen believes that "considerable pressure may have been brought to bear on those who resisted leaving," but I disagree. Although bureau officials may have wished they could force freedpeople out of the District, they could not. See Cohen, *At Freedom's Edge*, 81.

14. *Fourth Annual Report*, 12. The Freedmen's Bureau also encouraged families to migrate together, as it did not want to be responsible for caring for the dependent relatives of wage earners who had left the city. See Rogers to Griffing, January 28, 1867, Letters Sent, ACDC, BRFAL.

15. Oliver St. John to J. Miller McKim, March 14, 1866, Samuel J. May Anti-Slavery Collection, Cornell University.

16. Waity Harris to Samuel Austin, September 11, 1866, Records of the Rhode Island Association for Freedmen, RIHS.

17. C. H. Howard to Mrs. J. S. Talcott of the Cleveland Freedmen's Union Commission, January 21, 1867, Letters Sent, ACDC, BRFAL.

18. The fear of black competition for Northern labor is also addressed in the

preliminary and final reports of the American Freedmen's Inquiry Commission; see RG94, M619, Letters Received by the Adjutant General, Roll 199, National Archives and Records Administration. Northern public concern over African American dependency also appeared following proposals for emancipation after the American Revolution. See Joanne Pope Melish, *Disowning Slavery: Gradual Emancipation and "Race" in New England, 1780–1860* (Ithaca, N.Y.: Cornell University Press, 1998), chaps. 2–3; Schwalm, "Encountering Emancipation."

19. Laura Haviland, *A Woman's Life Work: Labors and Experiences of Laura S. Haviland* (Chicago: C.V. Waite, 1887), 450; Melish, *Disowning Slavery*, 77–79; David J. Rothman, *The Discovery of the Asylum: Social Order and Disorder in the New Republic* (New York: Little Brown, 1971, 1990), chaps. 7, 8; Michael B. Katz, *The Undeserving Poor: From the War on Poverty to the War on Welfare* (New York: Pantheon Books, 1989), 6–7, 11. Haviland continued to aid black migrants through the exodus to Kansas. See also Nell Irvin Painter, *Exodusters: Black Migration to Kansas After Reconstruction* (1976; New York: W. W. Norton, 1992), 231.

20. Emily Howland to Father and Mother, May 7, 1863, and to her father, December 10, 1866, Emily Howland Papers, Friends Historical Library, Swarthmore College. Read on microfilm at Kroch Library, Cornell University, Collection 2760, Reel 1 (hereafter referred to as Swarthmore).

21. Emily Howland to Hannah (probably Hannah Howland), December 14, 1869; see also Howland to Mother, July 14, 1867, Swarthmore.

22. Lucretia Mott praised the efforts of Mrs. L. M. E. Ricks, comparing her to the American Freedmen's Union Commission: "I want to hear what Miller M'K. & their Union are doing." Lucretia Mott to Martha Mott Lord, July 20, 1866, Mott Papers, Swarthmore. For more on Ricks's career with the Freedmen's Bureau see Ricks to C. H. Howard, March 9, 1866, November 14, 1866, February 2, 1867; A. F. Williams to S. N. Clark, February 13, 1867; Ricks to S. N. Clark, November 2, 1867; Ricks to C. H. Howard, April 13 and July 30, 1868, Letters Received, ACDC, BRFAL.

23. *National Anti-Slavery Standard,* February 7, 1863, December 5, 1863; Eugene H. Roseboom, "Frances Dana Barker Gage," *Notable American Women* (Cambridge, Mass.: Belknap Press, 1971).

24. Newspaper clipping, undated, Griffing Collection, Columbia University; *National Anti- Slavery Standard,* September 1, 1866.

25. Griffing to Isaac and Amy Post, January 10, 1866, Post Family Papers, Department of Rare Books and Special Collections, University of Rochester Library.

26. Sojourner Truth to Amy Post, July 3, 1866, Post Papers.

27. J. C. Thayer to Sojourner Truth, March 15, 1867; Theodore Backus to Truth, February 22, 1867; Davis Carpenter to Isaac Post, March 14, 1867; Mrs. James Annin to Truth March 15, 1867; Post Papers. See also Painter, *Sojourner Truth,* 217–19; Carleton Mabee, "Sojourner Truth Fights Dependence on Government: Moves Freed Slaves Off Welfare in Washington to Jobs in Upstate New York," *Afro-Americans in New York Life and History* 14, no. 1 (January 1990): 7–26.

28. Griffing to Sojourner Truth and Amy Post, March 26, 1867, Post Papers.

29. As quoted in Bentley, *History of the Freedmen's Bureau,* 125.

30. *Sixteenth Annual Report of the Rochester Ladies' Anti-Slavery and Freedmen's Aid Society* (Rochester, N.Y.: William S. Falls, 1867), 10.

31. Eliphalet Whittlesey to Griffing, May 26, 1870, Letters Sent, Office of the Commissioner, M742, BRFAL. By 1870, the Freedmen's Bureau had ceased providing employment agents and freedpeople with transportation expenses. Griffing continued her employment agency and still communicated with the Freedmen's Bureau.

32. For example, L. M. E. Ricks to C. H. Howard, August 14, 1867, Letters Received, ACDC, BRFAL.

33. Newspaper clipping "A Noble Charity" with letter of A. F. Williams to S. N. Clark, February 13, 1867, Letters Received, ACDC, BRFAL.

34. Josephine Griffing to Sojourner Truth and Amy Post, March 26, 1867; Truth to Griffing, March 30, 1867, Post Papers.

35. Henry M. Wilson to O. O. Howard, August 28, 1866; Sayles J. Bowen, President of the National Freedmen's Relief Association of the District of Columbia, to C. H. Howard, September 7, 1866, Letters Received, ACDC, BRFAL.

36. Mrs. Sarah A. Tilmon to C. H. Howard, August 13, 1867, September 30, 1867, Letters Received, ACDC, BRFAL. Tilmon had been operating an employment agency since at least 1860. One advertisement for her agency read: "All good colored help coming to this city in search of employment would do well to call. Every attention paid to strangers." *New York Anglo- African,* November 24, 1860.

37. Tilmon to C. H. Howard, February 6, 1867; Anna Lowell to C. H. Howard, December 9, 1866; Letters Received, ACDC, BRFAL.

38. Tilmon to C. H. Howard, February 6, 1867, Letters Received.

39. Mrs. L. M. E. Ricks to C. H. Howard, February 12, 1867, Letters Received.

40. Ricks to S. N. Clark, November 2, 1867, Letters Received.

41. Mrs. R. M. Bigelow to O. O. Howard, November 7, 1866, Letters Received, ACDC, BRFAL.

42. J. L. Roberts to Major Vandenburgh, June 13, 1867, Letters Received, ACDC, BRFAL. See also S. N. Clark to Waity Harris, December 20, 1866, Letters Sent, ACDC, BRFAL.

43. Agent Rogers to Josephine Griffing, July 18, 1866, Letters Sent, ACDC, BRFAL. For an analysis of black family reconstitution during Reconstruction see especially Herbert G. Gutman, *The Black Family in Slavery and Freedom, 1750–1925* (New York: Vintage Books, 1976), chap. 9; Ira Berlin and Leslie S. Rowland, *Families and Freedom: A Documentary History of African-American Kinship in the Civil War Era* (New York: New Press, 1997).

44. O. O. Howard to Griffing, September 23, 1867, Letters Sent, Office of the Commissioner, BRFAL.

45. Eliphalet Whittlesey to Griffing, July 13, 1868, Letters Sent, Office of the Commissioner, BRFAL.

46. Karin L. Zipf, "Reconstructing 'Free Woman': African-American Women, Apprenticeship, and Custody rights during Reconstruction," *Journal of Women's History* 12 (Spring 2000): 8–31.

47. Anna Earle to C. H. Howard, October 12, 1867, Letters Received, ACDC, BRFAL.

48. Earle to C.H. Howard, January 24, 1868, Letters Received, ACDC, BRFAL. Reformer E. H. Valentine tried to trace the movements of another girl, Ellen Green, who "had the prospect of a good home at Watertown and was full of bright anticipations in going to make herself useful at the north." But when Ellen arrived in Boston she was mistakenly taken to the "Institution at Cambridgeport," where she caught scarlet fever. After Ellen's bout of fever she was "subject to fits." She was then taken to the almshouse at Tewksbury and then forwarded to either Washington or Virginia. Valentine hoped that her information "will furnish a clue to her present abiding place." E. H. Valentine to C. H. Howard, June 15, 1868, and E. H. Valentine to Major Vandenburgh, September 21, 1868, Letters Received by the Commissioner, M752, BRFAL.

49. Anna Lowell to C. H. Howard, December 4, 1866, Letters Received,

ACDC, BRFAL. At the time of this letter Lowell was a member of the Soldiers' Memorial Society. The society, made up of prominent Bostonians, including Edward Everett Hale, was established at the end of the war to "keep close the ties which had united us in the charities of the war, that we might be ready for whatever exigency should still require charities rendered in a kindred spirit." Similar in structure and aims to the American Freedmen's Union Commission, the Soldiers' Memorial Society also devoted considerable energy to the relief of destitute freedpeople. Lowell left the society to dedicate herself fully to the Howard Industrial School. Significantly, Anna Lowell did not identify with radical abolitionists, but rather with moderate antislavery Republicans. *Reports of the Soldiers' Memorial Society Presented at Its Third Annual Meeting, June 11, 1867* (Boston: Soldiers' Memorial Society, 1867), 3, 12–13; Anna Lowell to C. H. Howard, February 6, 1867. See also Pleck, *Black Migration and Poverty*, 26–27. The dearth of servants may have been in the imagination of the employers, as the low status of domestic servitude made for a transient labor force. Employers constantly searched for more reliable and more pliable servants. See Faye Dudden, *Serving Women: Household Service in Nineteenth Century America* (Middletown, Conn.: Wesleyan University Press, 1983).

50. For African American women's resistance to the conditions of domestic service see Elizabeth Clark-Lewis, *Living In, Living Out: African-American Domestics in Washington, D.C. 1910–1940* (Washington, D.C.: Smithsonian Institution Press, 1994); Tera Hunter, *To 'Joy My Freedom: Southern Black Women's Lives and Labors After the Civil War* (Cambridge, Mass.: Harvard University Press, 1997). On the relationship between enslaved women and white women in the antebellum South, see Marli F. Weiner, *Mistresses and Slaves: Plantation Women in South Carolina, 1830–1880* (Urbana: University of Illinois Press, 1998); Elizabeth Fox-Genovese, *Within the Plantation Household: Black and White Women of the Old South* (Chapel Hill: University of North Carolina Press, 1988); Catherine Clinton, *The Plantation Mistress: Woman's World in the Old South* (New York: Pantheon Books, 1982).

51. Anna Lowell to C. H. Howard, December 4, 1866, January 13, 1867, February 6, 1867, February 27, 1867, Letters Received, ACDC, BRFAL. See also October 25, 1866, November 1, 1866.

52. Lowell to C. H. Howard, January 13, 1867.

53. Griffing to C. H. Howard, October 20, 1866, Letters Received.

54. A. F. Williams to O. O. Howard, January 21, 1867, Letters Received by the Commissioner, M752, BRFAL.

55. H. M. Wilson to C. H. Howard, September 27, 1867, Letters Received, ACDC, BRFAL.

56. Griffing to Whittlesey, August 29, 1868, Letters Received by the Commissioner, BRFAL.

57. For a brief discussion of the end of Griffing's marriage, see Stacey Marie Robertson, "Parker Pillsbury, Antislavery Apostle: Gender and Religion in Nineteenth-Century United States Radicalism," Ph.D. dissertation, University of California, Santa Barbara, 1994, 110–17. For Griffing's economic situation, see Josephine Griffing to O. O. Howard, September 15, 1868, and November 22, 1869, Letters Received by the Commissioner, BRFAL. Griffing probably divorced her husband as her daughters claimed she was a "femme sole" at the time of her death in 1872. See Estate of Josephine Griffing, filed March 16, 1876, No. 7679, RG21, National Archives.

58. Rogers to Griffing, April 18, 1866, Letters Sent, ACDC, BRFAL.

59. H. G. Stewart to C. H. Howard, April 24, 1867, Letters Received, ACDC, BRFAL. For another complaint against Stewart see Stewart to C. H. Howard,

August 30, 1867. However, fifty-three freedpeople also petitioned in support of Stewart and his intelligence agency in Providence. See Petition, November 15, 1867, Letters Received, ACDC, BRFAL.

60. Sojourner Truth, *Narrative of Sojourner Truth; A Bondswoman of Olden Time, with a History of Her Labors and Correspondence Drawn from Her "Book of Life"* (New York: Oxford University Press, 1991), 191.

61. *Fifth Annual Report of the National Freedmen's Relief Association of the District of Columbia* (Washington, D.C.: McGill and Witherow, 1867), 6–7.

62. *Fifth Annual Report*, 7–8.

63. Painter, *Exodusters*; James R. Grossman, *Land of Hope: Chicago, Black Southerners, and the Great Migration* (Chicago: University of Chicago Press, 1989).

Chapter 8. The Limits of Women's Radical Reconstruction

1. Josephine Griffing Petition, HR38A-G10.5, Records of the House of Representatives, Record Group 233, National Archives and Records Administration.

2. Jacqueline Jones, *Labor of Love, Labor of Sorrow: Black Women, Work, and the Family from Slavery to the Present* (New York: Vintage Books, 1985), 46; Leslie A. Schwalm, "'Sweet Dreams of Freedom': Freedwomen's Reconstruction of Life and Labor in Lowcountry South Carolina," *Journal of Women's History* 9 (1997): 9–38; Schwalm, *A Hard Fight for We: Women's Transition from Slavery to Freedom in South Carolina* (Urbana: University of Illinois Press, 1997), chap. 6; Catherine Clinton, "Reconstructing Freedwomen," in Clinton and Nina Silber, eds., *Divided Houses: Gender and the Civil War* (New York: Oxford University Press, 1992), 306–19; Noralee Frankel, *Freedom's Women: Black Women and Families in Civil War Era Mississippi* (Bloomington: Indiana University Press, 1999), 30; Tera Hunter, *To 'Joy My Freedom: Southern Black Women's Lives and Labors After the Civil War* (Cambridge, Mass.: Harvard University Press, 1997); Sharon Harley, "When Your Work Is Not Who You Are: The Development of a Working-Class Consciousness Among Afro-American Women," in Darlene Clark Hine, Wilma King, and Linda Reed, eds., *We Specialize in the Wholly Impossible* (New York: Carlson, 1995), 25–37.

3. As Jean Fagan Yellin notes, even before the Civil War the "anti-slavery feminist discourse became race specific." Yellin, *Women and Sisters: The Anti-Slavery Feminists in American Culture* (New Haven, Conn.: Yale University Press, 1989), 76, 24–25. Louise Michele Newman, *White Women's Rights: The Racial Origins of Feminism in the United States* (New York: Oxford University Press, 1999), 4–5; Peggy Pascoe, *Relations of Rescue: The Search for Female Moral Authority in the American West, 1874-1939* (New York: Oxford University Press, 1990). Thomas C. Holt has suggested that the realities of Reconstruction, including freedpeople's resistance to the tenets of free labor ideology, caused many white reformers to turn their backs on civil and political equality for African Americans: "Their racial attitudes and beliefs were not autonomous, discrete entities unrelated to other ideas and events; during the emancipation era racial attitudes were shaped by events even as they shaped events in turn." Thomas C. Holt, "'An Empire over the Mind': Emancipation, Race, and Ideology in the British West Indies and the American South," in J. Morgan Kousser and James M. McPherson, eds., *Region, Race, and Reconstruction: Essays in Honor of C. Vann Woodward* (New York: Oxford University Press, 1982), 306–7; Barbara Jeanne Fields, "Slavery, Race, and Ideology in the United States of America," *New Left Review* 181 (May/June 1990): 95–118; Thomas C. Holt, "Marking: Race, Race-Making, and the Writing of History," *American Historical Review* 100, no. 1 (February 1995): 1–20.

4. Undated Certificate of Commission (probably 1865), Lucy Salisbury Doolittle Papers, Library of Congress.

5. "Journal of Miss Susan Walker, March 3–June 2, 1862," *Quarterly Publication of the Historical and Philosophical Society of Ohio* 7 (1912): 21.

6. Saidiya V. Hartman, *Scenes of Subjection: Terror, Slavery, and Self-Making in Nineteenth-Century America* (New York Oxford University Press, 1997), 118, 135.

7. "Journal of Miss Susan Walker," 15–16.

8. Lucy Chase to Dear Friends, July 1, 1864, in Henry Swint, ed., *Dear Ones at Home: Letters from Contraband Camps* (Nashville, Tenn.: Vanderbilt University Press, 1966), 117–18. African American women did not enter the industrial sector in significant numbers until World War II. Jones, *Labor of Love, Labor of Sorrow*, 127–28, 235–40.

9. "Journal of Miss Susan Walker," 15–16. Deborah Gray White, *Ar'n't I A Woman? Female Slaves in the Plantation South* (New York: W.W. Norton, 1985); Schwalm, *Hard Fight for We*, 47–64; Jones, *Labor of Love, Labor of Sorrow*, chap. 1.

10. Laetitia Campbell to Mrs. Mary K. Wead, January 24, 1865, Wead Papers, Sophia Smith Collection, Smith College.

11. Carrie Lacy to Emily Howland, April 20, 1869, Emily Howland Papers, Cornell University.

12. Lacy to Howland, April 6, 1870.

13. Herbert Gutman, *The Black Family in Slavery and Freedom, 1750–1925* (New York: Vintage Books, 1976), chap. 9; Ira Berlin, Steven F. Miller, and Leslie Rowland, "Afro-American Families in the Transition from Slavery to Freedom," *Radical History Review* 42 (1988): 89–121; Ira Berlin and Leslie Rowland, *Families and Freedom: A Documentary History of African-American Kinship in the Civil War Era* (New York: New Press, 1997); Frankel, *Freedom's Women*, chaps. 5 and 6.

14. Gulielma Breed to Howland, April 2, 1860; M. Robinson to Howland, January 3, 1867; Emily Howland Papers.

15. Anna Searing to Howland, December 31, 1865, Emily Howland Papers.

16. On apprenticeship see Schwalm, *Hard Fight For We*, 250–54; Frankel, *Freedom's Women*, 135–45, 154–56; Karin L. Zipf, "Reconstructing 'Free Woman': African-American Women, Apprenticeship, and Custody Rights During Reconstruction," *Journal of Women's History* 12 (Spring 2000): 8–31.

17. During the Civil War, community leaders in both the North and South employed poor women to sew clothes for soldiers. See *First Annual Report of the Educational Commission for Freedmen*, May 1863 (Boston: Prentiss and Deland, 1863); LeeAnn Whites, *Civil War as a Crisis in Gender: Augusta, Georgia 1860–1880* (Athens: University of Georgia Press, 1995), 89. In July 1868, John Alvord noted the existence of forty-six industrials schools for freedpeople, with 1,873 pupils. Of these forty-six schools, six were located in Washington, D.C. These schools had 375 scholars and had produced or repaired 3,105 garments. In 1868, Samuel Armstrong Chapman opened a normal school at Hampton, Virginia, that would become famous for its focus on industrial education. John Alvord, *Sixth Semi-Annual Report* (Washington, D.C.: Government Printing Office, 1868). For antebellum manual labor see Robert H. Abzug, *Cosmos Crumbling: American Reform and the Religious Imagination* (New York: Oxford University Press, 1994), 116–24. On industrial education during Reconstruction, see Donald Spivey, *Schooling for the New Slavery: Black Industrial Education, 1868–1915* (Westport, Conn.: Greenwood Press, 1978), 19, 20, 22; James M. McPherson, *The Abolitionist Legacy: From Reconstruction to the NAACP* (Princeton, N.J.: Princeton University Press, 1975), 210–15; James D. Anderson, *The Education of Blacks in the South, 1860–1935* (Chapel Hill: University of North Carolina Press, 1988), chap. 2; August Meier,

Negro Thought in America, 1880–1915: Racial Ideologies in the Age of Booker T. Washington (Ann Arbor: University of Michigan Press, 1963, 1988), 85–87. Other nations also promoted industrial education as an integral component of the transition to free labor. For example, Thomas C. Holt, *The Problem of Freedom: Race, Labor, and Politics in Jamaica, 1832–1938* (Baltimore: Johns Hopkins University Press, 1992), 191–92.

18. Susan Walker to General Oliver Otis Howard, October 11, 1867, Letters Received, Records of the Assistant Commissioner for the District of Columbia (ACDC), M1055, Bureau of Refugees, Freedmen, and Abandoned Lands (BRFAL).

19. Walker to Howard, October 11, 1867, ACDC, BRFAL. See also, *Special Report of the Commissioner of Education on the Improvement of Public Schools in the District of Columbia, 1871. Section C: History of Schools for the Colored Population* (New York: Arno Press, 1969), 242–43.

20. S. S. Chamberlin to Major Vandenburgh, June 20, 1867, Letters Received, ACDC, BRFAL.

21. Susan Walker to C. H. Howard October 11, 1867, Letters Received.

22. Vandenburgh to Stuart Eldridge, May 2, 1868, Letters Received.

23. J. Major to Eldridge, May 4, 1868, Letters Received.

24. Walker to C. H. Howard, May 5, 1868, Letters Received. Schwalm, *Hard Fight for We*, 204–14.

25. Although it is impossible to know what went on between Johnson and her husband, it is likely that they reached a mutual agreement that she did not need to work for Walker. Frankel, *Freedom's Women*, 70–78; Jones, *Labor of Love, Labor of Sorrow*, 73–77. Anna Searing reported: "There is at present a greater call for women's labor than men's, so many have been thrown out of government service: a skilful woman can make more here now than a man. Such an one with whom we are well acquainted said that she could get $1.00 per day and her board while her husband only received $1.25 without board." Searing to Howland, December 31, 1865, Emily Howland Papers, Cornell.

26. Walker to C. H. Howard May 5, 1868, Letters Received, ACDC, BRFAL. The bureau's failure to censure Walker may have been due to her close connection with Salmon P. Chase, who had recommended her for the Port Royal Experiment. C. H. Howard even advised giving her larger quarters. See C. H. Howard to E. G. Townsend (notation of response), July 26, 1866, Letters Received. See also C. H. Howard to Walker, October 18, 1866, Letters Sent, ACDC, BRFAL.

27. O. O. Howard to Waity F. Harris, June 28, 1866; R. M. Bigelow to Samuel Austin, July 2, 1866; Records of the Rhode Island Association for Freedmen, Rhode Island Historical Society (RIHS). I have found no evidence that Harris was an "abolitionist-feminist." She came to her industrial school after working as a nurse in Washington hospitals during the war (a route also taken by Cornelia Hancock, a Quaker who I would describe as an abolitionist). I believe Harris was committed to helping freedpeople, although her actions clearly indicate an incredible level of self-interest.

28. Harris to Austin, September 11, 1866, RIHS.

29. Mr. Roberts to C. H. Howard, July 9, 1866, Letters Received, ACDC, BRFAL.

30. Testimony of Sophia Johnson, in Eliza Heacock's report of the committee, July 1866, Letters Received.

31. O. O. Howard to Waity F. Harris, June 28, 1866, RIHS.

32. Newman, *White Women's Rights*, 8, 12.

33. Charlotte Forten, "Life on the Sea Islands," *Atlantic Monthly* (May 1864);

86. Lisa A. Long discusses this ambivalence in her article on Charlotte Forten's experience in the Sea Islands of South Carolina. Long, "Charlotte Forten's Civil War Journals and the Quest for 'Genius, Beauty, and Deathless Fame'" *Legacy* 16, no. 1 (1999): 37–48.

34. Many of Brown's letters to Howland can also be found in Dorothy Sterling, ed., *We Are Your Sisters: Black Women in the Nineteenth Century* (New York: W.W. Norton, 1984), 191–202, 286–94.

35. Judith Colucci Breault, *The World of Emily Howland: Odyssey of a Humanitarian* (Millbrae, Calif.: Les Femmes, 1976), 36–37, 82.

36. Samuel Rhoades to Howland, April 14, 1859; S. J. Bowen to Howland, April 14, 1859; Howland to Samuel Rhoades (draft), April 27, 1859, Emily Howland Papers, Cornell.

37. Bowen to Howland May 31, 1862, Emily Howland Papers.

38. Emma Brown to Howland, July 14, 1859, Emily Howland Papers.

39. Brown to Howland, December 2, 1861.

40. Brown to Howland, November 19, 1859.

41. Brown to Mr. Hunnicutt, April 8, 1859, Emily Howland Papers.

42. Brown to Howland, May 22, 1860; April 30, 1860; November 29 1860.

43. Brown to Howland, April 30, 1860.

44. Brown to Howland, December 10, 1861.

45. Unidentified author to Howland, June 30, 1861.

46. Brown to Howland, December 10, 1861; March 19, 1868; May 27, 1870.

47. Brown to Howland, December 10, 1861.

48. Brown to Howland, July 18, 1864; see also Brown to Howland, November 19, 1862.

49. Brown to Howland, March 29, 1868.

50. Brown to Howland, February 8, 1867; December 10, 1861. When Brown arrived at Oberlin, she told Howland that when she first started working in the washroom (for her tuition and room and board), the other girls laughed at her because she washed awkwardly. See Brown to Howland April 30, 1860. According to Dorothy Sterling, Brown's mother, Emmeline Brown, was a dressmaker; see *We Are Your Sisters*, 191.

51. Brown to Howland, July 14, 1859; September 23, 1862.

52. Brown to Howland, September 23, 1862.

53. Brown to Howland, September 23, 1862; February 8, 1867; May 27, 1870. Deborah Gray White, *Too Heavy a Load: Black Women in Defense of Themselves, 1894–1994* (New York: W.W. Norton, 1999), 79.

54. Brown to Howland, April 9, 1861.

55. Brown to Howland, May 22, 1860.

56. Anna Searing? to Emily Howland, May 26, 1861.

57. Brown to Howland, September 23, 1862.

58. Brown uses the phrase "N.T.s," thus appropriating the derogatory phrase for white and black freedmen's teachers. Brown to Howland, February 3, 1867. Albion Tourgee, *A Fool's Errand* (Cambridge, Mass.: Belknap Press, 1961), 53–54.

59. Brown to Howland, February 3, 1867.

60. Brown to Howland, March 23, 1867.

61. Brown to Howland, November 19, 1862.

62. Brown to Howland, July 3, 1869, and May 27, 1870.

63. Eric Foner, *Reconstruction: America's Unfinished Revolution, 1863–1877* (New York: Harper and Row, 1988), 352–53; Brown to Howland, May 27, 1870.

64. Brown to Howland, February 8, 1867.

65. Brown to Howland, January 11, 1865, August 27, 1865.

66. Brown to Howland, March 29, 1868.

67. Darlene Clark Hine, "Rape and the Inner Lives of Black Women in the Middle West: Preliminary Thoughts on the Culture of Dissemblance," in Ellen Carol DuBois and Vicki L. Ruiz, eds., *Unequal Sisters: A Multicultural Reader in U.S. Women's History* (New York: Routledge, 1990), 292–97.

68. Brown to Howland, January 25, 1875.

69. Sterling, *We Are Your Sisters*, 293–94.

Conclusion

1. For example, Carol Tavris, "Misreading the Gender Gap," *New York Times*, September 17, 1996, A23; Joyce Purnick, "G.O.P. Quest to Narrow Gender Gap," *New York Times*, November 14 1996, B1; Frank Rich, "The G.O.P.'s Bitter Pill: Return of the Gender Gap," *New York Times*, February 12, 1997, A25.

2. Linda Gordon, ed., *Women, the State, and Welfare* (Madison: University of Wisconsin Press, 1990); Seth Koven and Sonya Michel, eds., *Mothers of a New World: Maternalist Politics and the Origins of Welfare States* (New York: Routledge, 1993).

3. George Fredrickson, *The Inner Civil War: Northern Intellectuals and the Crisis of the Union* (New York: Harper and Row, 1965); Lori D. Ginzberg, *Women and the Work of Benevolence: Morality, Politics, and Class in the Nineteenth-Century United States* (New Haven., Conn.: Yale University Press, 1990); Joan Waugh, *Unsentimental Reformer: The Life of Josephine Shaw Lowell* (Cambridge, Mass.: Harvard University Press, 1997); Elizabeth Leonard, *Yankee Women: Gender Battles in the Civil War* (New York: W.W. Norton, 1994); Judith Ann Giesberg, *Civil War Sisterhood: The U.S. Sanitary Commission and Women's Politics in Transition* (Boston: Northeastern University Press, 2000).

4. *The Revolution*, March 24, 1870.

5. Louise Michele Newman, *White Women's Rights: The Racial Origins of Feminism in the United States* (New York: Oxford University Press, 1999). For divisions among black women see especially Deborah Gray White, *Too Heavy a Load: Black Women in Defense of Themselves, 1894–1994* (New York: W. W. Norton, 1999), chaps. 1 and 2.

6. Kathryn Kish Sklar, "The Historical Foundations of Women's Power in the Creation of the American Welfare State, 1830–1930," in Koven and Michel, *Mothers of a New World*, 43–93.

7. "Remarks of E. D. Cheney at the meeting on Saturday Morning," Ms. A.10.1 no. 14, Boston Public Library; James M. McPherson traces the activities of abolitionists and their descendants, in *The Abolitionist Legacy: From Reconstruction to the NAACP* (Princeton, N.J.: Princeton University Press, 1976).

8. Glenda Elizabeth Gilmore, *Gender and Jim Crow: Women and the Politics of White Supremacy in North Carolina* (Chapel Hill: University of North Carolina Press, 1996), xxi.

9. Ellen Carol DuBois, *Feminism and Suffrage: The Emergence of an Independent Women's Movement in America, 1848–1869* (Ithaca, N.Y.: Cornell University Press, 1978); Roslyn Terborg-Penn, *African American Women in the Struggle for the Vote, 1850–1920* (Bloomington: Indiana University Press, 1998).

10. Newman, *White Women's Rights*, 12, 181, 183.

11. Newman, *White Women's Rights*, 8.

12. See especially Laura Edwards, *Gendered Strife and Confusion: The Political Culture of Reconstruction* (Urbana: University of Illinois Press, 1997).

13. Newman, *White Women's Rights*; David Roediger, *The Wages of Whiteness: Race and the Making of the American Working Class* (New York: Verso, 1991). For the connection between African American and women's rights see Jean Fagan Yellin, *Women and Sisters: The Antislavery Feminists in American Culture* (New Haven, Conn.: Yale University Press, 1989); Kathryn Kish Sklar, ed., *Women's Rights Emerges within the Antislavery Movement, 1830–1870* (New York: Bedford Books, 2000); Sara Evans, *Personal Politics: The Roots of Women's Liberation in the Civil Rights Movement and the New Left* (New York: Knopf, 1979).

14. Barbara Jeanne Fields, "Slavery, Race, and Ideology in the United States of America," *New Left Review* 181 (May/June 1990): 95–118.

15. For reconciliation and the unraveling of Reconstruction see Eric Foner, *Reconstruction: America's Unfinished Revolution, 1863–1877* (New York: Harper and Row, 1988), especially the epilogue; Nina Silber, *The Romance of Reunion: Northerners and the South, 1865–1900* (Chapel Hill: University of North Carolina Press, 1993).

Index

9 780812 219708